TRIBE, POVERTY AND EXPLOITATION

ABOUT COUNCIL OF ANALYTICAL TRIBAL STUDIES (COATS) KORAPUT, ODISHA

COATS is a premier Research-*cum*-Academic Institute in the field of Tribal Studies. It is affiliated to Berhampur University, Odisha. COATS is a Registered Body under Societies Registration Act of 1860 bearing Registration No. 712/82 of 1991-92. It is situated in Koraput town in the district of Koraput, Odisha which is the heart of central tribal belt of the country.

COATS mainly aims at acquainting and educating the students, scholars and development workers about the tribal life, culture and development programmes. Presently, it imparts M.A. and M.Phil. courses in 'Tribal Studies' and its academic staff guide research scholars who are doing research leading to M.Phil. and Ph.D. degrees in tribal affairs. The Institute also undertakes District Planning and other evaluation studies entrusted by Central and State Governments. It organizes seminars, workshops and training programmes from time to time.

About the Author

Jagannath Rath, M.A. (Economics) from Utkal University, Vani Bihar, Bhubaneswar; Ph.D. (Economics) from Berhampur University, Bhanja Bihar, Berhampur, Odisha, is Senior Lecturer (Group A) in Economics in Laxmipur College, Laxmipur. Dr. Rath, from his long practical experience in the field, has developed critical insight on issues of tribal development. In addition to this he knows Kandh language and culture as a practitioner. He is credited with a book on Kandh Folklore [*Tribal Folklore: A Study on Kuvis* (*Kandhas*) *of Koraput*], a number of seminar papers, and is an active member of Council of Analytical and Tribal Studies, Koraput which is committed to the cause of tribal upliftment. Dr. Rath can be contacted at Email: jagasriya@gmail.com

TRIBE, POVERTY AND EXPLOITATION
Kandhas of Koraput District in Odisha

Jagannath Rath

Published for

Council of Analytical Tribal Studies (COATS)
Koraput

by

CONCEPT PUBLISHING COMPANY PVT. LTD.
NEW DELHI - 110 059

ISBN-13: 978-93-5439-010-4

First Published 2022

Published and Printed by

Concept Since 1974

Concept Publishing Company Pvt. Ltd.
A/15-16, Commercial Block, Mohan Garden
New Delhi-110059 (India)
T : 25351460, 25351794, *41101460*
E: publishing@conceptpub.com, W: www.conceptpub.com

Cataloging in Publication Data--Courtesy: D.K. Agencies (P) Ltd. <docinfo@dkagencies.com>

Rath, Jagannath, author.
Tribal, poverty and exploitation : Kandhas of Koraput District in Odisha / Jagannath Rath.
pages cm
Includes bibliographical references and index.
ISBN 9789354390104

1. Kandh (Indic people)--India--Laxmipur (Block)--Social conditions. 2. Kandh (Indic people)--India--Laxmipur (Block)--Economic conditions. 3. Kandh (Indic people)--Employment--India--Laxmipur (Block) 4. Poverty--India--Laxmipur (Block) I. Council of Analytical Tribal Studies (India) II. Title.

LCC DS432.K192R38 2022 | DDC 305.800954133 23

FOREWORD

Dr. Jagannath Rath presents a vivid penetrating and empirical analysis of the triadic connections of tribe, poverty and exploitation with the Kandhs of Koraput district in Odisha as case study. Dr. Rath has examined the factors and the nature and extent of exploitation prevalent in the community under study. The condition of poverty is primarily a *priori* assumption based on the number of ration cards and composite development index developed by Council of Analytical Tribal Studies (COATS), Koraput. Poverty indicators are Block aggregates and as Kandhs are in majority in Lakhimpur Block of the district, the percentage of ration card holders of BPL families being 88.6 per cent in the Block, it is but logical to deduce that the Kandhs are poor. This assumption provides the background on the basis of which the relation between poverty — the dependent variable and exploitation — the independent variable is examined. The incidence of poverty though has economic content at the core, in its comprehensive meaning it is a state of deprivation in different non-economic areas also.

Precisely, Dr. Rath has examined the nature and types of deprivation inherent in the process of exploitation as indicators of poverty. In doing so, he has questioned the relevance of quantitative technique to measure the incidence of poverty in tribal societies in general and in Kandh community, the tribe under study, in particular.

Selection of the case of Kandh is theoretically grounded in that the trajectory of tribal poverty and their exploitation is typical of the broad class of the phenomenon to which theoretical explanations are available. Contemporary studies on tribe and poverty or tribal poverty and exploitation, or tribal marginalization, exclusion and deprivation in the process of integration with development agenda are abound. Dr. Rath's study is methodologically innovative in this regard and also from the point of view that he has combined both survey and ethnographic methods to examine cause-effect relationship between poverty and exploitation of the Kandhs. The study is primarily synchronic in nature as it has focused on contemporary period when the Kandhs have been exposed to national development agenda.

Exploitation and poverty of the Kandhs is a phenomenon of colonial legacy which perpetuates, unfortunately, even when the national government of post-colonial India is committed to tribal welfare. Two implications follow from the above statement.

First, during pre-colonial period, more particularly before any type of tribal interaction with non-tribals, incidences of poverty and exploitation were not characteristics of community mode of tribal production based on sharing ethics, subsistence needs, mutual reciprocation and dependence on foraging and hunting in common property resources. The proposition stands validated in Marshall Sahlins' conceptualization of hunter-gatherer societies as *original affluent societies*. As tribal communities exposed to non-tribal communities, their exploitation started and they were reduced to the state of poverty.

The second implication is theoretically crucial. Exposure and exploitation point to power inequality between tribes and those others they are exposed to. Max Weber considers power inequality as a source of exploitation of the powerless (subordinated) by the powerful (dominant). It is quite evident in Dr. Jagannath Rath's study of the Kandhs who are exploited by outside neighbours (Doms — a Scheduled Caste in Indian Constitution), *sahukars*, traders, moneylenders, petty *Mutadars*, police, revenue and excise officials and other Government officials and *Shundis* (wine vendors). Often the same person, like a *Shundi*, happened to be the moneylender and landlord. These agents had money power, wealth, connections, manipulative power (cunning, better informed than tribals) and power of their designation as government functionary.

When exploitation is a characteristic feature, potential and actual, in power inequality, it does not matter who is at the opposite end. James Woodburn records in the context of Africa that a tribe with improved technology dominates the neighbour with simple technology. I have also found in my study of Puroiks of Arunachal Pradesh who are hunter-gatherers and subordinate to cultivator neighbouring Nyishis and Mijis. The dichotomy of dominance and subordination has one or the other form of exploitation. It is an unwarranted consequence in the process of development that a few Kandhs have emerged richer and powerful than others. Dr. Rath has reported that comparatively better off Kandhs have started exploiting their own brethren.

As the subordinate section gets empowered, the extent of exploitation declines. This is quite evident when Dr. Rath reports that people around Laxmipur, the Block headquarters, were a little advanced — exposed, literate; they are not easily cheated by Doms; but, in Kumbhikota, where the Kandhs are unexposed, live in interiors often fell prey to exploitation by the Doms.

The study is empirically rich and theoretically grounded. I am sure; Dr. Jagannath Rath's study will incite further such tribe based micro studies so that grand theories on poverty, exploitation and marginalized communities emerge. In addition, such studies would help addressing the incidence of the global phenomenon of tribal poverty emerging in the process of their integration with State sponsored market oriented development agenda.

Dr. Maguni Charan Behera
Arunachal Institute of Tribal Studies
Rajiv Gandhi University
Arunachal Pradesh

Books from Council of Analytical Tribal Studies (COATS), Koraput, Odisha

Sl.No.	*Title of the Book*	*Editors/Authors/Publishers*
1.	Forest Management in Tribal Areas	P.M. Mohapatro & P.C. Mohapatro (Ed.) Concept Publishing Company (P) Ltd., New Delhi (1997)
2.	AmoGaon O AmoSasan (Odia)	J. Samal & N.N. Pradhan (Ed.) Hindustan Offset Printers, Jeypore, Koraput (2002)
3.	Dongar Katha (in Odia)	J. Samal Hindustan Offset Printers, Jeypore, Koraput (2002)
4.	Organisation and Management of Tribal Markets	K.K. Behera Independent Publishing Company, Delhi (2003)
5.	Tribes of Koraput	K.K. Mohanti P.C. Mohapatro & J. Samal Hindustan Offset Printers, Jeypore, Koraput (2006)
6.	Sustainable Development in Bonda Hills	P.M. Mohapatro K.K. Mohanti & P.C. Mohapatro Perfect Print and Graphics, Bhubaneswar (2009)
7.	Didayi — The Primitive Tribe	Gopinath Pradhan Hindustan Offset Printers, Jeypore, Koraput (2009)
8.	Law Preventing Land Alienation by Scheduled Caste and Scheduled Tribe	Jagannath Shroff Concept Publishing Company (P) Ltd., New Delhi (2013)
9.	Participatory and Sustainable Development among the Didayi	P.M. Mohapatro K.K. Mohanti & P.C. Mohapatro (Ed.) Concept Publishing Company (P) Ltd., New Delhi (2014)
10.	Shifting Cultivation in India — A Tribal Livelihood Alternative	N.K. Rath Concept Publishing Company (P) Ltd., New Delhi (2015)
11.	Watershed Management — Effective Tool for Sustainable Livelihood	A.K. Mohanty Concept Publishing Company (P) Ltd., New Delhi (2017)
12.	Tribal Folklore — A Study on Kuvis (Kandhas) of Koraput	Jagannath Rath Concept Publishing Company (P) Ltd., New Delhi (2019)

ACKNOWLEDGEMENTS

A study of available literature on tribals' livelihood, their poverty and exploitation provoked the scholar to make an in-depth study on the subject to know the nature and extent of exploitation of tribals in general and that of the backward Kandh tribe, in particular. In a period of more than sixty two years of independence and fifty-nine years of planning, a lot of schemes and projects have been implemented in the name of tribal welfare. Various rules and regulations have been framed and implemented to save the tribals from exploitation. The democratic and welfare Government is claiming to have come nearer or closer to the people. A large number of non-governmental organizations are working in tribal areas to create awareness among the people and to pave the way for socio-economic development of tribals in a time bound manner. Mass media including electronic media are now very active to make any sensitive issue public in no time. With this background, can one think of the exploitation of tribal people by outside (as well as inside) agencies in the same manner, as it was there before independence? Such thought provoking questions have compelled the scholar to go deep into the problem of exploitation, if at all it exists, in tribal areas of Koraput District and if it exists, then in what forms and to what extent? For an in-depth study of the problem the scholar has taken the case of the Kandh, a socio-economically quite backward tribe living in Laxmipur Block of Koraput District as the Sample.

The above question not only motivated the researcher to investigate the problem but also inspired him to work on it as a topic of Ph.D. assignment. However, the present book is the outcome of a research study at Ph.D. level which was undertaken under the guidance and supervision of Dr. Jagabandhu Samal, Professor, Council of Analytical Tribal Studies (COATS), Koraput. He is kind enough to write the foreword to this book. I humbly express my gratitude to him for his guidance and supervision both at M.Phil and Ph.D. level.

I am also grateful to Dr. P.C. Mohapatro, Director, COATS, Koraput for his comments and suggestions on my work and encouragement that helped a lot to complete the work. He also took special interest to publish the work in the form of a book.

I express my heartfelt regards and gratitude to Professor (Dr.) Maguni Charana Behera, Arunachal Institute of Tribal Studies, Rajiv Gandhi University, Itanagar, Arunachal Pradesh for his comments, suggestions and inspirations which helped improving the work before publication.

I am also thankful to all my colleagues of Laxmipur college and staff members of COATS, Koraput for their support to complete my work.

I express my deep sense of appreciation and thankfulness to my students Mr. Ramesh Jambeka, Miss Saibi Manding, and Mr. Kabish Hikoka and all other respondents of sample villages for helping me to collect required information.

I also express my thanks to my wife Sriya (Sabitree), loving daughter Shrim (Debansika) and son Shrit (Debashrit) for all those inconveniences they might have faced during my fieldwork and preparing MSS. I am also grateful to my elder sisters Kuni (Jagynaseni), Titi (Mana Mohini) and Mami (Jagat Mohini) who have constantly inspired me to undertake research works on tribal culture and livelihood.

Last but not the least, I take the opportunity to convey my sincere thanks to Concept Publishing Company Pvt. Ltd. who readily accepted the responsibility to publish the book and release it in time.

Jagannath Rath
Lecturer in Economics
Laxmipur College, Laxmipur
Dist: Koraput, Odisha

CONTENTS

LIST OF MAPS

LIST OF FIGURES

LIST OF TABLES

ABBREVIATIONS

ACA	:	Additional Central Assistance (for agricultural development)
AOBRC	:	Andhra Orissa Border Regional Committee
ANM	:	Auxiliary Nurse Mid-wife
APL	:	Above Poverty Line
ATMA	:	Agriculture Technology Management Agency
BBSR	:	Bhubaneswar
BC	:	Before Christ
BMI	:	Body Mass Index
BPL	:	Below Poverty Line
CAPART	:	Council for Advancement of People's Action and Rural Technology
COATS	:	Council of Analytical Tribal Studies
CD	:	Community Development
CMAS	:	Chasi Muliya Adivasi Sangha
CPI-ML	:	Communist Party of India-Maoist Liberation
CPRC	:	Chronic Poverty Research Centre
DDA	:	Deputy Director Agriculture
DTDP	:	Dispersed Tribal Development Programme
EGS	:	Employment Guarantee Scheme
EPW	:	Economic and Political Weekly
FLR	:	Female Literacy Rate
FAO	:	Food and Agriculture Organisation
GDP	:	Gross Domestic Product
GIPE	:	Gokhale Institute of Politics and Economics
GP	:	Gram Panchayat
HAL	:	Hindustan Aeronautics Limited
HH	:	Household
HINDALCO	:	Hindustan Aluminium Company
HQ	:	Head Quarter
IFAD	:	International Fund for Agricultural Development
IIPA	:	Indian Institute of Public Administration
IMR	:	Infant Mortality Rate
IOB	:	Indian Overseas Bank
IRDP	:	Integrated Rural Development Programme
ITDA	:	Integrated Tribal Development Agency
IWDP	:	Integrated Wasteland Development Project
KCCB	:	Koraput Central Co-operative Bank
KPGB	:	Koraput Panchabati Gramya Bank
LAMPS	:	Large Size Multipurpose Society
LI Points	:	Lift Irrigation Points
MADA	:	Modified Area Development Approach

MFP	:	Minor Forest Produces
MLA	:	Member of Legislative Assembly
MP	:	Member of Parliament
MSL	:	Mean Sea Level
NABARD	:	National Bank for Agriculture and Rural Development
NAC	:	Notified Area Council
NALCO	:	National Aluminium Company
NCAER	:	National Council of Applied Economic Research
NEFA	:	North-Eastern Frontier Agency
NFFWP	:	National Food For Work Programme
NGO	:	Non-Governmental Organisation
NICD	:	National Institute of Communicable Diseases
NIRD	:	National Institute of Rural Development
NREGS	:	National Rural Employment Guarantee Scheme
NREP	:	National Rural Employment Programme
NSS	:	National Sample Survey
NSSO	:	National Sample Survey Organisation
NTFP	:	Non-Timber Forest Products
OTDP	:	Orissa Tribal Development Project
PC	:	Percentage
PDS	:	Public Distribution System
PESA, Act	:	Panchayats (Extension to the Scheduled Areas), Act
PHC	:	Primary Health Centre
PLB	:	Poverty Line Basket
PPP	:	Purchasing Power Parity
PRH	:	Percentage of Rural Household
PRI	:	Panchayat Raj Institution
PTG/PVTG	:	Primitive Tribal Group/Particularly Vulnerable Tribal Group
QLI	:	Quality of Life Index
RBI	:	Reserve Bank of India
RI	:	Revenue Inspector
ROR	:	Record Of Right
RY	:	Real Income
SC	:	Scheduled Caste
SHG	:	Self-Help Group
SIDA	:	Swedish International Development Agency
SJGSY	:	Swarna Jayanti Gram Swarojgar Yojana
SMPT	:	Special Multipurpose Tribal Development Block
ST	:	Scheduled Tribe
TD Blocks	:	Tribal Development Blocks
THRTI	:	Tribal and Harijan Research-cum-Training Institute
TSP	:	Tribal Sub-Plan
UGPHC	:	Up-Graded Primary Health Center
UNDP	:	United Nations Development Programme
UNICEF	:	United Nations International Children's Emergency Fund
UPPL	:	Ultra Poor Poverty Line
URP	:	Uniform Reference Period
VHP	:	Vishwa Hindu Parishad

1

INTRODUCTION

1.0 Research Problem

Contemporary tribal situation in India reflects a paradoxical situation in which tribals are passing through a phase of economic transformation on the one hand and discontentment, unrest, deprivation, poverty, misery and in some cases armed rebellions on the other.

The state sponsored planning of the Central and State Governments, following democratic framework of the Constitution of independent India, has brought about significant changes in the socio-economic status and pace of development of tribal India. Several development and welfare programmes adopted so far such as universalization of primary education, provision of safe drinking water and sanitation, housing assistance for the homeless under Indira (now Pradhan Mantri) Awas Yojna, nutritional support to the needy women and children through Angan Wadi Centres (AWCs), primary health care support to the needy people through PHCs/Sub-centres, supply of subsidized food grains and other essential commodities to the tribals through the PDS, rural electrification and road connectivity to all villages with the urban market centres/district headquarter towns etc. have brought about profound changes in the tribal economy and society.

Obviously, the major factors and forces of change which resulted from those measures education, connection of tribal markets with big and urban markets, co-operative movements, spread of commercial and regional rural banks, impart of knowledge and awareness due to implementation of various schemes/projects for development of tribals and Constitutional safeguards and protective regulations like Land Mortgage Acts, Bonded Labour Acts, Land Alienation Act, New Forest Policies, National Rural Employment Guarantee Act (NREGA) etc. (see Vidyarthi and Rai, 1976).

These are the forces of national development agenda through plan programmes committed to tribal welfare and upliftment. Before independence, however, colonial contact released forces of change even though principle of isolation guided British interest in tribes.

In spite of planned intervention through several development and welfare schemes to raise the socio-economic standard of the tribals in India, the result is not satisfactory. Various studies have shown that the process of planned development has engendered several undesired consequences differentiating a few privileged sections of people with majority unprivileged or underprivileged sections of population (see Aiyappan, 1965; Behera, 1994 and 2018; Dev Nathan and Xaxa, 2012 and World Bank, 2011). The former section of people, being able to grab the larger share of the benefits of mainstream development, has become richer and richer while the later section is subjected to exclusion in the form of land alienation, marginalization, deprivation, subordination and subjugation. Under such a situation, the alienated poor and weaker sections of population have been lagging behind in the race of climbing the development ladder compared to their privileged counterparts and economic inequality between these two groups (privileged and underprivileged) of population have been widening over the years (Bijoy, 2003).

The scale of alienation of the tribal people from development process have been much more deplorable. Alienation of those tribal villagers can very well be gauged by witnessing their sufferings and limitations in their lives in the form of abject poverty conditions, livelihood insecurity, illiteracy and ignorance, living with deadly epidemic and killer diseases like cholera, malaria, TB, smallpox etc. Incapable of acquiring the art and abilities of getting assimilated into the market-based mainstream development process, the major section of the tribes are still compelled to live under subjugation of the people leading the market forces. Ever increasing influence of market-based economy has been appearing as the main bone of contention before the peaceful and sustainable living of the primitive tribes (see Bijoy, 2003; Panagariya and More, 2013; Nazer, 2004 and Mishra, 2002).

It follows that a great majority of the tribals still live in poverty and deprivation. They find it difficult to meet their basic necessities like food, shelter, health care etc. That tribal have not been benefitted from development interventions can be logically deduced from the fact that from among the tribal communities (STs) a new category called PTGs/ PVTGs (Primitive Tribal Groups/Particularly Vulnerable Tribal Groups) have been delineated for special treatment. Introduction of tribal sub-plan (TSP) in Fifth Schedule Areas since Fifth Five Year Plan is another indicator that earlier plan programmes did not benefit tribals as expected. Inter-tribe inequality in north-east reflects in the demand for special status. That is why a few tribes have been recently covered under the provisions of Sixth Schedule (like Bodos) and others under state regulations (like Mishing, Sonowal Kachari, Tiwa etc.). Still the demand by other tribes continues. It merits mention that by quirk of fate they have become "victims of progress" leading to discontentment, unrest and in some cases, rebellions (see Xaxa, 2018 and Anuradha and Dash, 2019).

Although awareness level among the tribals is gradually but slowly increasing through intervention of both government and non-government agencies, the major problem like poverty still remains there in its real form. Tribals are yet not free from exploitation. It is said to exist in one form or the other in the tribal areas of the country. It is regarded as one of the major hurdles in the path of their development.

What follows in general is that most of the tribals are backward both socially and economically. They are alleged to be more exploited than rest of the population in India.

What is generally true is also true to a large number of individual tribal communities in different states. It is to be mentioned that among various tribal communities found in Odisha "Kandhs" are numerically the largest tribal groups, numbering over one million, but economically backward. They are mostly concentrated in the districts of Koraput (undivided) Balangir, Phulbani and Kalahandi.

Precisely, it can be summed up in terms of that Scheduled Tribes in general and Kandhs in particular have remained mostly poverty ridden, illiterate, ignorant and depressed. They are more or less exploited too. Due to implementation of various anti-exploitative policies in tribal areas, the economic and social exploitation has been checked to a certain extent. Still the poor and technologically backward tribal people are falling prey to exploitative forces in several ways. It may not be always open, but hidden in nature.

In view of this, the present study has been designed to examine the nature and extent of poverty and associated exploitation of tribals with the Kandhs of Koraput region as case study.

1.1 Objectives of the Study

The objectives of the present study are to:

(i) study the present socio-economic status of Kandhs living in Koraput region;
(ii) find out the nature and extent of poverty in Kandh community;
(iii) examine the nature of exploitation both hidden and open and the agencies responsible for it;
(iv) know the impact of exploitation on socio-economic lives of the Kandhs; and
(v) to suggest measures to arrest the problem of poverty and exploitation.

1.2 Hypothesis

The study has tested the following two hypotheses:

(i) The incidence of poverty exists among the Kandhs despite state sponsored welfare measures.
(ii) The Kandhs have been exposed to forces of exploitation.

1.3 Significance of the Study

Tribes do not present homogeneity and their level integration with development process displays various degrees. Therefore, their situation cannot be comprehended with reference to macro statistics which is used to measure national economic growth. Due to heterogeneity, micro studies are useful to understand tribal situation which cannot be captured in macro aggregates. In this sense, the present study is an addition to existing knowledge in the field. The study has policy implications in that the findings will be useful to planners, NGOs and those others interested in tribal development in general and development of the Kandhs in particular.

1.4 Methodology

The work is empirical in nature and descriptive in analysis. Both secondary and primary sources of information have been taken into account in order to carry out the study. Primary data have been collected from field study which included personal interview, observation, case studies and focus group discussions. The interview was conducted by administering structured questionnaires to sample households. Besides semi-structured questionnaire was also used so that relevant details are not left out. Unpublished government documents were also consulted.

The investigator took enough care to record the observations as accurately as possible by participating in many of the community gatherings in Kandh villages. He has visited local hats, trading places and attended some Palli Sabhas organized in the villages to acquaint himself with problems of the people at the grassroots levels. The head of each sample household was administrated the main questionnaire containing questions on family particulars, occupations, different agricultural activities undertaken during the year, size of holding, the crops grown and output received etc. and also other related questions about exploitation.

Published books, articles and research papers on the tribal issues in general and on the Kandhs in particular, various Government reports and reports of other organizations constituted secondary sources which have been taken into account to supplement the information collected from the field.

Initially, in almost all sample villages the respondents were unwilling to answer to the questions relating to their movable and immovable property, their income and expenditure and especially to the oversensitive questions on types of exploitation (due to prevailing unrest in neighbouring Bondhugaon and Narayanpatana blocks of Koraput district). However, after establishing rapport with the respondents in Kandh villages and gaining their confidence the work became easier. The knowledge of Kandh language (Kuvi) of the researcher helped him a lot to gain their confidence and to collect information.

The data so collected were edited and suitably classified for presentation in tables and graphs. Simple statistical tools like percentage, ratio etc. have been used to analyse and interpret data.

1.5 The Census and the Sample

In the present study Koraput district of Odisha was taken as the universe and Laxmipur block as the sample frame of study. The block is a Kandh concentrated block in the district. Obviously, the Kandh families constituted sampling units and selected individuals sample respondents. Care had been taken to see that the sampling is done in such a manner that the socio-economic life of the Kandh community is appropriately represented and a meaningful conclusion is arrived at.

Laxmipur block of Koraput district is a tribal dominated block. The total population of the block was 55,268 out of which tribal population was 37,951 (2001 census).[1] This constitutes about 69 per cent (68.7% to be exact) to the total population of the block. Kandhs constitute more than 95 per cent of the total tribal population of the block. The other important tribal community found in the block is the Paraja, but they constitute a small percentage of total tribal population. So the Kandh tribe was selected for investigation. The Kandhs are poverty ridden and therefore are susceptible to various types of exploitation. Hence, Laxmipur block, therefore, was purposively taken as the sample in the present study.

Out of 13 Gram Panchayats in the Laxmipur block, the researcher selected purposively one village from each Panchayat for in-depth study where Kandhs constituted major portion of total population. Total number of villages selected was 13. From each sample village 20 Kandh households were randomly selected, except Kanapadi village from where 24 households were selected, for an in-depth study relating to their present socio-economic status, the developmental schemes implemented and the beneficiaries thereof and the degree of poverty and the agencies of exploitation, if any, and the measures taken to save them from exploitation and their impact. Total households selected from the Block were 264.

1.6 Methods of Sampling

Both probability and non-probability sampling techniques have been used in the study. Multistage sampling using non-probability technique was used. The Block was selected purposively as it is Kandh dominated Block in the district. From the Block, all the 13 Gram Panchayats were selected. The villages in the Panchayat are multi-ethnic in nature. Therefore, from each Gram Panchayat one village in which Kandh population is in majority was selected purposively. But from each village 20 households were selected randomly. Respondents from each household, whether head or any other member were selected randomly, on the basis of availability. The census data of 2001 were taken into consideration while selecting the village-wise population. The population details with SC and ST break-up is given in Table 1.1.

In sample villages total households are record 2500 out of which 264 households are sample households. This constitutes about 11 of the total households. As far as population is concerned it is about 67 (6,486 out of 9,687). The villages selected are tribal dominated is evident from Table 1.2. Table 1.2 shows distribution of ST population in sample villages. It can be seen from Table 1.2 that 8 villages have more than 60 of ST population and 7 villages more than 80. Only 2 villages have less

Table 1.1: Name of the G.P., Sample Villages with its Population Break-up in Laxmipur Block of Koraput District (2001 Census)

Sl. No.	*Name of the G.P.*	*Name of the Sample Village*	*Total No. of H.H.*	*Village-wise Sample H.H*	*Total Population*			*SC Population*			*ST Population*		
					T	*M*	*F*	*T*	*M*	*F*	*T*	*M*	*F*
1.	Bhitaragada	Charada	415	20	1590	796	794	89	56	33	733	368	365
2.	Burja	Bandikar	215	20	896	432	464	9	4	5	837	396	441
3.	Chimpii	Uparchampi	285	20	921	572	349	237	126	111	751	389	362
4.	Goudaguda	Lachhamani	219	20	872	426	446	78	41	37	763	367	396
5.	Kakiriguma	Kakiraiguma	569	20	2255	1096	1159	536	253	283	900	430	470
6.	Kusumaguda	Talachampi	76	20	322	151	171	5	4	1	289	135	154
7.	Kutinga	Minapai	147	20	577	273	304	131	63	68	439	207	232
8.	Laxmipur	Marbaiguda	87	20	385	198	187	96	51	45	229	119	110
9.	Odiapentha	R.P. Gura	111	20	449	227	222	41	17	24	383	197	186
10.	Panchada	Jodikhenda	99	20	347	174	173	7	5	2	326	165	161
11.	Pipalpodar	Mandalaguda	57	20	248	115	133	198	88	110	47	25	22
12.	Toyaput	Kanapadi	116	24	424	212	212	0	0	0	418	210	208
13.	Tunupar	Kainjhariguda	104	20	401	192	209	10	4	6	371	177	194
		Total	**2500**	**264**	**9687**	**4864**	**4823**	**1437**	**712**	**725**	**6486**	**3185**	**3301**

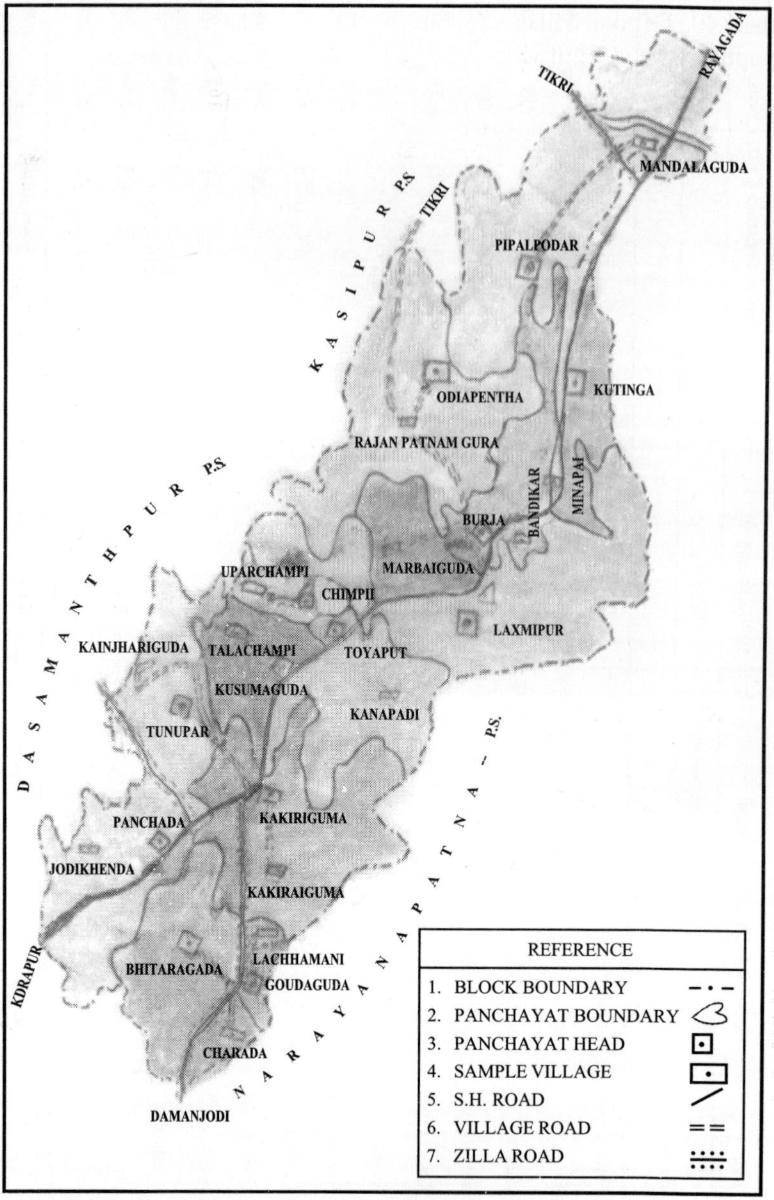

Map 1.1: Map of Laxmipur Block with Location of Sample Villages.

Source: Naba Krushna Chaudhury Centre for Development Studies.

than 40. Of total villages about 58 of villages have more than 80 of population and 62 of villages more than 60.

Table 1.2: Percentage Distribution of ST Population in Sample Villages

Distribution of Population (in %)	*No. of Villages*
Up to 20	1
20-40	1
40-60	3
60-80	1
80 and above	7

Source: Computed from census and field data.

As has been mentioned, only the village Kanapadi of Toyaput Panchayat has all the households belonging to Kandh community. All other villages are having Kandh families along with other multi-ethnic groups like Dom, Shundhi, Gouda, Kumuti, Brahmin and others. The multi-ethnic villages were selected to see if there was any instance of Kandhs being exploited by members of other ethnic groups in the village. Again, these villages were grouped under two categories, i.e. road-side villages and interior villages in order to find if there was any difference in socio-economic condition and extent of exploitation between these two groups of villages. Twenty Kandh households were selected from each village randomly with an exception to Kanapadi from where 24 households were selected purposively. So, in total 264 Kandh households were selected for an in-depth study.

Table 1.1 reveals that the total population of 13 sample villages, selecting one village each from a G.P. of the block, comes to 9687 which constituted of 4864 males and 4823 females. Of the total population, 6486 (67%) consisted STs and 1437 (14.83%) SCs. Hence, STs and SCs combinedly constituted 81.83 per cent to the total population. Females have outnumbered the males both in case of the STs and SCs.

Planning the Study

The researcher made several visits during a period of one year to the selected villages in order to collect required information from the sample Kandh families and other members.

In the 1st phase, a pilot survey of the sample households was made in the village named Kanapadi of Toyaput Gram Panchayat, with a structured questionnaire during March 2010. This exercise helped to reconstruct the questionnaire in order that reliability and validity of the investigation ensured. A structured questionnaire relating to the caste/tribe of the household, age, sex, education and marital status of the members of the household, their main and subsidiary occupations, movable and immovable property possessed by the households, their income and expenditure during the year 2009-2010, indebtedness and other related factors leading to exploitation were collected.

In the 2nd phase, during April-June 2010 data were collected from all the rest of the 12 villages in the similar fashion as mentioned above. In addition to this, participatory observation, case study and focus group discussions were conducted from time to time to support and supplement the information collected from sample households.

Tabulation and Analysis

After the collection of data/information, these were posted and tabulated in a neatly meaningful manner. These were analyzed by using simple statistical techniques like averages, median, mode, range etc. The report was written on the basis of the date and information collected from the field and supported by secondary sources of information.

Limitations

The study is not free from limitations. The term "tribe" has been defined variously by various authors and scholars, but no single definition is adequate. Even the Constitution of India has not given an adequate definition of the term. Only the Constitution basing on certain socio-economic characteristics has included certain community as the Scheduled Tribes.

Without going into the debate who is a tribe, the researcher simply accepted Kandh (Kuvi) as a tribe, as they have been scheduled in the Constitution of India. The researcher has not gone through the complex axiomatic refinements for poverty measurement, but measured poverty as per the "poverty line" defined by the expert group set by Planning Commission of India in November 2009.

Moreover, the term "exploitation" is not easy to define. It is a relative concept based on various socio-economic parameters defined from time to time. However, an attempt has been made to analyze the problem of exploitation among the Kandhs in the changing socio-economic scenario.

Furthermore, the head of households were answering the questions from their memory which cannot be claimed to be fully authentic. Many a times it was found that they were trying to avoid the questions particularly relating to the nature of exploitation. It was quite difficult to extract quantitative information as morality characterizes their life ways. So utmost care has been taken to collect the information through participatory observation, focus group discussions and in this way by counter-checking the information collected from the heads of the households.

However, with the limited time and resources at the disposal of the researcher, a bigger sample size could not be attempted. An attempt has been made to select the sample in such manner which will represent adequately the universe and focus objectively to explain the research problem.

1.7 Structure of the Study

The study contains in all, eight chapters. The first is the chapter on *Introduction* to the research problem, objectives, hypothesis, precisely the research design.

The second chapter is on *Review of Literature*. An attempt has been made to review the available literature dealing with the tribes, their poverty and exploitation in three sections. While reviewing the relevant books and articles the topic, the methodology adopted by the scholar, area of this study and conclusions or findings arrived at are dealt with as far as possible.

The chapter three is entitled *Tribe, Poverty and Exploitation: A Conceptual Analysis*. In this chapter an attempt has been made to conceptualize tribe, poverty and the incidence of exploitation with regard to tribal communities.

The fourth chapter is entitled as *Land and People: A General Profile*. It introduces to the land and people in general. In other words, it introduces to the universe in order that the research problem explained with reference to the sample is understood meaningfully. The chapter is divided into two broad sections. Section-I deals with a profile of Koraput region and Koraput district and Section-II deals with the Kandh tribes of Koraput. It introduces to geographical area of the district, location etc.; tribals of Koraput in general and the Kandhs in particular. Society, economy, traditional political organization etc. have been presented in this chapter.

The chapter five is entitled *Tribal Exploitation*. In this chapter a brief historical account of the tribal exploitation has been presented. It has discussed nature of exploitation, mechanism and agencies of exploitation in the region. It is to be mentioned that tribes do not live in isolation; they interact with intra- and inter-village non-tribals. The interaction is marked by exploitation which is discussed with reference to Kandhs' relation with Doms. In addition 10 case studies have been presented to examine the nature of exploitation.

The sixth chapter is entitled *A Profile of Sample Villages and Issues of Exploitation*. The chapter deals with the field survey and its findings. Here the economic life of the sample families along with the incidence, nature and extent of poverty and exploitation has been discussed. Poverty of the sample household is compared with the poverty measurement by the new expert group set by Planning Commission to measure poverty line of India in November 2009. The nature and extent of exploitation and its changing scenario in the present context have been explained.

The chapter seven is entitled *Protection, Failure and Reaction*. In this chapter a brief note on constitutional safeguards meant for the protection of tribal interest is discussed. With reference to the present study and other studies it is argued that tribal development has not been satisfactory. Therefore, it is further argued that plan policies aimed at tribal development failed in realizing desired goals. The tribals have reacted to the failure which is reflected in tribal unrests.

Tribal unrest and important Kandh uprisings in Odisha have been discussed in this chapter briefly. The tribal unrest in Koraput in general and armed rebellion by "Chasi Mulia Adivasi Sangha" of Narayan Patna and Bondhugaon blocks in particular is discussed.

The last and concluding chapter gives a brief summary of the study. It summarizes the present condition of the Kandhs, new dimensions of their exploitation, causes and effects of such exploitation. Finally, a humble attempt has been made to suggest certain measures to protect the Kandhs from exploitation and to raise the status of the tribals both socially and economically in general and the Kandhs in particular.

NOTE

1. The work was designed to study the impact of schemes and programmes. Obviously, their completion was required. Roughly, data were collected up to 2009/2010 so that the impact can be examined objectively. That is why figures of census, 2001 have been used.

2

REVIEW OF LITERATURE

2.0 Introduction

The terms like "tribe", "poverty" and "exploitation" are closely related to each other. In the present study, the researcher has accepted "tribe" as the ethnic group, identified by the Constitution of India as "Scheduled Tribes". Poverty is measured in absolute terms and an egalitarian approach has been undertaken to study poverty of the Kandh tribes. Similarly, exploitation is judged by the effects on socio-economic life of the people with ethical considerations. Attempt has been made to see the exploitation prevalent among the tribals in general and that of Kandhs of Koraput in particular. To find out the cause and effect relationship between poverty and exploitation is the prime objective of the study.

In this chapter an attempt has been made to review the available literature on tribal studies in India with reference to their poverty and exploitation at the national, state and at the district level. "Literature" mainly refers to the published and unpublished works of anthropologists, economists and other social scientists published in different books, journals, Government Documents, News papers and popular Media; as conference papers, dissertations, theses; and available in Internet and electronic data base etc. The literature review is a critical look at the available writings on related subject mostly focusing on the objectives, methodology and findings.

Keeping this in view, this chapter on Review of Literature is divided into three sections. Section-I deals with tribes and development interface in general and that of Kandhs in particular. Section-II deals with the literature related to poverty, poverty level and poverty estimates in general and that of the tribals in particular. Section-III deals with studies on exploitation with special emphasis on tribal exploitation.

SECTION – I

2.1 Tribes and Development Interface

The tribals constitute the core of the poor in our country. Poverty, poor health and sanitation, illiteracy and other social problems including exploitation prevalent among the tribals are exerting a dragging effect on Indian Economy. A plethora of literature is available on tribal economy, problems of land alienation, forest and tribe interaction, their socio-economic development, culture etc. It is highly imperative to have a look at these studies by various scholars in the disciplines of Anthropology, Economics and other social sciences.

Herskovites (1940) was one of earliest scholars of the world, who for the first time tried to establish a relationship between Anthropology and Economics. His analysis was based on the observation of tribal cultures from different regions of the world. He had made an attempt to differentiate indigenous tribal economy from the modern economy. He opined that tribal economies were marginal with simple technology; there existed co-operative support in economic pursuits, exchange of labour and a universal sex-based division of labour. Children from very early age entered into the work force. Barter system was prevalent in tribal economy. In the field of production, tribals' economic life resolves around their natural environment. The characteristics of tribal economy as identified by Herskovites are more or less found in the present day world. It is true that there have been a lot of transformations in the economic pursuits of the tribals.

S.C. Roy (1912), known as father of Indian Anthropology, dealt extensively with agrarian system of Chotanagpur in the beginning of last century and the nature of land relationship among the tribals. He gave an account of how the land in tribal areas in the past belonged to the community and how the system broke down, in course of time, and tribal lands were alienated by the Rajas, Dikus (outsiders) and Zamindars.

A new trend in ethno methodology which came during British period was a theory given by Varrier Elwin (1943) who suggested that the tribals should be kept isolated in their hills and forests. In order to guarantee this situation, he suggested that non-tribal people should not be allowed to enter into tribal pockets without permission of state government. But later on he admitted that he did not mean to keep the tribals as museum species. But he was against too much interference of non-tribals in tribal areas. So, in his *Philosophy for NEFA* (1959), he emphasized on integrationist approach to tribal development.

However, G.S. Ghurye (1943) challenged the theory of Public Park. He argued that the tribals were backward caste Hindus and hence, they should be treated as Hindus. D.N. Majumdar (1944), following Ghurye's arguments gave a slightly different opinion. He feared that if isolation is broken then the tribals will lose their ethical identity. So, there should be a "Selected Integration" of the tribals. Only those elements of civilization should be allowed to enter in the tribal areas which have relevance with tribal life. Such a policy will keep the tribals away from the vices of urban and so called civilized society. Similar writings of the anthropologists like Hutton (1933), Majumdar (1944) and Roy (1912), were labeled as "Isolationists" and "no-changer". The critics of Isolation model came forward with their own version. Condemning the policy of segregation, on the basis of the arguments that it can never lead to progress and advancement of the tribal people, the scholars opined that the civilization has been built mainly through constant contact and interaction among people. It was further argued that India being characterized by the multiplicity of races and cultures, flourishing together, the phenomenon of isolation would not be able to run counter to the facts of Indian situations. The difficulty lies with putting iron bar between the tribals and the non-tribal communities. Isolation was further criticized on the plea that the tribals could be of great service to the country, more so by bringing their rich treasures into common life.

Thakkar (1944, see Gandhi, 2019) also criticized isolationists. He stated "to keep these people confined to isolation in their inaccessible hills and jungles is something like keeping them in glass-cases of museum for the curiosity of purely academic persons". Separation and isolation, he considered, are dangerous as they struck at the root of national solidarity. Unless the aboriginals realized, he said, through contacts with more advanced people, their own backwardness in the economic, social and political fields, they could not make any progress. This approach was accepted neither by anthropologists, nor by the Government.

The Christian missionaries, the Hindu social workers, reformers and others were engaged in the task of tribal development and uplift through "assimilation" mostly by converting the tribals. However, the greatest psychological handicap in assimilation is the element of inferiority complex among tribals about their culture and religion. Therefore, in the last century "tribal development" was a matter of concern in almost all writings on tribals. However, the tribal problems remain unsolved and they still live in their world with their primitive technologies and limited sources of living.

Tribal studies in India will remain incomplete without a thorough review of the works undertaken by Varrier Elwin in his number of writings (1939, 1943, 1950, 1959, 1964 & 1965). Though his writings were mostly anthropological in nature, but socio-economic life of tribals were also reflected in his scholarly works. His book "A Philosophy for NEFA", as mentioned earlier, gives a description of land tenure system prevalent in the north-east tribal region. The ownership of land in those areas varies from tribe to tribe. He categorized it into three categories like the land owned by individuals, comprising all cultivable lands, irrigated rice fields, lands for dry crops garden plots, fruit trees and groves of bamboo etc. Secondly, the clan land consisting of meadow land near the village used for pasture, burial grounds, and tracks of forests where members of a particular clan has the right to trap and collect minor forest produces. Finally, the common village lands are confined to one or two stretches of pasture and forest tracks. The land used for shifting cultivation belongs to the whole village and the area was established by tradition and agreement with other nearby villages. Boundaries of lands were demarcated by streams, hills and big rocks and trees etc.

During his tours in the tribal areas of present Odisha he studied the life of tribes like Juangs, Sauras, Kuttia Kandhs and Bondas. He reported the misery of Juangs after the reservation of Malayagiri.

Elwin (1965) in his article "The Fundamental Needs of the Tribal People" laid stress on agriculture, communication, medical facilities, education, and generation of employment opportunities and so on which was common to the tribals living in India. Five other points which were more complex were cited like a special class called "Tribal" who were labeled as "Backward" in order to get material benefit from Government. "Unintelligent benevolence can be as great a danger as intelligent exploitation". A sense of inferiority complex should not be created among the tribals and nothing should be imposed upon them. Also, he pointed out that they should not loose their freedom and their zest for living and the motto should be, in the words of Spenser:

> "What more facility can fall to creature
> Than to enjoy delight with liberty"

Vidyarthi in his epoch-making works (1957, 1960, 1963, 1971, 1976 & 1981) categorized tribal studies in India in terms of meaningful chronological phases. He developed three historical phases of development, *viz*. formative (1774-1919), constructive (1920-1949) and recent (1950 onwards). These three stages of development, however, do not mean that one phase completely replaces the other. In general he made a strong plea that Indian Social Science should not overlook what may be termed its "Indianness". This refers to our distinct cultural milieu and value system as well as ideas reflected in ancient scriptures. He laid emphasis mainly on the importance of cultural factors in economic development of various tribal communities. Vidyarthi classified tribals into seven categories on cultural background and historical experience of the community concerned. There have been strikingly different rates of development of tribal researches in various parts of India, and an acquaintance with this fact has been emphasized and a generalization on all-India level with their respective distinctiveness and delimitations.

He also examined through his writings the impact of urbanization on tribal culture. He studied the impact of the emergence of a heavy engineering complex in a tribal belt of Chotanagpur and analyzed the changes occurred in the socio-economic life of the tribals due to large scale industrialization.

In the process of modernization, Roy Burman (1973), rightly pointed out that tribals live among the non-tribals, hardly share a common life. The contacts are few and formal. Tribals in urban areas live in fully neither of the two worlds. His studies point out to some of the few instances of modernization, like imparting education and creation of awareness etc., but he expresses his dissatisfaction regarding the strategies adopted for tribals' modernization.

K.S. Singh's study (1982) also relates to the transformation of tribal economics with introduction of new technology into agriculture. This change started from the colonial period and again being intensified since independence. However, he further observed that the process of transformation is not yet complete.

N.K. Bose (1977) made a typological study of the tribal communities of India. He classified the tribes, on the basis of their economic pursuits, such as, hunting, fishing, gathering, *jhum* cultivation with animal and plough, nomadic cattle keepers, artisans, labourers and those working in plantations and industries. He then went on to analyze the nature and scope of such activities and the tribal communities depending on these. He also gave some insight to tribal social life, "tribes differ from others in their social system. They have retained their own marriage regulation. Almost all marry within their restricted local groups and sometimes guided by their own elders or political chief in internal and external affairs. In other words, they form socially distinct communities who have been designated as tribes and listed in the schedule for special treatment, so that within a relatively short-time they can come within the mainstream of political and economic life in India". The scholar cited the examples of tribes like Juangs of Odisha, Gonds of Madhya Pradesh, Santals of Bihar and Bengal to show their social life basing upon economic pursuits. Several observations made in the book are the outcome of personal experience of the author.

Industrialization, entry of outsiders into tribal land due to communication, forest policies and lack of tribal leadership are described as the various conditions which have led to an increase in discontent among the tribal communities of India after independence. The author cautioned any kind of special provision by preparing the tribes for taking a due share in economic and political development, for that would weaken national solidarity rather than its strengthening.

The scientific study of tribal economy was first undertaken by two scholars, D.S. Nag and R.P. Saxena. Nag (1958) made an extensive field tours in the areas of Madhya Pradesh like Mandla, Bilaspur, Durg, Balaghat and studied the Baiga economy in the context of general economic theories laying emphasis on the sources of economy of Baigas. He selected a sample of 350 tribal families and basing on other available secondary data, found that the order of primitive tribal economy based on food gathering and shifting cultivation had undergone a radical change on account of modern forces. Acquisition of new assets after coming in contact with market and the ignorance of Baiga villagers about the external economy and the terms and costs of transportation led to widespread exploitation of these tribals by moneylenders, middle men and traders. Saxena (1964) followed the model of Nag and studied the tribals of western hills of Madhya Pradesh and presented the economy of five tribes. The authors have some limitations like exclusion of socio-cultural conditions of the tribes on their study areas.

N.N. Vyas (1967) presents the historical, social and economic life of the Baniyas of Rajasthan, Andhra Pradesh, Punjab and Gujarat. The methodology seems not suitable but this study has a good comparative background of Baniyas of different states in their social customs, practices and their economic pursuits.

By selecting a sample of 1120 rural households from 28 villages Vimal Saha (1969) studied the tribal economy of Gujarat based on the All India Rural Development and Investment Survey of the RBI (1961-62) and concluded that tribals were living in a subsistence economy with little diversification in occupation. Agriculture continued to be the main stay of tribal population. Banking and institutionalized credit facilities were still far from the reach of the tribals.

Some of the other studies at the national level basing mainly on tribal economy and about the process of modernization in the sixties and seventies include "A Socio-economic Study of Shifting Cultivation in Tripura" (Ganguly, 1968), "Santal Rural Economy" (1973), a study based on village survey in Santal Praganas by Agro Research Centre, the helplessness of the tribals after modernization and dissatisfaction (Roy Burman:1973). Dean Joros (1973), in his study presents his view on the relation between political socialization of the tribals and integration process. This view also explained by P.R.G. Mathur (1977) in "Accountraction and Integration in Tribal Life". S.L. Doshi (1978) takes a case study of Bhils in the process of unification and integration.

Dube and Murdia (1977) in the edited entitled "Land Alienation and Restoration in Tribal Communities in India" examines the process of transfer of land from tribals to non-tribals and various factors influencing such transfers. Similar studies were also undertaken by N. Gopal Rao (1978) by taking case study of Mondem Khal, a mixed village of tribes and castes at Parvatipuram taluk of former Srikakulam district. Land has a tremendous prestige value in the rural context and it stands as a security for borrowing and lending. Roy Burman (1979) pointed out the urgent need of integration of tribals into the mainstream, where integration meant four things, *viz.*, independent thinking, democratic style of life, secularism and planned economy.

All these studies mentioned above deal with different aspects of tribal life and economy, such as, tribal agriculture, shifting cultivation, indebtedness, tribal education, land alienation and political awareness. Most of them suggested that the tribal economy as well as the social and political attitudes of tribals is largely governed by their access to resources and technology. The process of adaptation and adjustment is not yet completed.

Similar kind of tribal studies were also found during the last part of the last century (1980-2000). Alock Kumar (1986) has attempted to analyze and interpret the socio-culture organizations and economic structures of Mal Paharias in Santal Praganas district of Bihar in the light of regional geographical complex. The responsiveness of the tribals to different projects and programmes undertaken during different plan periods were discussed by taking case study of Santhals in Bihar by Devendra Thakur (1986).

In his works, M.L. Patel (1984 & 1987) has dealt with the rationale of regional planning, micro planning and integrated area development with a view to build a viable model for Mandla district in Madhya Pradesh. In his book "New Dimensions of Tribal Development" a number of research papers dealing with different dimensions of tribal development at the National level were compiled.

The impact of Development Programmes on tribals was discussed in "Tribal Development in India" by Dr. A.K. Singh (1984) with special reference to the problems of isolated tribes in the state of Bihar. R.S. Singh (1986) in another study highlighted some significant issues with regard to impact of development efforts in Chottanagpur region of West Bengal in changing occupational structure as a result of industrialization and regional social economic prosperity. The scholar collected data by Sample Survey and observation methods from the tribal inhabitants of 15 villages around Ranchi city and also took the help of secondary sources. He found that percentage of tribal cultivators in Chottanagpur region had declined because of transfer of land from tribals to others, establishment of industries and other non-agricultural projects. To him, the industrialization and industrial prosperity of the region do not ensure prosperity to the tribal population living in it.

V.S. Ramamani (1988) presents a descriptive analysis of the main features of tribal economy. She dealt with the disparities between tribals and non-tribals and protective and promotional measures to reduce it. The author reviewed the policies and programmes for tribal development while dealing with the main features of tribal economy of Danubai Panchayat in Srikakulam District.

In the process of Random Sampling she collected information from 260 tribal households in Sithampetta block in Srikakulam District of Andhra Pradesh. She found that the economic activities have their social constraints as tribals spend more time and money on socio-religious activities. In her comparative study she found that the top layers (having 5 acres or more) enjoy a surplus than those having land less than 5 acres.

L.C. Mohanty (1989) has reminded the necessity of evaluation of tribal development and their integration into the larger Indian society. He opined that giving tribals full freedom to manifest their genius would help their integration.

Nirmal Sengupta (1990) opined that the process of industrialization after independence has added a new dimension to the tribal problem.

Displacement of tribals due to industrialization without proper compensation and difficulty to accommodation with the new environment added to tribal misery.

Verma (1990) in his treatise made an attempt to present a glimpse into the historical perspective of the Indian tribes, their demography, constitutional and legal provisions relating to their protection and development, working of the safeguards as well as problems and challenges of tribal development. Tribal problems in general have been discussed nicely and the author has tried to point out more realistic aspects of tribal problems. The study is mainly based on field observation by the scholar during his frequent visits to tribal areas. He concluded that, tribals mainly depend on agriculture and forests. Due to unauthorized alienation of tribal land and deprivation of tribals of forestry rights, the tribal economy has been seriously affected resulting migration of tribals to urban areas and other states to earn their livelihood.

Various causes of unrest among the Scheduled Tribes have been identified and analysed. Discontentment among tribals has been surfacing time and again either in the form of separate state or an agitation for better deal for development.

Evaluation of various developmental programmes, according to Verma, shows dissatisfaction for not receiving desired results. Enforcement of protective measures to safeguard the tribals is not satisfactory. This work also provides interesting informative material concerning anthropological, socio-economic and constitutional aspects on Scheduled Tribes. Finally, he concluded with the words of Pandit Nehru that the tribals would be allowed to develop on their own genius without imposing anything on them.

By taking case studies of Bhils of Rajasthan, Madhusudan Trivedi (1991) presents his views regarding entrepreneurship among the tribals; the economic transformation and introduction of capitalistic economy in tribal areas, and class-stratification among the tribals. Fruits of all developmental activities were swallowed-up by the top layers having better entrepreneurial skill. Sometimes they do not hesitate to exploit their poor brethren.

Buddhadeb Choudhuri's series of five edited volumes (1992) mainly deal with changing scenario of tribal development relating to the issues to tribal economy, agronomy, politics, ethnicity, ecology, education, technology transfer, social political movement, religious faiths and rituals with both diagnostic and remedial models. The authors, who have contributed to these volumes, have made a fresh look at micro and macro level dynamics of the tribal situation in India.

S.S. Shasi (1994) edited twelve volumes in the name of "Encyclopedia of Indian Tribes". The companion volumes 1 to 12 is a collection of articles, papers, notes and commentaries on tribal people of India, their way of life, customs and traditions, cultural characteristics and artistic inheritance. It is a meaningful addition to contemporary literature in anthropology and sociology. The editor tried to touch almost all aspects of a number of tribal life. All the efforts to give protection and support to the extent possible, by both Government and a host of voluntary agencies were discussed. The helplessness of tribals due to exploitation by vested and greedy interests of outside forces such as moneylenders, traders, forest contractors and petty Government officials were pointed out and regarded as the most important cause which led to turbulence and turmoil ultimately leading to a series of disturbances and unrest among tribal groups in the article "Saving Tribals from Exploitation". Wide variations in psychological, cultural, social, economic and political backgrounds of the tribal group pose a challenge to planners, administrators, social scientists and other thinkers. The introduction and undue insistence on adoption of improved technology are liable to offend their psychological, cultural and religious susceptibilities.

S.G. Deogaonkar (1994) in his ethnographic profile of selected tribes traces the origin and growth of the efforts for development of tribal population in India apart from examining various approaches to tribal development. It enumerates the administrative structures and organizational strategies adopted during the last many years of planning, the outlay on tribal development during the plans and the priorities adopted have also been indicated. The tribal sub-plan strategy and its implementation have been examined elaborately and an evaluation of the schemes therein has been attempted. Brief ethnographic notes on Gonds, Bhils, Santals and Nagas of representative nature have also been given. Dealing with tribal problems he concluded "Much has been done, but a lot more could have been done, had these hurdles been properly tackled. Planning should be from below and implementation honest, fool-proof and timely".

A.K. Pandey (1997) presents a thought-provoking study, where a correlation to the tendency of Western researchers and conservative scholars has been examined. He tried to find out the problem of underdevelopment, the culture of powerlessness and culture of poverty among tribals *vis-à-vis* the Indian society.

Jnanendra Kumar Rout (1963-64) in his article "Tribal Welfare of Orissa" critically evaluated the tribal population of Odisha and their education, economic upliftment, health, housing and other schemes, Grant-in-Aid and other measures were undertaken for tribal development by giving special emphasis on T.D. Blocks.

In the "Tribals in Transitions", S.N. Tripathy (1999) edited selected contributions from eminent authors relating to various issues and problems of tribals along with policy options. Basing on field data and data from secondary sources, this work portrays the evaluation and analysis of tribal problems and policy recommendation to tackle the problem of backwardness in tribal regions.

P.C. Jain (1999) gives some insight into the Bhils and Minas of Rajasthan. The objective was to find out the benefits derived from different plans by the tribals. Similar studies have been made by S.R. Bakshi and Kiran Bala in 2000 and Basanta Meheta and Prakash Chandra Meheta in 2000 also. They tried to review the overall tribal development on account of the adoption of different protective and development measures by Government and non-governmental agencies during the last century.

In almost all studies, briefly stated above, the scholars tried to locate the tribal problems and suggested certain recommendations. In these studies, it is clear that the Government failed to provide basic minimum needs to the tribals for subsistence. In the first half of the last century, British Government and local rulers who administrated the country were not bothered about their needs and welfare. Another issue pointed out by many scholars is that tribal exploitation stands in the mid-way of their economic progress. Most of the tribals living still in the hills and forests continue to fight for their economic survival and maintain most of their primitive characteristics.

The new Economic Reforms were introduced in the year 1991 through the process of stabilization and structural adjustment, but, how it failed in the tribal context is discussed in "Impact of Economic Reforms on SCs and STs" edited by K.P. Kumaran (2000). This book is an outcome of seminar proceedings and papers. The seminar was organized on *New Economic Reforms and Development of SCs and STs* at the NIRD on 16th and 17th March, 1998. Laxminarayan in his paper "Impact of New Economic Reforms on STs in India" critically evaluated the socio-economic scenario, land reforms and its implications, tribals and forests displacement of tribals, consumption pattern, health and education and tribals and reservation policy and suggested recommendations to safeguard the tribals from the adverse impact of New Economic Reforms.

The book "Two Tribal Friendly Acts and their Implementations" edited by Ota and Patnaik (2009) contain articles by various scholars critically analyzing the two recently implemented policies of the Government , i.e. Implementation of Panchayats' (Extension to Scheduled Areas) Act, 1996 and The Scheduled Tribes and Other Traditional Forest Dwellers (Reorganization of Forest Rights) Act, 2006. The authors opined that if these two Acts are implemented in letter and spirits, they would redress all the core issues of tribal people of the country.

Ota also has edited another book entitled "Development Induced Displacement and the Tribals" (2009). The papers given by various scholars in the book deal with multiple problems faced by displaced persons due to establishment of projects mostly in tribal areas. It has been revealed from the empirical studies that majority of the people displaced because of development projects have invariably failed to restore and regain their former standard of livelihood.

Another scholarly book is edited by Behera and Basar (2010) entitled "Interventions and Tribal Development — Challenges before Tribes in India in the Era of Globalization". The scholars, who contributed to the volume, have critically dealt with various problems relating to socio-economic life of tribals and their development particularly in the field of agriculture, folklores, culture and on impact of globalization.

A very similar type of book has been edited by S.R. Padhi and Biswajita Padhi (2010) entitled "Tribal Development in India — Contemporary Issues and Perspectives". The scholars have contributed articles on economy and tribal development, social issues of tribals, forest and other natural resources, problems of education, health, agriculture, watershed and irrigation etc. with special reference to Koraput region.

There are also some scholarly publications on tribes of Odisha, their socio-economic and cultural life. Similarly, there are studies on specific tribes living in different parts of the state. So far as the Kandhs are concerned, it is believed that the Kandhs came to the notice of the so called civilized society for the practice of human sacrifice (Mariah or locally known as "toki puja"), one can get some historical information about the district of Koraput and about its indigenous inhabitants from D.F. Caramichaels' manual of the Vizagapattam District published in 1869. This socio-religious practice of human sacrifice was supposed to be prevalent among the Kandhs in order to satisfy the supernatural power mainly the Mother Earth for good harvest, particularly of turmeric.

The *Vizagapattam District Gazetteers* by Francis (1907) also covered the profile of Koraput and its inhabitants including the Kandhs. It may be mentioned here that the undivided Koraput region was a part of Vishakhapatnam district in the past. The two District Gazetteers available on Koraput are by Bell (1945) and Senapati and Sahu (1966). In these Gazetteers, they deal with location, population, cultural practices, geology, forests, lands, minerals, communications etc. They also gave a note on the socio-economic practices of its inhabitants, particularly that of the tribals.

The British officials like Macpherson and Campbell came to know about this community as early as the middle of 19th century when they were deputed to the Kandh country for the suppression of human sacrifice that was alleged to be prevalent. The accounts given by these officers serve as valuable source of information regarding the culture of Kandhs. Elwin was the first anthropologist in the country to give a systematic impression about the tribe in the year 1943. Niggemeyer had published detailed ethnographic account of the Kutia Kandhs in the year 1964, but it was written in German language, many scholars cannot have access to it.

As far as the origin of the term Kandh is concerned, Macpherson (see his report of 1838 and 1842) prefers to connect the term with the Tamil word "Kondhs" meaning thereby the inhabitants of the hills. Dalton (1872) holds a similar view. But Risley (1891) does not agree to it. "Thus, the origin of the name Kondha still remains obscure" (Patnaik, 1986:2-3).

Therefore, origin of the term "Kandh" is obscure. The most likely suggestion which is widely accepted is the one that is put forward by Captain Macpherson in his original report (C.R. 1846-A, p. 25), submitted to the British Government in 1842, where the word "Kondh" is used to identify the tribal group.

L.N. Sahu (1942) gave some useful information about the economic life of Koraput tribals. Their economy which is mainly dependent upon shifting cultivation is unable to support the tribal families. Only 4 to 5 months they got food from such cultivation and rest of years the tribals had to live on fruits, roots, leaves, tubers and seeds, he stated.

Kiran Bala Devi (1964) in her article "Kondh" laid emphasis on the derivation of the word "Kandh" from the Telugu word "Konda" meaning a hill as stated earlier by Macpherson. Their demography, nature, language, social organizations, individual life cycle, important festivals, material culture and economy etc. were discussed briefly basing on the 1961 census reports. Their economic pursuits, consumption pattern, production pattern, indebtedness and exploitation by the Panos (Harijans) in the course of providing loans, purchasing and selling of their agricultural products were dealt in the study. She expected that due to special protective and developmental measures undertaken by the government, the Kandhs would very soon improve their standard of living.

U.N. Patnaik (1964-65) took a case study of Baliguda taluk of Phulbani District and discussed the life cycles of Kandhs. The author laid emphasis on tribal education, its model curriculum and pointed out that *adivasi* students should know their cult first before they are made to improve on it. He made a request to all orthodox educationists to ponder over the problem of education and child psychology. Problem of teachers mainly belonging to non-tribal communities and that of Panos have been discussed by the scholar. Origin of obscure term "Kandh" has also drawn the attention of the author including their marriage practices and trial by ordeal for resolution of disputes among the tribals.

In another study, U.N. Patnaik (1984) shows his findings through the eyes of an administrative officer in the Kandh Hills in the early forties. He throws light on their village pattern, drainage system, layout of a village, house, food & food habits, drinking habit and covered almost all aspects of the economic life of the Kui Kandhs of Phulbani District and their practice of Dalli hunt was presented.

Patnaik (1970) in his study entitled "Religious Ceremonies, and Ordeals of the Kandh", has stated about a legend about Oriya infiltration in Kandh Hills. Kandhs' beliefs, rituals, their drinking habits, prevalence of Mutha Panchayat in Kandh villages of Baliguda area of Kandhmal District and the ordeals undertaken to punish the culprit were discussed in his writings. They have their own world with their own, political, social and economic systems, he says.

Neville A. Watts (1970), in his book "The Half Clad Tribes of Eastern India", had given a clear picture of the socio-economic life of Dongaria Kandhs living in the Niyamgiri hills of Bisam Cuttack.

The Harijan and Tribal Research Centre of Orissa has made a number of studies on various aspects of the tribals of the state. One of such studies was on "Gotti" system (Bonded Labour System) in Koraput District (1966-67) mainly in Laxmipur, Narayanpatna, Kakiriguma, Semiliguda and Pottangi areas of the district.

Rout's (1963-64) study on "Dom" exploitation in Tribal Kandh Villages in Koraput District, mainly in Kumbhikota and Laxmipur areas focuses on the extent of exploitation by "doms".

Behuria's Final Report on the major settlement operations in Koraput District (1965) deals, along with settlement reports, the tribal communities and their economies in the region. In this survey and settlement operations of Koraput District, he stated, the lands were classified as cultivated land and uncultivated land. The cultivated lands further were classified under four categories, *viz.*, paddy land, dongar land, river-side lands and land growing vegetables as *bari* (garden) land. Uncultivated lands were classified as cultivatable waste land and uncultivatable waste land. As such lands and their possession provides highest social and exchange values to the tribals.

N. Patnaik, F. Bara and A. Mall (1986) in their work "Herbal Medicines of Dongrias" showed the access of tribals into the nature. They stated that the herbal medicines used by the tribals sometimes excelled the advanced medical science. However, they concluded that with the introduction of modern allopathic medicines, the importance of some of the herbal medicines is decreasing.

P.C. Mahapatro (1980) in his doctoral Dissertation which has been published under the title of "Economic Development of Tribal India" gave a detailed description of the tribal economy in general and that of the tribals of Koraput district in particular. He adopted multi-staged random sampling method and took 373 sample households from 17 villages of three different blocks of Koraput District. He gave emphasis to developmental aspects of the area and the people at regional level. His regional approach to spatial dimensions of tribal development based on secondary data collected from different agencies of Government is noteworthy.

Jagabandhu Samal's (1992) research study was based on ecology based economic study of the tribals of Koraput origin. It was a micro-level analysis of 365 days of engagement of the tribal households (1983-84) living under three different ecological situations; tribals living on the hills with some forest cover, tribals living on hills denuded of forests and tribals living in the plateaus and plains and adopting settled agriculture. His study made a detailed analysis of the agricultural and non-agricultural pursuits of the tribals. The relative efficiency and productivity of various activities, the level of income and poverty and also seasonality of their operations were also discussed by him.

The book "Tribes of Orissa" (2004), published by SC and ST Research and Training Institute, Bhubaneswar, Government of Orissa, contains ethnographic account of different tribal communities of Orissa. Various scholars who contributed articles in this volume dealt with tribal traditions, customs, social and cultural institutions of various individual tribes living in Orissa.

In the book referred to above P.S. Daspatnaik contributed on the distinctiveness of "Kondha" tribes and tried to give a bird's eye view on their language, social organization and rituals and festivals and also their dress pattern, adornments and art and craft. He pointed out that there are two linguistic groups, 'Kui' and 'Kuvi'. The Kuttia Kandha inhabited in the area of Kandhmal district speak the 'Kui'. But the people living in Koraput and Rayagada district identify themselves as "Kuvis". The 'Dongaria' Kandhs also identify themselves as 'Kuvis' and speak "Kuvi Hada".

In the said volume "Tribes of Orissa", B.B. Mohanty in his article "Tribal Culture in Orissa", and K. Mahapatro in his article "Tribal Languages of Orissa" gave importance on their culture and language. Mahapatro gave emphasis on the necessity of tribal language survey to minimize the confusion over the status of language and reduce the demo-linguistic complexities and the long array of languages to manageable sub-groups. Once the languages are clearly identified and properly classified into cognate groups, due attention can be given for their study, preservation and promotion at administrative, academic and socio-cultural spheres.

The book "The Kondh" edited by N. Patnaik (1989) deals with socio-economic characteristics and cultural profile of the Kandhs. This is a presentation of ethnographic and development accounts of Kandh tribe. The author shows the distinct characteristics of Kandhs in their language and culture, religion and society, occupation and mode of life and habits and customs. The cultural relativism of Kandhs is directed by their cultural background and geographical conditions. This book deals in detail about the habitat, economic and material existence, health, nutrition, social life, beliefs, political organization, aesthetic life and the development and change of the Kandhs. Exploitations in the form of debt, trade and middlemenship by the Panos, Dombs and non-tribals in Kandh areas were analyzed. Infrastructural development and employment generation are the prime concern for their development, he concluded. He says that the Kandhs are in transitional phase. Acceptance to change is very remarkable but slow for various reasons.

The book "Economic History of Orissa" edited by Nihar Ranjan Patnaik (1997) in a similar fashion dealt with various aspects of tribal life of Orissa. In the chapter "Economic Life of the Tribals of Orissa", emphasis has been given on their economic pursuits. Agriculture stood as the main stay of the tribals. Their methods of shifting cultivation and cropping pattern were discussed. Trade and commerce, cottage industry, taxation system, communication and their related problems were also discussed. He also gave a deep insight into their economic exploitation, their nature, kinds and dealt with some of the causes and agencies of exploitation. He concluded in a similar fashion that they (i.e. the tribals) began to prosper, though in very slow and small degrees.

Proceeding of a seminar edited in a book-form by P.M. Mahapatra and P.C. Mahapatro (1997) under the title of "Forest Management in Tribal Areas" mainly deals with the problem of inseparability of tribals from forest. The paper writers gave emphasis on relation between forests and tribals, forest policy and tribal development in general and the forest problems faced by the Koraput tribals in particular.

Mahapatro and Samal (1999) in their book "Adibasi-Reeti, Neeti O Arthaniti" (Odia) have dealt with various aspects of tribal life and economy in general and that of Koraput tribals in particular. They have dealt with the tribal problems relating to shifting cultivation, forests, economic pursuits, industrialization, indebtedness, weekly markets, role of tribal women in economic pursuits and tribal development schemes etc.

Behera (2000) conducted a research study on the marketing habits of the tribals and the role of weekly markets in the tribal areas of Koraput. It was found that almost all the marketing activities of the tribals were carried on in the weekly hats only. The tribals are often cheated in these markets by the foul play of middlemen in weights and measurement. Due to their ignorance about the prevailing market prices and metric system of measurement etc., they are exploited.

To conclude, several studies thus have been made by different scholars out of whom some were anthropological in nature and conducted by Eastern and Indian anthropologists and some by the tribal research centres in India. They studied on the tribes inhabiting their respective areas, their demography, economic, educational and hygienic condition etc. Manifold tribal problems are reflected sympathetically and appreciations made for the development programmes. Various recommendations and suggestions were made from time to time. But the tribal problems remain unsolved and rather, still persist. Most of the authors cited exploitation as one of the cause of their poverty and misery. It is assumed that there exists cause and effect relationship between exploitation and poverty. Some of the studies dealing exclusively on poverty and exploitation have been reviewed in following paragraphs.

SECTION – II

2.2 Poverty: A General Review

A brief analysis of the poverty related literature with special reference to tribal and rural poverty in rural India/Odisha has been made in the following paragraphs.

Poverty in India (1971) by V.M. Dandekar and Nilakanth Rath was perhaps the first systematic work in the country to conceptualize poverty. They dealt with the problems of poverty in India with particular reference to rural India. In their view low income, unequal distribution of resources and slow pace of development are the great threats to rural India. They attributed rural poverty to mainly landlessness and small and marginal landholders. So, rural poor consists predominantly of agricultural labour households and small landholders. The urban poor are only an overflow of rural poor into the urban area.

Authors criticized the process of development during the past decade which benefited only the middle, upper middle and the richer sections much more than the middle, the lower middle and the poorer sections. They maintained that the Planning Commission's perspective for the coming decade was out of line and could not abolish poverty. Even a high growth, beyond the range of feasibility, could not lift the bottom of the society. They warned that high growth rate would not be a substitute for deliberate policies to ensure equitable distribution of the gains of development.

They suggested three crucial areas in the policy matters. These were redistribution of land, adoption of labour intensive technology and guaranteeing the right to gainful employment.

> "There is little doubt that the poor in the country have been grossly neglected in the past and that the economic development during the past two decades has been taken a wrong course. A mid-course correction is urgently needed" (Dandekar and Rath, 1971: 144).

The scholars rightly pointed out the pitfalls of the then poverty alleviation programmes and suggested certain measures which could reduce rural poverty.

Similarly, Rath (1985) in his article "Garibi Hatao — Can IRDP do it" opined that "the problem of rural poverty is old and massive" and the efforts of Government through giving cattle and assets too has yielded little. He cautions and argues that subsidy lies at the centre of attraction of the IRDP. He observed how the Government programmes were based on statistics by showing the example that 5 million cattle were given during the plan period (Fifth Plan), spread over all the 5000 blocks in the country. He questioned and proved that such huge amount of high breed buffaloes and cross-breed cows were not available to purchase in India. So, the target had been achieved by buying anything that was available. Such a purchase resulted in, without any doubt, wastage and corruption. Everyone involved in it gained from it; the seller through high-price for non-descript cattle and all others including the beneficiary, from subsidy, insurance and even the loan underpaid. Similarly, he questioned the foresight of the planners. Rath pointed to non-availability of raw-materials, infrastructure, and markets as most important drawbacks of the scheme. His conclusion was that the poor wanted income, but not land, animals etc.

The critical role of employment creation was also emphasized by Dr. Rath. He suggested for greater income and employment opportunity to the bulk of the poor to enable them to rise above poverty, at least, at the basic subsistence wage rate. He showed his dissatisfaction to design a programme which gave secondary place for wage employment during the period of seasonal unemployment like NREP during the Sixth Plan.

Amartya Sen's "On Economic Inequality" (1973) mainly focuses on economic inequality and its measurement. This book makes a systematic treatment of the conceptual framework as well as the practical problems of measurement of inequality. He suggested to express technical measurement of inequality in purely non-technical terms to make this effort simpler and make usable by general economists and layman. In the second part of the book, the author discuses inequality with reference to India. Sen has provided a mixture of descriptive and normative analysis regarding concept of inequality.

Sen (1981), in his book "Poverty and Famine: An Essay on Entitlement and Deprivation" mainly emphasizes on the cause of starvation in general and famines in particular. He has given a brief account of the concept and approaches to poverty and its measurement. He had illustrated some of the case studies of famine and poverty situations from different parts of the world: the Great Bengal Famine of

(1943) and the Ethiopia famines of 1973-75, famine in the Sahel regions of Africa during early 1970s and the Bangladesh famines of 1974.

Abdul Azis's (1983), work "The Rural Poor: Problems and Prospects" examines the need for and possibility of organizing the rural poor and also outlines the manner in which they should be organized. He identified their socio-economic problems and evaluated their existing practices and suggested for a single organization to work for all sections of rural poor. The strategies and methods of organizations are outlined in details. He also categorically differentiated the rural poor from the urban poor.

Jaganath Pathy in his work *Underdevelopment and Destitution: Essays in Orissan Society* (1988), has given a historical analysis of the nature of underdevelopment and deprivation in Odisha. In the later part of the book, he analyses the production relations that exist in tribal and rural villages of Odisha. He examines the political economy of Kandh tribe by focusing on their inner working on existing mode of production relations. Political economy of tribals during pre-colonial period, colonial period and present day were discussed. The present economic life of the Kandhs have been analyzed on the basis of information collected from two Kandh villages. He concludes that Kandh is a class community, where limited feudal and semi-feudal relations dominate the economy. He suggests creating awareness among the tribals about their rights and responsibilities otherwise progressive legislations enacted for them cannot work properly in tribal areas.

The book "Poverty, Unemployment and Rural Development", edited by Baidyanath Mishra (1991) is a similar kind of study where concept of poverty, extent of poverty and unemployment in Odisha have been critically analyzed. Papers included in the volume make an assessment of anti-poverty programmes, point out bottlenecks and suggest remedial measures to make the programmes of rural development more viable. This study also shows contradictions in the strategy of development and suggests how rural development can be all embracing to improve the well-being of rural poor and bring about integration between rural and urban areas.

K.N. Prasad (1991), while dealing with rural poverty and inequality focuses on the meaning, concept, approaches to rural poverty and on specific regions in various states in which rural poor are concentrated and also among various occupational groups. Among the rural poor, he emphasized, the members of tribal groups were not properly streamlined in the production process. The ranks of rural poor are manned substantially by the people of low caste or ultra-caste tribal groups, who are discriminated against in a numerous ways in rural society. The major weakness of Indian agriculture, however, happens to be the main focus of this work.

"National Development and Tribal Deprivation", edited by Walter Fernandes (1992), envisages the fact that four decades of planning era only transferred the resources from traditional communities to corporate sectors. The tribals living in the resource rich regions are worst affected. He has asserted that the tribal traditions have kept a balance between environment and human needs and analyzed the factors responsible for marginalization and possible solutions to it. His study is an important contribution on the present state of the tribals who have been deprived of their livelihood due to so-called national development programmes. Several paper writers in the book have concluded that the tribals have been induced to be integrated into the mainstream but as subordinates. Displacement of tribals without proper compensation, ongoing forest policies and its negative implication on tribal rights and colonization by non-tribals were critically analyzed.

G.K. Srichandan, in his book *Tribal Development and Welfare Legislation in Orissa* (1998), makes an attempt to show the gradual evolution of welfare policies and schemes in Odisah for the upliftment of tribal communities. He analyzed different legislative measures undertaken by the Government on education, employment, land etc. He also made an attempt to focus on different income generating schemes for the socio-economic development of STs in Odisha. The author has suggested certain measures for the meaningful implementation of welfare programmes meant for the tribals in Odisha.

To tackle the problem of poverty in rural areas, various policy-mixes are being tried out, yet the problems seem nowhere near solution. One of the problems points to the absence of clear and concrete knowledge of structural parameters of rural life. In view of this, B.C. Meheta (1993) adopted a structural approach in his study, prepared structural profiles of the regions as a supplementary study and developed appropriate measures of poverty. In most of the studies, poverty is measured based on a unidimensional measure of nutritional inadequacy. His study deviated from other studies and captured other aspects of poverty like income insufficiency, resource deprivation and low quality of life etc. Like this seventeen poverty indicators were used by him. Poverty profiles of 64 regions were prepared on the basis of these indicators. An attempt was made to understand these poverty situations with the help of structural (agrarian), geophysical and policy variables, multivariate regression method is also used as the tool of analysis, for preparing a typology of poverty and its correlates using cluster analysis. His work is an exercise to understand the processes which generate poverty in all its dimensions like geophysical, demographic, historical and structural. The study also focuses on the substantial differences in the level and nature of poverty between states/regions.

This study recommended that the policies for poverty alleviation needed be regionally differentiated, mainly in the 13 poverty clusters which were classified in his study. He concluded that the poor are not only economically deprived but also politically isolated and unorganized and hence, along with the structural changes, institutional agencies for the poor should be strengthened with urgent land reform measures.

Gail Omvedt, in her article "Worst in a Hundred Years: The Kalahándi Drought" (1996) analyzed the causes of poverty and the sources of livelihood of the poorer people of Kalahandi district. In her study she shows that these poor people mainly depend on forest collection like *kendu* leaves, *sal*, bamboo and other minor forest produces. The author also explains the aftermath of 1965 drought, how the poverty ridden *Adivasi* started migrating to Raipur in search of work. She explained how the tribal people of Kalahandi were even exploited during such situation. People suffered from food insecurity, starvation and in some instances, people lost their lives. Finally, the author suggested that in addition to income and employment generating measures there should be adequate empowerment of the people to save them from poverty.

P. Sainth's "Everybody Loves a Good Drought: Stories from Indian Poorest Districts" (1996), is a well organized work related to poverty and hunger victim people of Bihar, Tamil Nadu, Madhya Pradesh and Odisha. The author has highlighted some of the poorest districts in southern parts of Odisha. He has highlighted the poverty scenario of Malkangiri, Koraput, Kalahandi, Bolangir and Nuapada Districts.

The poverty estimates have generated considerable debate in the official and academic circles. The estimates of poverty, occasionally conflicting, have raised serious questions in regard to adequacy and reliability of the database and also appropriateness of the traditional indicators, *viz*. per capita consumption expenditure (PCE) and per capita/household income in identifying the poor and thus measurement of poverty levels. K. Hanumantha Rao and S. Balakrishna (1998) edited the papers of the workshop on "Database on Rural Poverty Indicators" held at the National Institute of Rural Development, Hyderabad during April 17-19, 1996, with the objectives to identify suitable indicators of rural poverty and to discuss the available database for the above indicators.

Arjan de Haan and Sakti Padhi in their article "Monitoring of Poverty in Orissa" (2003) described poverty as a multidimensional phenomenon. They suggested the need of reliable measures that allow for comparisons across regions and over time to tackle the situation. Strengthening monitoring mechanism would also work in favour of decentralized planning. So, a two-day brainstorming workshop on methodological and empirical aspects like instruments, agencies and problems of monitoring was organized by the Naba Krishna Choudhury Centre for Development Studies, Bhubaneswar during February 26-27, 2003. In household survey: Income Poverty Method of Measurement was suggested to be monitored from various angles. This article also guides how to measure livelihoods.

In another article, K. Sundaram and Suresh D. Tendulkar (2003), examined the levels and changes in poverty indicators of the rural and urban population in India. This analysis is based on the comparable estimates of poverty for the mixed reference period computed from the unit record data for the 50th (1993-94) and 55th (1999-2000) rounds of the Consumer Expenditure Surveys conducted by National Sample Survey Organization. In terms of changes in poverty in the 1990s, it is found that while SCs, agricultural labour (rural) and casual labour (urban) households experienced decline in poverty on par with the total population, Scheduled Tribe households fared badly in both the segments. So, the study highlighted inter-group disparities in poverty and disparity-adjusted measures of poverty.

In the seminar paper presented at CPRC-IIPA Seminar on "Chronic Poverty: Emerging Policy Options and Issues" held during 29-30, September, 2005 at Indian Institute of Public Administration, New Delhi by Sakti Padhi, Nilakantha Panigrahi, Aswini Kumar Mishra, on the topic "Tribal Population and Chronic Poverty in Orissa: The North-South Divide", made a comparative analysis of tribal poverty in north and southern Odisha. The NSSO has divided the state into three agro-climatic zones, *viz*. North, South and Coastal plains. They tried to find out the causes of disparities among different regions and communities. Therefore, they suggested for providing priorities in southern (Eastern Ghats) mainly in Kalahandi, Kandhmal and Koraput regions. They focused on the priority areas of policy intervention as a whole.

Bajpai, Bhandari and Sinha (2005) in their book "Social and Economic Profile of India", provided a first point reference on socio-economic condition of India. It is based on census report of 2001, surveys conducted by N.S.S.O., various Government sources and other literatures based on socio-economic condition. This is mainly a statistical reference on the heterogeneity of India. For example, the book pointed out that Koraput District in Odisha is among one of the poorest in India. However, there are large intra-state variations. In U.P. for instance, poverty incidence ranges from 1 (one) per cent in Ghaziabad to over 61 per cent in Rai Bareli District.

Santosh Mehrotra and Enrique Delomonica (2007) in their book "Eliminating Human Poverty" focused on the provisions of basic social services like access to education, health and water supplies as the central point of any development strategy. The author concentrated on how these basic social services can be financed and delivered more effectively to achieve the internationally agreed Millennium Development Goals. The study is mainly based on the results of UNICEF and the UNDP, findings and investigating the records on basic social services of some thirty developing countries. They suggested measures to expand human capabilities and to fulfil human rights. The combination of governance reforms and fiscal and macroeconomic policies outlined in this book can eliminate human poverty in the span of a generation.

Ruddar Datt and K.P.M. Sundharam's (2009) 60th fully Revised Edition of the book "Indian Economy" is the most valuable contribution which presents a comprehensive survey of the Indian Economy in terms of GDP Growth, saving and investment with allocation of growth to various sectors. The failure and success aspects of different plan periods have been analyzed. The promises of Globalization, Privatization and Liberalization were critically examined. Human development in India and current challenges like poverty and unemployment in rural areas have been discussed. The study of poverty in general, its concept, studies of poverty in India, its estimation and relevant comparisons were discussed in a lucid manner. The suggestions made by eminent authors on poverty alleviation were discussed.

"Report of the Expert Group to Review the Methodology for Estimation of Poverty" (2009) provides official estimates of poverty released by the Planning Commission of India. The expert group under the chairmanship of Professor Suresh Tendulkar has suggested new methodology to arrive at state-wise and all India rural and urban poverty lines for 2004-05.

In the present study, the researcher has accepted the new methodologies adopted by the expert group.

SECTION – III

2.3 Tribal Exploitation — A General Review

It is quite interesting to note that there have been considerable amount of writings on tribal problems and their social and economic life in recent years. Many a scholars discussed these problems from different angles. Presently, brief review of available literature on tribal exploitation is made in this section. However, while dealing with tribal exploitation special references have been made on Koraput tribes in general and that of the Kandhs of Koraput District in particular.

One would find vivid description of exploitation of tribals in Ganjam and Koraput districts by the Scheduled Caste Doms, Patro landlords, Kumuti businessmen and Sundhi wine vendors and also officials of the Forest Department in the epoch making writings of Elwin (1943, 1950, 1958, 1964 and 1965). The scholar while writing on tribal situations in the country has expressed concern over the exploitation of tribals in the hands of the socio-economically dominant groups, mainly the non-tribals.

The maxim that literature reflects society is true when novels have depicted the poverty, exploitation and tradition of tribals. Though they are not scientific studies, they are not unreliable as far as they reconstruct the tribal life of the time. In this context, Gopinath Mohanty's two novels are noteworthy who had spent long time among the tribals.

In his novel "Paraja" (1946), Gopinath Mohanty tried to show the naked pictures of tribal exploitation. The protagonist of the novel, Sukuru Jani, represents the tribal community — in fact, all the tribes to whom the mountains and forests historically belonged to. The problems of tribal exploitation by moneylenders, land alienations, sexual harassment, judiciary matters, dom exploitation and consequent bonded labour (Goti), in fact, almost all types of tribal exploitation were described by the author in his novel. Though the narrations and events in the novel go back to the forties of the last century, still tribal exploitation of such kinds more or less, persists even today.

Another classic entitled "Amrutra Santan" (1949) by the same novelist depicts the lifestyle, and agricultural practices of the Kandhs and adjustment of Kandh tribals to their natural surroundings, rituals, marriage practices, blind beliefs, taboos of the tribals of Koraput region. Exploitation by Forest Department Officials and other government officials, social-exploitation by their own clan members and the like, were also narrated elaborately by the author.

Shrivastava (1968), in the book "Exploitation in Tribal Areas", briefly highlighted various types of exploitation of the tribals. He discussed the issue with regard to various agencies of exploitation coming from different socio-economic strata. The helplessness of the tribals, despite legislative measures to protect them has been discussed by the scholar. The scholar observed that the British Policy of keeping the tribal people in isolation and treating the tribal areas as separate entity outside the purview of normal administration did more harm to the tribal than good. It resulted in their exploitation in the hands of land lords, moneylenders, traders, contractors and unscrupulous people. Their poverty pushed them into the debt trap and which ultimately lead to exploitation. He estimated that the percentage of indebted tribal families in various states ranged between 43 and 77. The author stated that the consequences of indebtedness were mostly land alienation and bonded labour. Though there are legislations to save the tribals from exploitation, but the exploiters succeeded in manipulating the regulations due to certain loopholes in them.

L.M. Shrikant, while writing the "Foreword" of B.N. Shrivastava's book commented:

> "Let us hope that the active social workers in the field of tribal welfare will study this booklet and may be able to find out some remedies for removing this blood-sucking germ nullifying all the good efforts of the various welfare workers of different agencies in the field of tribal welfare".

Raghaviah (1971) in his book "Tribal Revolts" narrates the protests of the tribal people of India against the exploitative non-tribals over a period of one hundred and ninety three years. Most of the revolts broke out in the states of Bihar, Assam, M.P. and A.P. He remarked that though Indian Government tried to provide them education, freedom, sanitation, medical care and adult franchise etc., but it failed to stop effectively economic and political exploitations. It has failed to restore their lost land, put a stop to the calculated cruelties of Mahajans, the Sahukars, the greedy moneylenders, landlords and the petty Muttadars etc.

In the "Preface" he says "the tribals ask for bare justice and nothing more. Whether we compensate him for past neglect or not, we are bound to redress his grievances with sympathy and understanding that are due to him".

Haimendorf (1982) studied the tribal economy of India during his extensive tours and through personal observations. The scholar was particularly concerned with tribal exploitation in the hands of outside agencies. The non-tribal moneylenders, traders and liquor vendors from the plain entered the tribal pockets, made tribals easy prey of indebtedness and finally grabbed their land on the plea of non-payment of loan amount. He estimated that the percentage of tribal cultivators declined from 68 to 57 between 1961 and 1971 and the percentage of agricultural labourers increased from 23 to 33 during the same period in Adilabad district of Andhra Pradesh. Due to exploitation by various agencies, the poverty status of the tribals either remained unchanged or still deteriorated.

Siba Prasad Rout's (1964-65) "Dom Exploitation in Tribal Areas" is a notable contribution on the subject. He through field study and personal observation explained the extent of exploitation of tribal Kandhs in Laxmipur area of Koraput district, particularly in the hands of Scheduled Caste "Doms".

G. Prakash Reddy (1987) described how the tribal communities were passing through a critical phase resulting in unrest and discontentment. Tribals in general and that of the tribals of Andhra Pradesh in particular, were inclined towards extremism forces with a belief that their age-old grievances and sufferings might be mitigated. He has dealt with the precarious economic life of tribals of Adilabad district (AP) immigration of non-tribals into tribal pockets and its socio-economic impacts, problems of indebtedness and land alienation and the role played by the extreme elements in mobilizing the tribals to join them. He concluded "there is no use of blaming the extremist groups, that they are unscrupulous and misleading the innocent tribals. One has to blame the Government for providing opportunity to these elements to increase their influence among the tribal communities of the area by failing again and again to understand the basic problems of the tribals and gearing up the machinery to solve them".

S.G. Deogaonkar (1990) in the book "Tribal Exploitation" made his study on victimology. It is rather a new origin which has got momentum in countries like USA and Europe during the last 50 years. The study is based on criminal-victim relationship. It also deals with the social and economic status of the victims and the aspects of compensation. This book is a study based on the Gond-madia Tribe. The study deals with the tribal victims of crime and their consequences.

N.K. Vaid (2004) reviewed the whole developmental process in the country basing on the Report of the VIII Plan Working Group for STs, the Annual Reports (1991-92) of the Ministry of Welfare and the 29th Report of the Commissioner for SCs and STs etc. Most of the Planners and administrations reacted and called the study as "biased", "Lop Sided", "One Sided" etc., but none has the guts to denounce inference drawn by the author. He made a vivid description of state's failure in the field of tribal development on all counts. Official claims regarding tribal development had been mostly proved faulty by another. He used harsh words like "tribal development — my foot" and he criticized the Government laws, forest policies and explained how it adversely affected the tribals. The cause and effect relationship between poverty and exploitation among the tribal have been critically examined. He suggested to shift development policies statistical account to the one suggested by Pt. Nehru in his Tribal Panchasheel. One of the most important suggestions made by him, may be difficult, but not impossible, is that tribals who have attained the requisite limits of development must be strictly debarred from availing assistance any further so that the limited resources could reach the real target groups.

He suggested that the priorities must be reidentified, policies reoriented and programmes redesigned, to meet with the actual needs of the tribals. This needs more sympathy and sincere efforts on the parts of the Government and the implementing agencies. He states:

> "When we talk about as sensitive an issue as tribal development, the questions that automatically comes; whose desire — those of planners, of implementers or of tribal themselves. The questions become more relevant when we realize in the name of 'Tribal development' others have tried and have imposed their will on tribals".

"Bonded Labour System in India" (1995) is a study by Y.R.H. Reddy in the state of Andhra Pradesh. The study identifies the existence and incidence of bondage and reveals the causes behind the origin of this system in the state of Andhra Pradesh. Prevalence of "Goti" in the district of Koraput has also been identified by Mahapatro (1980). It has been extensively dealt with in the "Report in Goti System in Koraput

District" (1996). It may be stated here that "Goti" (bonded labour) is the most exploited person in the sphere of tribal exploitation.

Joe Madiath and Deborah Nelson (2009) in their article (Posted in the Internet) as "Dignity, Not Charity — Empowering Tribal Communities" critically evaluated Government works. The study is mainly based on survey of Madanguda village of Kalahandi district of Orissa, a region commonly referred to as "Poverty Basket of India". They state that tribals are victimized by the very institutions which are supposed to help them to improve the quality of their lives. They criticize the ongoing forest policy and cited how the benefits of tribal development go to the unscrupulous exploiters from the majority culture. There are people who "skim the icing" from the development cake and the uneducated and uniformed tribal people are helplessness to stop them. They suggest for rigorous re-examination of the current policies of development. The Government should be an ennobling institution and should create the conditions for dignity and not charity, they concluded.

Surendra Nath Dash (2001) produced a doctoral thesis on "A study of the Problem of Land Alienation in Tribal Areas — with special references to the District Koraput". His findings show that transfer of land to others is taking place in a number of ways, *viz.* transfer of land in accordance with law, acquisition of land to capital projects, acquisition for secondary and tertiary activities, illegal transfer by fraud or forceful occupation and encroachment. The study was undertaken to examine the nature and extent of land alienation and factors responsible for it. He also examined different legal, administrative and other measures taken by Government to check the incidence of land alienation. The scholar adopted purposive stratified sampling method in selecting the blocks, N.A.C. and villages of Koraput District to undertake the study.

Mr. Dash made his study on a sample of 128 land alienated families which had 1629.19 acres of land by 1990; but, within a period of 5 years, i.e. 1994, it came down 1405.56 through land alienation. It means 13.72 per cent of landholdings were alienated during the said period. Only 53.13 per cent of lands were alienated legally and the rest were alienated either through mortgage or transferred orally or encroached. The causes of such alienation were mainly due to expenditure on marriages of members of the households, repayment of old debts and purchase of plough and bullock etc. The author suggested adopting appropriate legal and administrative measures to check the incidence of land alienation in tribal areas. He also suggested that the government should adopt a more cautious policy in this regard. The poverty alleviation progress and other developmental policies for employment generation should be effectively and honesty implemented otherwise discontentment among the tribals may lead to explosive consequences, he suggested.

From the review of available literature made above, it is enough to conclude that the authors more or less, opined that the tribals even today are living in misery and poverty. Tribals are often exploited by various agencies with the passage of time, the nature, type and agencies of exploitation are also changing. Tribal exploitation seems to be both the cause and effect of their poverty and misery. The tribals are still living away from mainstream of development. Even these comments of the Commissioner for SCs and STs are more shocking. It reads:

> "What should one say about a system in which the constitution itself bestowed on the President and the Governors unlimited powers for protection and welfare of the tribal people, yet they have not been able to save the people, from exploitation and oppression of their own servants and this historic task has been accomplished only by the Naxalites in some areas".

The literatures reviewed clearly indicate the magnitude and nature of poverty and exploitation among the tribes in their process of integration with national development agenda. It also justifies the study of Kandhs to examine the trend of poverty and extent of exploitation as prevails during first decade of 21st century.

3

TRIBE, POVERTY AND EXPLOITATION: A CONCEPTUAL ANALYSIS

3.0 Introduction

It is axiomatic that tribal people in India epitomize social and economic backwardness. They are poverty ridden. A crude estimate would place about 90 per cent of them living below the poverty line. Similarly, they are educationally backward. Illiteracy, ignorance, subsistence mode of living by using simple technology, and above all their credulous nature expose them to their exploitation in the hands of non-tribal money-lenders, traders, intermediaries and even by some of their own community members who are socio-economically and/or politically powerful (see Anuradha and Dash, 2019). It has been alleged that the tribals, very often, are exploited by various government agencies; and by virtue of their link with the power corridor in the process of national development (See Behera, 2018; Padel and Das, 2010; Behera and Basar, 2014; and Pati, 2011). Hence, their poverty and resultant indebtedness, leading subsequently to exploitation, have become great concern for planners and policy-makers. Therefore, it is not a surprise to find right from the beginning of the First Five Year Plan that policies are adopted and strategies formulated to eradicate poverty and associated maladies. Broadly, the policies, programmes, and schemes directed towards eradication of poverty and elimination of exploitation have two interrelated objectives. These are:

(a) to raise the socio-economic status of the tribals; and
(b) to save them from exploitation of various types.

Before going to deal with the problems of exploitation of the tribals in general and that of Kandhs of Koraput district in particular, it is in fitness of things to throw light on the terms of *tribe*, *poverty* and *exploitation* which conceptualize the thematic frame of discussion in this investigation. Keeping this in view, the present chapter is divided into three sections. Section-I deals with definition of Tribes, Geographical distribution of tribes in India and Odisha in general and of Koraput district in particular. Section-II deals with Poverty, its concept and meaning, the poverty line, measurement of poverty, approaches to poverty and poverty among the tribals in India. Section-III deals with Exploitation, its concept and meaning, theories of exploitation, and tribal exploitation in India.

SECTION – I

3.1 The Tribe

3.1.1 *Definition of Tribe*

In common parlance, in the context of India, tribes are usually taken to be highlanders or the dwellers of hills and forests. This notion, however, is not adequate to understand the tribes properly. Moreover, this type of approach is rather offensive one, as it implies that the tribes are nothing but hill people or jungle men. In this context we can take up the dictionary meaning of tribe. Chambers Twentieth Century Dictionary *inter alia* defines a tribe "as an aggregate of stocks — a stock being an aggregate of persons considered to be kindred — or an aggregate of families, forming a community usually under the government of a chief". The underlying idea behind this definition is that a tribe is an isolated small group dependent mainly on itself in the matters of economic and non-economic facets of its activities.

The Dictionary of Anthropology mentions tribe, as a social group usually with a definite area, dialect, cultural homogeneity and unifying social organization. A tribe ordinarily has a leader and has a common ancestor as well as patron deity. The families of small communities making up the tribe are linked through economic, social, religious, families or blood ties (see Bhowmik, 1971). It is often very difficult to define the tribal population in terms of any single set of formal criteria because of the variation of the cultural and social values from one tribe to another.

The term "tribe" has been derived from English term "TRIBUZ" which has a Latin root. The term means three divisions into which the early Romans were grouped. The meaning of the term thus varies from nation to nation. The Romans conceived the term as a political division, while the Greeks seemed to have equated the term with fraternities and in Irish History, the term means families of communities having the same surname (Roy, 1972).

Etymologically, the term refers to a group of 'primitive' or 'barbarous' clans under recognized chiefs (*Oxford Encyclopedic Dictionary*, Vol. 3, 1983). The western scholars used the said concept with a slight modification. In first half of the twentieth century western scholars tried to attempt at the definition but arrived at what a tribal community characterizes. Perry, (quoted in Pathy, 1984:22), for example, thinks that a tribe is a group of people speaking a common dialect and inhabiting a common territory. W.H.R. Rivers[1] adds that the members of a tribe have a single government and act together for some common purposes such as warfare etc. Wissler (1923) includes certain criteria like specific name, unity of a speech etc. as a feature of the tribe. No single definition mentioned above gives a clear and comprehensive idea about the tribe. It is difficult to distinguish the tribe from the caste through such references. None of the above mentioned definitions envisage tribe as a politically or socially coherent and autochthonous group. The same has been highlighted in *Notes and Queries in Anthropology* (1951). Like other definitions, this definition of tribe does not include anything about division of labour. Das (1945) on the basis of his study on Purum-Kuki has pointed out that the tribe does not have any economic specialization so as to produce or nourish class stratification. However, many folk tales of the Indian tribes depict that intra tribal economics specialization is evident even in a traditional set up.

A tribe is variously described in Indian history. The term "JANA", i.e. a community of people is applied profusely in the Buddhists, Puranic and secular literature of early or medieval period just to designate many communities whom we often refer to as the tribe. Risley (1933) designated the tribe as 'aboriginal', i.e. man of the soil. Hutton (1933) coined the term primitive tribe, while Shoobert (1933) designated the tribe as a true aboriginal community. Ghurye (1959) has referred to tribe as *Backward Hindus*. According to him, the tribe of central India is neither isolated from the Hindu Caste of the plains in terms of distribution and tradition nor they are true autochthonous in their present habitat. They are imperfectly integrated with the caste system.

The following seven criteria are proposed by T.B. Naik (1968) by which a tribe can be recognized: (1) a tribe has the least functional interdependence within the community; (2) it is economically backward; (3) it is geographically isolated; (4) it speaks a common dialect which may, however, be subject to original variations; (5) It is politically a unit under a common tribal authority; (6) the tribal members are averse to change; (7) A tribe has its own traditional laws which often differ from those of majority communities. All characteristics together or a part designate a community to become a tribe. It might be undergoing acculturation; but with a high degree of acculturation, it would cease to be a tribe. However, if these criteria are applied to the tribes as 'scheduled' by the Indian Government, many would be disqualified.

Majumdar (1950) has defined a tribe as social group with a territorial affiliation, endogamous, with no specialization of functions, ruled by tribal officers, hereditary or otherwise, united in language or dialect, recognizing social distance with other tribes or castes, without social obloquy attaching to them it does in the caste structure, following tribal traditions, beliefs and customs, illiberal of naturalization of ideas from alien sources, above all conscious of a homogeneity of ethnic and territorial integration.

Bell (1945) places tribe as a community of people without any individual rights over the community sense of belonging, without any sense of accumulation of property and concern for future. The people work only for bare subsistence, the work that would bring him food sufficient for the day. According to his definition tribals are concerned with present than the future.

Hence, in brief, the obscure concept "tribe" may be defined as a social group usually within a definite area, dialect, cultural homogeneity, ordinarily having a leader, mostly living in the hills and forests, economically backward, geographically isolated, following the traditional laws, having a least functional interdependence with community, often exploited by other ethnic groups due to their simplicity and ignorance, little care for their individual rights and adverse to any change that may be social, political, cultural or economic.

Unfortunately, neither the anthropologists nor the Constitution of India could give a concrete definition of tribe by which they can be distinguished from other ethnic groups. So, academically we are nowhere near a comprehensive method of identifying the "tribes", simply, accepting the ethnic groups, identified by the Constitution of India as Scheduled Tribes. Singh (1982) points out echoing in the same line that in India the notion of tribe proceeds from the assumption that a tribe is an administrative and political category.

The Kandh community selected for the purpose of study is therefore a tribe in Constitutional sense, an administrative and a political category. The underpinning notion that Kandh is a social category is not altogether ruled out.

3.1.2 *Tribal Groups in India*

The Constitution of India initially identified 427 groups as Scheduled Tribes (Bose, 1971), and the number has gone up to 698 (including sub-tribes) at present (Draft National Plan on Tribals, 2006). They are found mostly in 27 States and four Union Territories. The Scheduled Tribes have not been specified in two States of India, i.e. in Punjab and Haryana and three Union territories, i.e. in Chandigarh, Delhi and Pondicherry. Mizoram has the highest percentage of (94.75%) of ST population and undivided Uttar Pradesh, the lowest percentage (0.21%) of the total population of the States.

3.1.3 *Tribal Typology*

Guha (1935) has tried to divide Indian tribes into 3 groups:

1. The proto Austroloids, who are smaller to wider group.
2. The Mongoloids, who are found among the Naga tribes of Assam and Nagaland etc.
3. The Negrito, with curly hair found in Andamans.

Bose (1967) has divided the tribal people into three principal categories, basing on the manner in which they primarily make their living. These are (a) hunters, fishers and gatherers; (b) shifting cultivators; and (c) settled agriculturists using plough and plough cattle. He lists two other categories, *viz.* nomadic cattle keepers, artisans and labourers; and workers in plantation and industries, Similarly, Vidyarthi (1968) while explaining the categories of tribes based on sources of livelihood has given seven types, i.e. (i) forest hunting type, (ii) hill cultivation type, (iii) plain agricultural type, (iv) simple artisan type, (v) the pastoral and cattle herder type, (vi) the agricultural non-agricultural labour type, and (vii) the skill and white collar-job-type working in offices, hospitals, factories and so on.

Among these, the settled agriculturists using the plough and plough cattle account for the overwhelming majority of the tribal people. The workers in plantations and industries are also recruited mainly from their ranks.

3.1.4 *Tribal Concentration*

India has the second largest concentration of tribal population next to African continent. According to 2001 Census tribal populations accounted for 8,43,26,240 (4.26 crores Male and 4.16 crores Female) and it represented 8.19 per cent to the total population of India which accounted 102.7 crores. About 67 per cent Scheduled Tribes population is concentrated in Central belt of older hills and plateaus along the dividing line between peninsular India and Indo-Gangetic plains. This zone begins where the Gangetic plain ends and extended up to 16 latitude in the South covering Eight States (Undivided Madhya Pradesh, Odisha, Bihar, Maharashtra, Gujarat, Rajasthan, Andhra Pradesh and West Bengal) (Vidyarthi and Rai, 1976).

3.1.5 *Geographical Distribution of the Tribes*

Geography and tribal demography of India permit a regional grouping and zonal classification of the tribal people. Three tribal zones have been demarcated by Guha (1951, 1955:28). These are as follows:

(i) the northern and north-eastern area in the mountain valleys and eastern frontiers of India;
(ii) the central belt which occupies the older hills and plateaus along the dividing line between Peninsular India and the Indo-Gangetic plains. This zone also includes the hills and the converging lines of the western Ghats; and
(iii) That falls in the peninsular India, i.e. below 16° N latitude.

Majumdar and Madan (1956:253) also referred to these zones and presented a somewhat similar distribution. They have rather termed them Northern and North-eastern zone, the Central or Middle zone and the Southern zone.

Taking into account all classifications as well as geographical, ecological, social, economic, administrative, ethnic and racial factors, Vidyarthi and Rai (1976:66) proposed a four-fold geographical regions along with one distinct sub-region of the islands. These are:

(i) Himalayan Region, with three sub-regions, *viz.*:
   (a) North-Eastern Himalayan region,
   (b) Central Himalayan region, and
   (c) North-Western Himalayan region.

Assam, Meghalaya, the mountainous region of West Bengal, i.e. Darjeeling, Arunachal Pradesh, Nagaland, Manipur, Mizoram, and Tripura fall in the north-eastern Himalayan region, whereas the Tarai areas of Uttar Pradesh (presently in Uttarakhand) and (undivided) Bihar come in the Central Himalayan region. Himachal Pradesh and Jammu & Kashmir constitute the north-western Himalayan region. More than one third of the region's population is made of tribals which is one-eighth of the tribal India.

(ii) Middle India region: It comprises Bihar (including present Jharkhand), West Bengal, Odisha and Madhya Pradesh (including present Chhattisgarh) with more than two crores of tribal people, i.e. 55 per cent of the total tribals in the country (1971 census).

(iii) Western India Region: It includes Rajasthan, Gujarat, Maharashtra, Goa, and Dadra and Nagar Haveli with about one crore tribal population.

(iv) South India Region: It comprises Andhra Pradesh, Tamil Nadu, Karnataka and Kerala with a meagre tribal population (1.66% of the region), constituting one-sixteenth of the Country.

(v) The Island Region: The Islands of Andaman and Nicobar in the Bay of Bengal and Lakshadweep in the Arabian Sea with 54.3 per cent tribal population constitutes a distinct Sub-region.

3.1.6 *Tribes of Odisha*

Odisha occupies a unique position among the States for highest concentration of Scheduled Tribes numbering 81.45 lakhs (40.66 lakhs male and 40.78 lakhs female) (2001 census), constituting 22.13 per cent of the total population of the state. The regions of Koraput, Mayurbhanj, Phulbani and Sundargarh are inhabited by a larger number of tribes than other districts of the state. The Kandhs of Odisha alone are the seventh largest tribal group in India and they are twice the size of the better known Naga people of Nagaland. In number and group, the tribal population is very significant here.

Odisha had as many as 62 varieties of Scheduled tribes but the number has increased to 68 recently (Draft National Policy on Tribals, 2004). Territorially, the tribes of Odisha may be broadly divided into three divisions and they are as follows:

(i) Those living in Southern Region of Odisha such as Kandhs, Parajas, Gadabas, Gonds, Saoras, Koyas etc.

(ii) Those living in Northern Region of Odisha such as Munda, Santal, Kolha (Ho), Oraon, Kisan and Bhuiyans etc.

(iii) The tribals living in Central Odisha such as Juangs and some Bhuiyans.

Odisha comes under the central tribal belt of the country.

The tribals and natural resources constitute the real cultural and economic strength of Odisha. Tribal villages of Odisha found in different ecological, economic and cultural environments have been differently affected by modern forces of change. These villages are found to have often different types of economic organizations and economic problems which need to be considered in the light of their cultural characteristics and age-old traditions. In some cases customs and traditions stand in the way of economic changes.[2] However, with accelerating impact of urbanization and industrialization tribals' economic and cultural life is undergoing considerable transformation.

Tribal areas are mostly the backward areas of the State. The Scheduled Areas of Odisha fully cover former six districts (Mayurbhanj, Sundargarh, Koraput, Rayagada, Nowrangpur and Malkangiri) and seven districts partially (*viz.* Balasore, Keonjhar, Sambalpur, Kalahandi, Gajapati, Ganjam and Phulbani). More than 50 per cent of tribal population of the State is found in undivided Koraput district, Mayurbhanj and in Sundargarh districts, out of which 25 per cent of tribal population is found in undivided Koraput districts alone (i.e. present Koraput, Rayagada, Nabarangpur and Malkangiri districts).

In absolute terms, the tribal population of the State has increased from 42.24 lakhs to 81.45 lakhs during 1961-2001. But the percentage of tribal population to total population of the State has declined from 24.07 per cent in 1961 to 22.13 per cent in 2001 Census. This may be due to high mortality rate among tribes and also due to low standard of living and difficult environment.

3.1.7 *Tribes of Koraput*

Koraput district of Odisha is a tribal concentrated district. Tribes of Koraput in general and that of Kandhs in particular are discussed elaborately in Chapter IV.

SECTION – II

3.2 Poverty

3.2.1 *Meaning and Concept of Poverty*

Poverty rips the very social fabric of a society. Its victims are apparently divested of some universally accepted human quality of life. Poverty exists since time immemorial with its complex and multidimensional features. It has various manifestations that include a person's inability to fulfil his/her basic requirements for subsistence living.

Fundamentally, the concept of poverty is associated with socially perceived deprivation with respect to basic human needs. Poverty is deprivation (Shanti, 1985) and such deprivation has four essential features. First, it is deprivation of the basic necessities of life like food, clothing, and housing, from which all other accompanying deprivations flow, *viz.* educational and intellectual deprivation, cultural and such other aspects to which anthropologists call as "Culture of Poverty". Second, deprivation means being deprived of what one is entitled to. Everyone is entitled for a decent standard of living and deprivation neglects this entitlement and right. Third, there are various degrees of deprivation which we in this country have covered by inventing such terms as the poorest of the poor, very poor and the poor. Fourth, deprivation involves its antinomy which is abundance. That is, many are deprived of because some have abundance; many are denied their entitlement because some have more than their entitlement (Adiseshaiah, 1990).

3.2.2 *Definitions of Poverty*

The term 'poverty' has its origin from the old French word 'poverte' that implies a level of living which is so low that it inhabits the physical, mental and social development of human personality. Poverty is defined as the total absence of opportunities, accomplished by high levels of undernourishment, hunger, illiteracy, lack of education, physical and mental ailments, emotional and social instability, unhappiness, sorrow and hopelessness for the future. Poverty is also characterized by a chronic shortage and hopelessness for the future.

Here follows some of the definitions of poverty given by eminent authors, organizations and world bodies. According to World Bank (2011):

Poverty is an income level below some minimum level necessary to meet basic needs. This minimum level is usually called the "poverty line". What is necessary to satisfy basic needs varies across time and societies. Therefore, poverty lines vary in time and place, and each country uses lines which are appropriate to its level of development, societal norms and values. But the content of the needs is more or less the same everywhere. Poverty is hunger. Poverty is lack of shelter. Poverty is being sick and not being able to see a doctor. Poverty is not having access to school and not knowing how to read. Poverty is not having a job, is fear for the future, living one day at a time. Poverty is losing a child to illness brought about by unclean water. Poverty is powerlessness, lack of representation and freedom.

Poverty is the deprivation of common necessities such as food, clothing, shelter and safe drinking water, all of which determine our quality of life. It may also include the lack of access to opportunities such as education and employment which aid the escape from poverty and/or allow one to enjoy the respect of fellow citizens (Wikipedia).

According to Mollie Orshansky who developed the poverty measurements used by the U.S. government poverty is a stage of deprivation, for "to be poor is to be deprived of those goods and services and pleasures which others around us take for granted" (quoted in Addae-Korankye, 2014:148; see Orshansky, 1969).

The definition of poverty agreed by the World summit on Social Development in Copenhagen in 1995, is that:

Poverty is a condition characterized by severe deprivation of basic human needs, including food, safe drinking water, sanitation facilities, health, shelter, education and information. It depends not only on income but also on access to services. It includes a lack of income and productive resources to ensure sustainable livelihoods; hunger and malnutrition; ill health; limited or lack of access to education and other basic services; increased morbidity and mortality from illness; homelessness and inadequate housing; unsafe environments and social discrimination and exclusion. It is also characterized by lack of participation in decision making and in civil, social and cultural life. It occurs in all countries: as mass poverty in many developing countries, pockets of poverty amid wealth in developed countries, loss of livelihoods as a result of

> *economic recession, sudden poverty as a result of disaster or conflict, the poverty of low-wage workers, and the utter destitution of people who fall outside family support systems, social institutions and safety nets.*

This definition focuses on the characteristics of poverty, its nature across countries along with its various manifestations.

The UN definition (1998) of poverty (quoted in Gordon, 2005) is given as follows:

> *Fundamentally, poverty is a denial of choices and opportunities, a violation of human dignity. It means lack of basic capacity to participate effectively in society. It means not having enough to feed and cloth a family, not having a school or clinic to go to, not having the land on which to grow one's food or a job to earn one's living, not having access to credit. It means insecurity, powerlessness and exclusion of individuals, households and communities. It means susceptibility to violence, and it often implies living on marginal or fragile environments, without access to clean water or sanitation.*

All these definitions focus on health, education, sanitation, decent living etc., whose absence is a condition of deprivation and thus marks the existence of poverty.

David Gordon (2005) in his paper, "Indicators of Poverty and Hunger" has outlined certain special features relating to poverty.

According to him, poverty is the absence of any two or more of the following eight basic needs:

- Food: Body Mass Index must be above 16 (if weight status is under 16 it is considered as seve underweight).
- Safe Drinking Water: Water must not come from solely rivers and ponds, and must be available nearby (less than 15 minute's walk each way).
- Sanitation Facilities: Toilets or latrines must be accessible in or near the home.
- Health: Treatment must be received for serious illnesses and pregnancy.
- Shelter: Homes must have fewer than four people living in each room. Floors must not be made of dirt, mud, or clay.
- Education: Everyone must attend school or otherwise learn to read.

- Information: Everyone must have access to newspapers, radios, televisions, computers, or telephones at home.
- Access to services such as education, health, legal, social, and financial (credit) services.

According to Peter Townsend (1979:31):

Individuals, families and groups in the population can be said to be in poverty when they lack the resources to obtain the types of diet, participate in the activities and have the living conditions and amenities which are customary, or are at least widely encouraged or approved, in the societies to which they belong. Their resources are so seriously below those commanded by the average individual or family that they are, in effect, excluded from ordinary living patterns and activities.

He looks poverty in terms of exclusion from resource use.

If we analyze these above definitions of poverty one thing that becomes clear is that persons who are unable to secure their bare necessities of life are poor. This is due to their lower level of earnings and therefore corresponding lower level of expenditure which is not enough to meet the basic necessities of life. However, the concept of poverty is a relative term and it changes from time to time, person to person and country to country. Needless to say, an attempt has been made here to give a brief analysis of the concept, measurement and different approaches to study of poverty as defined in previous paragraphs.

3.2.3 *Concept of Poverty*

Poverty is generally analyzed with reference to (i) Absolute poverty, and (ii) Relative Poverty (see Foster, 1998). A brief analysis of these terms is given below:

Absolute Poverty: Absolute poverty refers to the inability of a person or a household either through the level of income or expenditure to fulfil even the basic means of subsistence. So, it may be referred to the condition of inabilities to fulfil minimum physical wants with resultant starvation and malnutrition etc. It is reflected through want of food, clothing, and shelter and total lack of medical care. Poverty leads not only to the lack of well-being but also the denial of opportunities and choices most basic to human development in order to lead a long, healthy creative life and enjoy a decent standard of living with freedom, dignity, self-esteem and the respect of others.

Relative Poverty: A comparison between rich and poor generally indicates relative poverty. The term 'relative poverty' suggests that a person's access to basic needs of life is relatively low, as compared to some reference groups of people. Between two groups or persons or households, one may be considered as poor, while the other rich even through both may be in a position to fulfil their basic material needs. Relative poverty is more a matter of subjective element than of objective condition. A person may have everything what a normal human being requires, i.e. food, clothing, shelter, entertainment but he/she may have uncomfortable feeling that he/she is 'poor' in comparison to the person living next door. For measurement of relative poverty, different societies have different standards; hence, it is not possible have a universal measurement of poverty in relative terms. Poverty will remain as long as there is social stratification and inequality prevailing in the society.

3.2.4 *The Poverty Line*

Generally poverty is explained with reference to poverty line. Poverty line may be defined as a cut-off point on the line of distribution, which divides the population as poor and non-poor. The simplest method of determining the poverty line is to agree upon a certain level of income or a level of consumer expenditure as necessary to meet the minimum needs of life of an individual and his family.

Different studies have made use of different methodologies to determine the 'poverty line'. They may broadly be classified as follows:

- determination of the minimum nutritional level of subsistence,
- estimating the cost of their minimum diet, and
- by estimating the per capita consumption expenditure.

Dandekar and Rath (1971) were the scholars who made the first systematic work in India to determine poverty. They mainly dealt with the problem of low national income and its unequal distribution. They identified slow pace of development and inequitable distribution of the small gains of development as the main cause of poverty in India. To measure the poverty line in India they based their study on calorie intake of individuals living in both rural and urban areas. A food intake of 2250 calories was treated as the minimum level of nutrition required for an individual. At the 1960-61 prices, the people with an income per head per annum below ₹ 180 in rural areas and below ₹ 270 in urban areas were considered to be living below the poverty line.

International organizations often refer to $1 and $2 a day to determine the poverty line for the world as a whole. People with income below $2 are "poor" and people with income below $1 are "very poor".

In case of India, "Task Force on Projections of Minimum Needs and Effective Consumption Demand of the Planning Commission" (1979) used an average nutritional energy requirement norm to define the poverty line. Since the calorie is the unit of energy, the norm used was in terms of calories. The nutritional expert groups in 1968 recommended 2400 calories per person per day for rural areas and 2100 calories per person per day for urban areas. The people below this measure were said to be living below the poverty line.

3.2.5 *Measurement of Poverty*

The simplest and most commonly used way to measure poverty is to calculate the percentage of the population with income or consumption levels below the poverty line. This is also known as the Head-Count-Ratio of poverty.

$$\text{Head-Count-Ratio} = \frac{q}{n} \times 100$$

where q is the total number of persons below the poverty line and n refers to the total population.

Amartya Sen (1981) discusses two stages of poverty measurement: identification and aggregation. The first stage involves the method of identifying a group of people as "poor" (Identification) and the second stage, a method of aggregating the characteristics of the set of poor people into an over-all image of poverty (Aggregation).

Gutkind (1986) conceptualizes poverty as a condition which involves severe "deprivation, intensified by associated adverse of occurrences and usually, but not exclusively, associated with inadequate resources. It embodied an element of inequality of income and wealth as well as inequality in opportunities and in access to different markets". So, Gutkind concluded, poverty can't be treated as a unique category. It can be defined in various ways.

Mehta (1993) conceptualized poverty in following four ways, where poverty may be considered in absolute or relative terms:

- poverty of resources or resource deprivation,
- income insufficiency,

- nutritional deficiency or nutritional deprivation or food inadequacy, and
- poverty in terms of low quality of life.

The above aspects need a little more elaboration as follows:

1. Resource Deprivation: Generally, when we talk about rich and poor, one refers to wealthy and non-wealthy persons. People earn their livelihood by utilizing their physical and financial capacities available. Returns from these depend on many factors. One of the most important factors which influence human capital is the probability of getting employment. The following indicators are used to reflect poverty in terms of resource deprivation:

- Physical Resources (Land and other assets) deprivation,
- Human capital Deprivation,
- Rate of unemployment, and
- Measures of inequality in the distribution of land and other assets which depict relative poverty.

2. Income Insufficiency: Income insufficiency can be considered to be a derivative resource inadequacy. Perfect correlation between the two, i.e. income and resources cannot be granted, because income is a flow concept and resources are the stock.

The National Sample Survey (NSS) has chosen *average per capita consumption expenditure* (APE) as a proper proxy. It is also the best proxy of permanent income on which the consumption pattern is supposed to depend (Cramer, 1968)

It will be proper to take the real per capita expenditure instead of nominal per capita expenditure. This is necessary in cross-section studies because there are inter-state differences in consumer prices.

Average expenditure of the region can be found out by dividing nominal average per capita expenditure (APE) and expenditure required to attain a calorie norm of say 1920 (Ultra poor poverty line).

$$RY = \frac{APE}{UPPL}$$

where RY stands for Real Income and APE stands for Average Per Capita Expenditure (in ₹) and $UPPL$ for Ultra Poor Poverty line.

Measures of distribution on Income/expenditure, and used to represent relative poverty.

3. Nutritional Inadequacy: This can be either a food based poverty line (Greer and Thorbecke, 1986) or a food adequacy standard of living

(Lipton, 1983). Food based poverty line is defined as the minimum expenditure on food to acquire necessary calories. And food adequacy standard of living is the total expenditure level (or income level) with which an individual, when left to himself/herself, will meet the calorie need for an active and healthy life.

Different indicators of poverty, ranging from simple percentages to highly complicated formula, have been suggested by the experts from time to time. Complications arise when equity aspects are considered. Some of the widely used indicators are: (i) Head-Count Ratio, (ii) Poverty gap, (iii) Sen's Index, and (iv) The Lorenz Ratio.

The simplest method as discussed earlier to measure poverty is Head-Count-Ratio.

Sen's Index and its variants satisfy the Criteria (axioms) almost fully. Lorenz curve measures the inequality qualitatively.

However, Panda (1987) concedes that most of these complex poverty indicators are highly correlated with the simple Head-Count-Ratio. This Head-Count-Ratio can be used to measure absolute nutritional poverty.

So, Dandekar (1981) concluded, "In Indian situations, in fact, concentration on effort on axiomatic refinements will only divert attention from the basic questions regarding poverty".

4. Low Quality of Life Index: There are indicators used for constructing a measure of quality of life — individual states, technological development, individual equality, living conditions, economic status, agricultural production, education, development etc. These indicators are both subjective and objective. Hence, there is a problem of indicator overload (Mehta, 1993).

In this analysis, Morris (1979) used four indicators to define quality of life. They are as follows:

(i) Percentage of rural households living in houses with 'Kutcha' Walls (PRH).
(ii) Infant Mortality Rate (IMR).
(iii) Survival Ratio: Since the data about IMR and expectation of life are not complete and reliable, a proxy variable is adopted. This is defined as the ratio of 1961 rural population surviving to 1971. Since migratory ratio is not calculated it reflects mortality as well as migration. Moreover, it does not help in measuring infant mortality.
(iv) Literacy among rural females (FLR).

3.2.6 *Expert Group Review on the Methodology for Estimation of Poverty by Planning Commission, Government of India (November-2009)*

Planning Commission of India set up an expert group under the chairmanship of Professor Suresh Tendulkur to examine the issue of Poverty estimate and suggest a new poverty line for 2004-2005 and estimates.

The new Poverty Line Basket (PLB) represents some low enough but (socially acceptable) reasonable standard of living, recommended by this expert group is choice of mixed reference period over Uniform Reference Period (URP) is based on the observation that 365 day recall captures better than 30-days recall.

The revised minimum calorie norm for India recommended by FAO (Food and Agriculture Organization) is currently around 1800 calories (1770 calories per capita) per day which is very close to the average calorie intake of those near the new poverty lines in urban areas (1776 calories per capita) and higher than the revised FAO norm (1999 calories per capita) in rural areas as recorded in the 61st round of NSS.

The new poverty line happens to be close to, but less than, the 2005 PPP $1.25 per day poverty norm used by the World Bank in its latest world poverty estimates.

In comparison to the earlier 1993 expert group, the recent approach makes four major departures. They are as follows:

- They consciously move away from calorie anchor but test for the adequacy of actual food expenditure near the poverty line to ensure certain aggregate nutritional outcomes.
- Secondly, they do not discriminate between the urban and rural population and recommended to provide a Uniform PLB based in the latest available observed household consumption data to both the rural and urban populations.
- Thirdly, they suggest a price adjustment procedure that is predominantly based in the same data set that underlines the poverty estimation.
- Fourthly, they incorporated an explicit provision in price indices for private expenditure on health and education which has been rising over time and to verify their adequacy to ensure certain desirable educational and health outcomes.

Expert Group suggested a monthly expenditure of ₹ 407.78 in rural areas and ₹ 497.31 for urban areas (for 2004-05) in Odisha as the poverty line as against the all India average of ₹ 446.68 and ₹ 578.68 respectively for rural and urban areas.

3.2.7 *Approaches to Poverty*

The different approaches to the problem of poverty in India and the developing countries have been classified into three broad categories (Mehta, 1993): (i) Structural, (ii) Developmental, and (iii) Egalitarian.

The structural approach focuses on the causes of poverty. According to this approach, poor is not an economic class. Poverty is a common outcome of a variety of economic relationships and circumstances. So, categorization of poor and non-poor is operationally not relevant. In this approach, the main question taken up is about the causes of poverty, underemployment and low productivity, low wages, unequal exchange and in general exploitation. So, structural approach does not accept the conventional poverty measures.

In contrast, the developmental approach argues that rapid rate of growth reduces inequalities and poverty after a time lag. This approach also does not need a concrete measurement of poverty. Such approach was accepted by Indian planners during initial periods of planning and latter on discarded.

In the egalitarian approach, the focus is neither structured nor developmental but attention is paid to the problems of specific backward regions, sectors and groups of the poor. Now-a-days this is most popular approach to poverty as it attempts direct and immediate attack on poverty. It necessitates use of a poverty measure.

3.2.8 *Poverty among the Tribals in India*

As discussed earlier, India has the second largest concentration of tribal population next to African continent. Nearly 8.19 per cent of the total population of India is tribals. They lead relatively isolated life living in highlands, hills and forests. Lack of communication and interaction with outside world kept them mostly illiterate and ignorant. Due to their subsistence outlook, illiteracy and ignorance they use primitive technology in productive pursuits. More than 94 per cent are staying in rural areas and 90 per cent of them are poverty ridden (Samal, 1992).

The preceding discussion gives us an understanding of what poverty means among the tribals. It means hunger and the real hunger. Poverty to them is lack of shelter. Poverty is being sick and not being able to see a doctor. Poverty is living one day at a time. Poverty among the tribal may also be characterized by a shortage of economic, social and political participation.

Tribes in India, more or less, have retained their separate social identity but economically their unfamiliarity with market economy, less sense of acquisition of wealth, lack of profit motive and inability to negotiate and cope with the consequences of their forced integration with the mainstream economy, society, cultural and political system perilously, sometimes hopelessly, grapple with the tragic consequence of poverty.

During historical period they were pushed into a situation, where they had to depend upon nature and forest for their survival. They remained backward both economically and socially. But after independence our national leaders were very eager to help and uplift the tribals. In the Constitution of India, tribals were given all special care (Article 46). Huge amounts were earmarked in different Five Year and Annual plans. As a result the tribals are now passing through a phase of transformation with the rest of the country. The developmental activities and industrialization have helped some of the tribals get alternative jobs. They are gradually developing higher aspirations. However, their development process is very slow. Majority of the tribals are still poverty ridden. They have very inadequate access to natural resource endowment. They are primitive in technology and therefore, generally very poor in their living. Because of their poverty and ignorance, they are often more exploited by different private and even some public agencies than rest of the rural population.

SECTION – III

3.3 Exploitation

3.3.1 *Exploitation: Meaning and Concept*

The term exploitation may carry two distinct meanings. In the simple sense, it is the act of using something for any purpose. In this case, exploitation is a synonym for "Use". And the other, it implies act of using something in an unjust or cruel manner, simply an "unjust benefit" (Wikipedia, 2009). According to Oxford's Advanced Learner's Dictionary, the term "exploitation" means using somebody or something selfishly and unfairly for one's own advantage or own profit.

In the disciplines like Political Economy, Economics and Sociology, exploitation involves a persistent social relationship in which certain persons are being mistreated or unfairly used for the benefit of others. This corresponds to one ethical conception of exploitation, that is, the treatment of human beings as mere means to an end or as mere "objects". In other words "exploitation" refers to the use of people as a resource, with little or no consideration of their well-being. Exploitation may take the following basic forms:

- Taking something off a person or group that rightfully belongs to them,
- Short changing people in trade,
- Directly or indirectly forcing somebody to work,
- Using somebody against his/her will or without his/her consent or knowledge, and
- Imposing an arbitrary differential treatment of people to the advantage of some and the disadvantage of others (as inscriptive discrimination).

3.3.2 *"Exploitation" as Understood in Economics*

In economics most often, the word exploitation is used to refer to economic exploitation which refers to the act of using another person's labour without offering him/her an adequate compensation. There are two major perspectives on economic exploitation. They are as follows:

- In the broad tradition of liberal economic thinking, most of the theories of exploitation center on the market power of economic organizations within a market setting. This may be termed as "organizational" or "micro level" exploitation.
- Neo Liberal theories[3] focus on exploitation by large sections of society even (or especially) in the context of free markets. Marxist theory points to the entire capitalist class as an exploitative entity and to capitalism as a system based on exploitation. This may be termed as "structural" or "macro level" exploitation.

3.3.3 *Socio-economic Exploitation*

Theories of exploitation tell about the existence of exploitation towards human beings in the socio-economic process where people trade their labour or allegiance to a powerful entity, such as the state, a corporation or any other private company or entity. They take unfair advantage of person's characteristics or their situation. However, it is difficult to specify the nature of unfairness of the advantage, and the ways in which the opportunity to take advantage arises. Therefore, in this context it is useful to discuss, in brief, some of the theories of exploitation.

3.3.4 *Marxist Theory of Exploitation*

In Marxian economics exploitation[4] refers to the subjection of producers (the proletariat) to work for passive owners (bourgeoisie) for less compensation that's equivalent to the actual amount of work done. The proletarian is forced to sell his or her labour power, rather than a set quantity of labour, in order to receive wage for survival, while the capitalist exploits the work performed by the proletarian by accumulating the surplus value of their labour. Therefore, the capitalist makes his/her living by passively owning the means of production and generating a profit, which is really the product of the labour and which is entitled to all its produces. The kinds of exploitation described by other theories are usually called "super exploitation", meaning exploitation which goes beyond normal standards of exploitation prevalent in capitalist society. The Marxist theory is primarily concerned with the exploitation of an entire segment or class of society by another. This kind of exploitation is seen as being an inherent feature and key element of capitalism and free markets.

Marx typically assumed the existence of purely competitive markets in general. It is argued that the greater the "freedom" of the market, the greater the power of capital, and the greater the scale of exploitation.

In Marxist view, "normal" exploitation is based on three structured characteristics of capitalist society:

- Inability of the workers (proletarians) to survive without selling their labour-power to the capitalists.
- Workers have little or no choice but to pay the capitalists surplus value (profits, interests and rent) in exchange for their survival.
- Workers are threatened by the capitalists by the "reserve army of the unemployed".

Some Marxian theories of imperialism extend this kind of structural theory of exploitation further, posing exploitation of poor countries by rich capitalist ones.

3.3.5 *Theories of Neo-classical Economics*

In neo-classical economics, exploitation is organizational in nature and is generally explained by using microeconomic theory. It is a kind of market failure, a deviation from the abstraction of perfect competition. The most common scenario is a monopsony or a monopoly market situation. These exploiters have bargaining power. This kind of exploitation is supposed to be abolished by the spread of competition and markets.

Other neo-classical theories go beyond simple organizational exploitation. First, another type of exploiter is the hired "agent" (employee) who takes advantage of the "principal" (employer) who hires him/her, under conditions of asymmetric information. This kind of exploitation is beyond the scope of markets, this can be solved by monitoring of employees and management, risk sharing agreements bonding and the like.

Another type of neo-classical exploiter is "free rider", who unfairly uses a public goods or resource. Non-payment of tax is an example of such kind of exploitation. Such exploitation of public goods or resources is known as the "Tragedy of Commons" (see Hardin,1968). Many neo-classical economists believed that introduction of private property rights would alleviate the overconsumption, i.e. exploitation (Wikipedia, 2009).

3.3.6 *New Liberal Theories of Exploitation*

According to the theories of some new-liberals, exploitation co-exists with free markets, as in the Marxist theory, the problem is structural rather than organizational. Such exploiters do have a special position in the society by controlling important assets that can shift the distribution of income in its direction improvising the rest, even though their role serves no reasonable purpose. Henry George pointed to "land-owners" (see Pullen, 2001), J.M. Keynes to "rentiers" (non-working owners of financial wealth) (see Jensen, 1983) where the former receives rent and the latter interest, even though they do contribute nothing to society. They simply own certain assets and have the ability to make money from that asset without actually doing any work themselves. While George argued for a single tax on land rent to solve this problem, Keynes hoped that interest rates could be driven to zero. In some way, these theories are similar to the Marxist one discussed earlier, where Marx advocated that abolishing rent or interest would make everyone better-off.

3.3.7 *Exploitation in Developing Nations*

In the context of Global economy, much debates are going on over the issue of exploitation of developing nations or "Third World Countries".

Third World countries generally pay their workers far lower than those prevail in developed nations, which is insufficient to attain minimum standard of living and also working hours much longer than in the first world. It is also argued that work conditions in these developing world factories are much less safe and much more unhealthy than that in the first world. In these countries people choose to work for low wages and unsafe conditions because it is their only alternative to starvation and they have no "free choice" to opt any other alternative. This is pointed out by Marx in his theory discussed earlier.

3.3.8 *Exploitation in Tribal India*

As discussed earlier in Section-II of this chapter, the tribals in India have very inadequate access to natural resource endowments. They use primitive technology and, therefore, generally very poor in their living. Because of their poverty, ignorance, illiteracy, simplicity and not having positive motive for acquisition of wealth, they are often more exploited by different private and even by some public agencies than that the rest of the rural population. Poverty and need lead the tribals to go for loans from private agencies. Indebtedness lead to the exploitation of various types starting from land alienation and ending with bonded labour. Economic problems of the tribals and their exploitation and agencies of exploitation etc. are elaborately discussed in Chapter-V of this dissertation.

NOTES

1. See *Encyclopaedia Britannica*, Vol. 22, Encyclopaedia Britannica Inc. Willam Bengton (Publishers), London/Chicago, Torento, p. 465.
2. See the debate on "The Relations between Cultural Values and Economic Growth and Development in Ntibagirirwa" (2009); also see UNDP, 2004.
3. See Phillips-Fein, 2009; Mirowski and Plehwe, 2009; Stedman-Jones, 2012 and Polanyi, 1957 for an idea of neo-liberal theories.
4. See Wolff, 1999 and Shishkov, 1993 for An Understanding of Marxist Theory of Exploitation.

4

LAND AND PEOPLE: A GENERAL PROFILE

4.0 Introduction

The present chapter[1] is divided into two broad sections. Section-I deals with a profile of Koraput region and present Koraput district; the section-II deals with the Kandh tribe of Koraput, the subject of investigation for an understanding of poverty, and exploitation of the tribal people.

SECTION – I

4.1 A Profile of Koraput and Its Tribes

4.1.1 *Koraput — A Brief Historical Background*

The then second largest district of the country, i.e. Koraput, was divided into four districts, i.e. Koraput, Rayagada, Nabarangpur and Malkangiri in 1992 for administrative convenience. Koraput region (undivided Koraput district) has a large tribal concentration, as nearly 54 per cent of its inhabitants are the tribals. The district-wise distribution of population of former Koraput region along rural, SC and ST status is presented in Table 4.1.

Koraput region, a part of Dandakaranya, as described in the holy epic *Ramayana* has a hoary past and rich cultural heritage. History records that this area was known as "Trikalinga" which formed parts of the empires of Satvahanas, Vakatakas, Nalas, Marathas, Eastern Gangas, Chalukyas, Somavamsis, Gangas, Kalachuris, Chindikanagas, Matsya dynasty, Silavamsis and lastly the Surya Vanshi (solar dynasty). The 32 stepping throne (Battisa Simhasana) at Nandapur is ascribed to the rulers of Sila dynasty who with their power and self emulated the glory of the famous king of Ujjain. The Matsya and Sila dynasties merged into one in the early 15th century and the monarchs were acting as the "Chief Feudal Lords" of the southern dominions of the Gajapati Kings of Kalinga (Odisha). As many as 25 rulers belonging to the solar dynasty ruled over Jeypore estate (undivided Koraput district) from 1443 A.D to 28.12.1952. Then the estate was vested in the state government under the provisions of the Orissa Estates Abolition Act 29.12.1952. Ten "Anchals" were formed for managing the affairs of the estate and regular Ryotwari system of administration was introduced with effect from 14.11.1957 (COATS, NFFWP, 2005).

4.1.2 *The Demography of Koraput Region*

The total population of undivided Koraput district, i.e Koraput Region was 35,47,710 of which 53.74 per cent were tribals (2001 census). Out of the four districts Malkangiri has the maximum percentage of tribals, i.e. 57.53 per cent followed by 55.71 per cent in Rayagada, 55.02 per cent in Nabarangpur and 49.66 per cent in Koraput. As 88.47 per cent of the people of the region lives in the villages, the region is mostly rural in character.

Table 4.1: District-wise Distribution of Total Population, Rural Population, SC and ST Population of Koraput Region (2001 Census)

Sl.No.	*Name of the District*	*Total Population (000 Nos.)*	*Rural Population (000 Nos.)*	*SC Population (000 Nos.)*	*ST Population (000 Nos.)*
1.	Koraput	1180	982 (83.22)	154 (13.05)	586 (49.66)
2.	Malkangiri	504	469 (93.05)	108 (21.42)	290 (57.53)
3.	Nabarangpur	1025	966 (94.24)	145 (14.14)	564 (55.02)
4.	Rayagada	831	715 (86.04)	116 (13.95)	463 (55.71)
	Region Total	**3540**	**3132 (88.47)**	**523 (14.74)**	**1903 (53.75)**

Note: Figures in brackets indicate percentages to respective totals.

4.1.3 *The Scheduled Tribes*

There are as many as 62 Scheduled Tribes found in Odisha. Most of these tribes in varying numbers are found in the erstwhile Koraput region. Varieties of the tribes inhabited in different areas in Koraput district is presented in Table 4.2.

Table 4.2: Block-wise habitation of Important Tribes in Koraput Region

Sl.No.	*District*	*Subdivision*	*Block*	*Name of the Tribes*
(1)	*(2)*	*(3)*	*(4)*	*(5)*
1.	Koraput	Koraput Subdivision	1. Koraput	(a) Paroja, (b) Kandh
			2. Semiliguda	(a) Paroja, (b) Kandh, (c) Gadaba
			3. Pattangi	(a) Kandh, (b) Paroja, (c) Gadaba
			4. Nandapur	(a) Paroja, (b) Kandh, (c) Kotia
			5. Lamataput	(a) Gadaba, (b) Paroja, (c) Kandh
			6. Dasamanthpur	(a) Paroja, (b) Kandh
			7. Laxmipur	(a) Kandha, (b) Paroja
			8. Narayanpatna	(a) Kandh
			9. Bandhugaon	(a) Kandh
		Jeypore Subdivision	1. Jeypore	(a) Paroja, (b) Gadaba, (c) Bhumiya, (d) Dharua, (e) Halva
			2. Boipariguda	(a) Bhumiya, (b) Paroja, (c) Dharua
			3. Kundra	(a) Bhumia, (b) Paroja, (c) Bhatra, (d) Kandh, (e) Dhurua, (f) Pentia
			4. Kotpad	(a) Bhatra, (b) Dhurua
			5. Borigumma	(a) Paroja, (b) Bhatra, (c) Amanatya, (d) Pentia
2.	Malkangiri	Malakangiri Subdivision	1. Malkangiri	(a) Koya, (b) Madia, (c) Paraja, (d) Dhurua, (e) Santal
			2. Korkunda	(a) Koya
			3. Khairput	(a) Bondaparoja, (b) Gadaba (c) Kandh, (d) Didayi
			4. Kalimela	(a) Koya, (b) Konda Dora (c) Halva
			5. Kudumuluguma	(a) Paraja, (b) Kandh, (c) Didayi
			6. Podia	(a) Koya
			7. Mathili	(a) Bonda, (b) Koya, (c) Bhumia, (d) Kollar, (e) Dhurua, (f) Gundia, (g) Halva
3.	Nawarang-pur	Nawarangpur Subdivision	1. Nowrangapur	(a) Bhatra, (b) Paroja, (c) Dhurua
			2. Kosagumuda	(a) Bhatra
			3. Nandahandi	(a) Bhatra, (b) Paraja, (c) Amanatya
			4. Tentulikhunti	(a) Paroja, (b) Bhatra, (c) Dhurua
			5. Papadahandi	(a) Bhatra, (b) Paroja, (c) Halva
			6. Dabugaon	(a) Bhatra, (b) Paroja
			7. Umarkote	(a) Bhatra
			8. Raighar	(a) Gond, (b) Halva, (c) Banjara
			9. Jharigaon	(a) Bhatra, (b) Paroja, (c) Gond, (d) Kandh, (e) Bhunjia, (f) Halva, (g) Santal
			10. Chandahandi	(a) Gond, (b) Bhunjia, (c) Banjara

(*Contd.*)

Table 4.2 (*Contd.*)

(1)	*(2)*	*(3)*	*(4)*	*(5)*
4.	Rayagada	Rayagada Subdivision	1. Rayagada	(a) Kandh, (b) Jatapu Dora
			2. Kashipur	(a) Kandh, (b) Paroja
			3. Kalyanșingpur	(a) Kandh
			4. Kolnara	(a) Kandh
		Gunupur Subdivision	1. Gunupur	(a) Kandh, (b) Saura, (c) Dhurua
			2. Gudari	(a) Kandh, (b) Saura, (c) Jatapu
			3. Ramanaguda	(a) Saura, (b) Jatapu, (c) Kandh, (d) Dhurua, (e) Muda
			4. Padmapur	(a) Soura, (b) Kandh, (c) Jatapu
			5. Chandrapur	(a) Kandh
			6. Bissamcuttack	(a) Kandh
			7. Muniguda	(a) Kandh

Source: Tribal Museum, Koraput.

The major tribes with population more than one lakh are the Kandh in Koraput and Rayagada, the Paraja of Koraput, the Koya of Malkangiri and Bhottada and the Gonds of Nabarangpur The tribes with population more than 50,000 and less than one lakh are the Bhottada and the Gadaba of Koraput, the Bhumia of Malkangiri, the Paraja of Nabarangpur and the Saora of Rayagada district. On the other hand, the Bhumia of Koraput, the Paraja of Malkangiri, the Kandh of Nabarangpur and the Sabara of Rayagada have a population more than 20,000 but less than 50,000. The tribes with the population size between 10,000 and 20,000; 5000 and 10,000; 1000 and 5000; 500 and 1000; 100 and 500 and less than 100 can.be studied from Table 4.3. There are about 54 numbers of tribes, both large and small from numerical point of view in Koraput district. Similarly, there are 56 groups of tribes in Malkangiri, 53 in Nabarangpur, and 45 in Rayagada districts of the region. These tribes live under varying ecological situations and their economy is conditioned accordingly.

4.1.4 *Profile of the Present Koraput District*

The district is located between 18°13' to 19°10' North latitude and 82°05' to 83°23' east longitude in the southern part of Odisha. Total geographical area of the district is 8807 sq.km. which covers 5.66 per cent of the total geographical area of state. It is bounded by Bastar district of Chhatishgarh state and Malkangiri district of Odisha in the west; Rayagada of Odisha and Srikakulam district of Andhra Pradesh in the east; Vizayanagrarm and Vishakhapatnam of Andhra Pradesh in the south; and Nabarangpur and Rayagada districts of Odisha in the north.

Table 4.3: Tribes with Population Size

Sl No.	Range of ST Population	Districts with Name of Tribes: Koraput	Malkangiri	Nabarangpur	Rayagada
1.	1 lakh and more	Kandh, Paraja	Koya	Bhottada, Gond	Kandh
2.	50,000 & more but less than 1 lakh	Bhottada, Gadaba	Bhumia	Paroja	Saora
3.	20,000 & more but less than 50,000	Bhumia	Paroja	Kandh	Shabar
4.	10,000 & more but less than 20,000	Kondadora, Omanatya, Parenga	Gadaba, Kandh	—	Paraja, Jatapu
5.	5000 & more but less than 10,000	Kotia, Pentia	Bondo, Dharua, Didayi, Kondadora, Kotia	Omanatya, Saora	—
6.	1000 & more but less than 5000	Bhumij, Holva, Kandha, Gouda, Santal, Saora	Bhuiya, Bhumij, Holva, Kandh Gouda, Matya Santal	Banjara, Bhunjia, Gadaba, Holva, Kandh Gouda, Munda, Santal, Shabar	Kondadora
7.	500 & more but less than 1000	Bhuiya, Dharua, Matya, Oraon, Shabar	Banjara, Gandia, Parenga, Saora, Shabar	Bhumia, Dharua, Kondadora	Gadaba, Kandh Gounda, Kolha Loharas, Munda
8.	100 & more but less than 500	Pathudi, Bondo, Ganda, Kawar, Kharia, Kissan, Kolha, Madia, Mahali, Munda	Bothoda, Gond, Kora, Munda, Oraon, Kisan, Kolha	Bagata, Bhuiya, Bonda, Gandia, Kolha Loharas, Lodha, Mahali Oraon, Sounti	Kharia, Koya, Matya, Santal
9.	Less than 100	Bagata, Baiga, Banjara, Bhuiya, Binjhal, Dal, Didayi, Gandia, Ghara, Ho, Jatapu, Juang, Khawar, KOI, Kolha Loharas, Koli, Kora, Korua, Koya, Kulis, Lodha, Mundari, Sounti, Tharua	Bagata, Baiga, Bathudi, Bhunjia, Binjhal, Binjhia, Chenchu, Desua Bhumij, Ghara, Ho, Jatapu, Juang, Kawar, Kharia, Kol, Kolha Loharas, Koli, Korua, Kulis, Lodha, Madia, Mahali, Mirdha, Omanatya, Pentia, Rajaur, Sounti, Tharua	Balhudi, Bhumij, Binjhar, Birhor, Desua, Ho, Jatapu, Juang, Kawar, Kharia, Kharwar, Kisan, KOI, Kolha, Koli, Kora, Korua, Kotia, Koya, Kulis, Madia, Mankidi, Mirdhas, Mundari, Parenga, Pentia, Rajuar, Saunti, Tharua	Bagata, Bonjara, Bhottoda, Bhuiya, Bhumia, Bhumij, Bhunjia, Binjhal, Binjhia, Bondo, Dharua, Didayi, Gandia, Gond, Ho, Kawar, Kol, Kolha, Kora, Kotia, Kulis, Lodha, Madia, Mirdha, Mundari, Omanatya, Oraon, Sounti, Tharua

Source: Compiled by Dr. J. Samal basing on 2001 Census Reports.

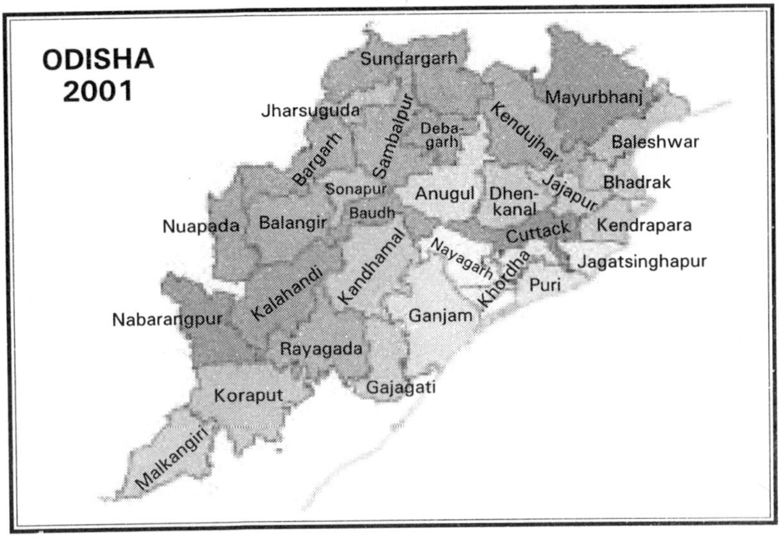

Map 4.1: Location of Koraput District in Odisha.

Source: Census of India.

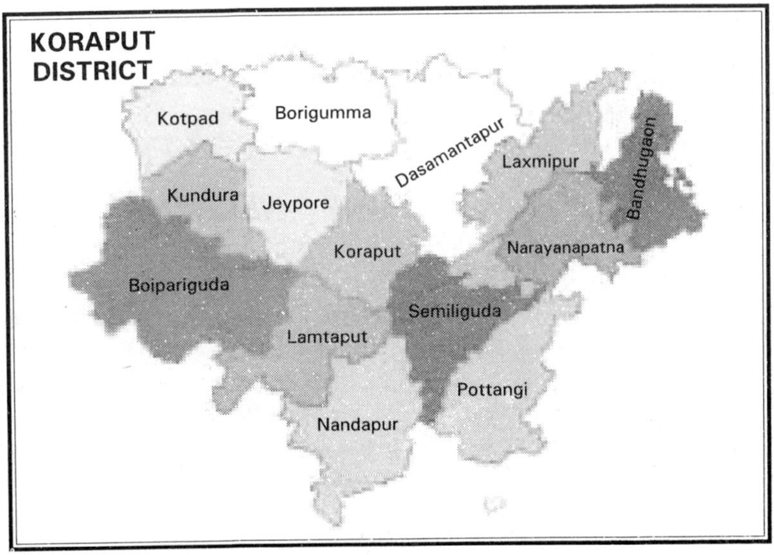

Map 4.2: Location of Blocks in Koraput District.

Source: Census of India.

(A) *Physiography*

The district is located on a section of Eastern ghats in two agro-climatic zones namely eastern ghat high land (entire Koraput sub-division and Kotpad block) and south-eastern ghat zone (Jeypore, Borigumma, Kundura and Boipariguda blocks). The district has altitude ranging from 300 meters to 1000 meters above MSL. The blocks namely Koraput, Semiliguda, Pottangi, Nandapur, Lamtaput, Dasamantapur and Laxmipur are having altitude over 900 meters above MSL. Narayanpatna and Bandhugaon blocks have altitude ranging between 300 meters and 600 meters above MSL. Jeypore subdivision has altitude up to 600 meter above MSL. The major rivers flowing across the district are Kolab, Jhanjabati and their tributaries.

(B) *Demographic Profile*

As per the 2001 census, the population of the district was 11,80,637; out of which the male population was 5,90,743 (50.04%) and female population was 5,89,894 (49.66%). The sex-ratio (number of female per one thousand male) is 999 which is more than the state figure (972). The rural population of the district is 9,82,188 (83.19%) and urban population is 1,98,499 (16.81%). The density of population per one square km is 134.

The combined ST and SC population of the district form 62.66 per cent of the total population. The ST population is 5,85,830 (49.62%) and SC population is 1,53,932 (13.04%).

The total population in the age group of up to 6 years is figured at 2,00,689 which forms 17 per cent of the total population.

(C) *Literacy*

The overall literacy rate of the district is 35.72 per cent with 3,50,044 persons out of which males are 2,31,055 (47.20%) and females 1,18,989 (24.26%) with a gender gap of 22.94 percentage point. The urban literacy rate is 74.9 per cent whereas the rural literacy rate is 27.30 per cent. Bandhugaon block has the lowest literacy rate of 19.85 per cent and Koraput has the highest literacy rate of 36.49 per cent.

(D) *Man Power and Employment*

The overall unemployment level in Koraput has remained significantly high. Total number of workers is numbered at 5,70,435 which is 48.32

per cent to the total population of the district, out of which 3,32,014 (56.20%) are males and 2,38,421 (40.42%) are females.

The main workers are 3,53,377 in number which is 61.94 per cent to the total work force. The distribution of main workers is shown in the Table 4.4.

Table 4.4: Occupational Distribution of Main Workers in Koraput District

Category	*Total Number of Persons*	*Percentage*
Cultivators	1,48,578	42.05
Agricultural Labourers	79,975	22.63
Workers in HH I	7,474	2.11
Other Workers	1,17,350	33.21
Total	**3,53,377**	**100.00**

Source: Economic Survey of Orissa, 2004-05.

Table 4.4 reveals that 64.68 per cent of the total workers are engaged as cultivators and agricultural labourers. Dependence of workers purely on primary sectors would be still more, if we add the workers engaged in livestock, forestry and agro-forestry based cottage works.

(E) *Climate*

The climate is warm and humid with mean summer maximum temperature of 34.1°C and winter minimum temperature of 7.5°C. During winter, in high altitude area of Semiliguda and Pottangi, the temperature goes down to 20°C and 30°C. To sum up, the monsoon is wet and humid; the winter is cool and prolonged, and the summer is mild and pleasant.

(F) *Rainfall*

The district is affected by depressions from Bay of Bengal. It causes widespread heavy rainfall and high wind. The average rainfall of the district is 1,521.8 mm. About 80 per cent of the rainfall is received during June to September. Rain the district actually received during 2000 and 2001 was 1,398.7 mm and 1,528.9 mm respectively. In 2001, Boipariguda block received the highest amount of rainfall whereas Nandapur block received the lowest amount with 2,739 mm and 965 mm respectively.

(G) *Predominant Economic Activities*

Agriculture is the mainstay of the people in the district. Traditionally, people take up agriculture along with animal husbandry, collection of minor forest produces, petty business and transport operations. Of late farmers have switched over to cultivation of vegetables, spices, sugarcane and maize.

(H) *Major Food/Commercial Crops and Plantation/Horticulture Crops*

Coffee and cashew are emerging as major commercial plantation crops. Along with coffee plantation, other activities like sericulture, oil palm, mango, guava, citrus, banana, commercial vegetables, spices like ginger/ turmeric etc. are also being taken up on moderate scale. In addition to these, there is good potential for medicinal and aromatic crops, spawn production unit, cattle breeding farms, organic vegetable production and coffee processing in the district (Potential linked credit plan, 2009-10, NABARD, Orissa Regional Office, BBSR). Paddy, raggi, and other minor millets are the food crops which are traditionally grown in the district.

(I) *Land Utilization Pattern*

The district has a forest area of 1,879.53 sq.km. The net area sown, otherwise called as cultivated area, amounts to be at 2,40,897 hectares. The area with miscellaneous trees and groves not included in net area sown is 20,900 hectares, permanent pasture and other grazing land 16,149 hectares, cultivable waste land 12,078 hectares, land put to non-agriculture uses 32,211 hectares, barren and uncultivable lands 11,493 hectares, current fallows 74,114 hectares and other fallows 18,382 hectares (*District Statistical Handbook*, Koraput, 2001).

(J) *Major Crops and Agricultural Productivity*

Paddy is the major crop of the district. Raggi is the second major crop from the non-paddy section, which constitutes an important food item of rural households. The total area under paddy cultivation is 1,52,442 hectares (2000-2001) having the production of 34,50,385 qtls with a yield rate of 22.63 qtls per hectare. The yield rate of paddy had been increased to 27.06 qtls/ha. during 2003-04 (*Economic Survey*, Orissa, 2004-05).

The coverage of Raggi in the district is 37,598 ha. having production of 2,05,515 qtls with the yield rate of 5.47 qtls/ha. The other crops include wheat, maize, green gram, black gram, horse gram, niger, groundnut, mustard, potato, sugarcane etc.

The overall agricultural productivity per worker is 4.68 qtls/year The average size of tilling per cultivator is 1.62 qtls/ha, i.e. 4 acres (2000-2001).

SECTION – II

4.2 The Kandh Tribe

4.2.1 *A Socio-Economic Profile*

The "Kandhs", (or the "Kuvi", as they call themselves), are the largest tribal group in Odisha, numbering over one million. Out of 62 groups of tribes numerically the "Kandha" is the largest group and in the present Koraput region, their population was 5,55,231 persons. Their population in the present Koraput district is 1,68,172; out of which 83,403 are males and 84,769 are females (2001 Census). Although they are scattered throughout the State of Odisha, the main concentration is in the central region of the Eastern Ghats covering Phulbani and Koraput districts. The undivided Koraput district contains about 40 per cent of the total Kandh population of the State. The Kandh population in undivided Koraput district, i.e. Koraput region, is 5,55,231 which is 39.78 per cent of the total Kandh population of the State. There are as many as 13,95,643 Kandh persons in Odisha (2001 Census). Total population of Kandh tribe in the present Koraput district is 1,68,172 (2001).

4.2.2 *Origin of the Word "Kandh"*

Opinions are as varied as they are vague concerning the origin, spelling and derivation of "Kandh" (Khond, Khand or Kandha, Kondh), the name by which both the tribal people and the hills inhabited by them are known to the plains people of Odisha and India. The most likely suggestion is that put forward by captain Macpherson in his "Original Report" [C.R. 1864(a), p. 25], submitted to the British Government in 1841 following two campaigns and surveys in the area: that the word "Kond" (Plural "Kondulu") means 'mountaineer' from the Telugu word signifying "a hill". Hence, the term, "Kandh" literally means the inhabitants of the hills.

The Kandhs have racial affinity with Proto-Australoid stock with Mongoloid admixture. They have dark brown to neatly black skin, medium structure and broad nose and broad head. The Kandhs are a Dravidian stock, but no mythology or legend has yet discovered to furnish any clue to their origin or place of descent.

4.2.3 *Division of the Tribe*

The Kandh tribe is divided into five different sub-groups. These are as follows:

The Maliah Kandhs:	They comprise the great majority; they live in villages throughout Phulbani District and West Ganjam district.
The Kutia Kandhs:	The Kutia Kandhs dwell in remote hills in the extreme south-west of Phulbani district. They occupy six out of seven Panchayats of Tumudibandh Block and parts of Kotogarh block.
The Dongria Kandhs:	They inhabit the steep slopes of the Niyamgiri Range of Rayagada District bordering Kalahandi district. No flat cultivatable land is generally available in these hill tracts.
The Kuvi Kandhs:	They are spread widely over the hills and valleys of north Koraput district. Kuvi, the mother tongue, is an extremely nasal form of the Kandh language and also contains a few Telugu words being alongside the State of Andhra Pradesh.
The Desia Kandhs:	The Desia Kandhs are migrant groups of Malliah Kandhs. They are influenced by the language and culture of the Odias and Hindu Religion. They are found mainly below the Eastern Ghats and on the coastal plains or in Central Kalahandi, Balangir and Dhenkanal Districts.

Recent studies of some of the scholars indicate that the roots of a number of "Kui and Kuvi" words are closer to Tamil than to Telugu, despite the much greater distance between the two language areas. They may throw interesting lights on the pre-history of both of them who claim that the Kandhs are a pre-Dravidian people.

However, variations in belief and cultural practices between the sub-groups make it far more likely that the one and a half-million Kui-Kuvi speaking people have grown together from groups on the plains who retreated first from Dravidian and then from Aryan invaders at different time since 4000 B.C.

Concentration of Kandhs and their sub-groups in Odisha can be studied from the Map 4.3 (Concentration of Kandhs in Odisha) and Map 4.4 (Concentration of Kandh Sub-Groups) respectively.

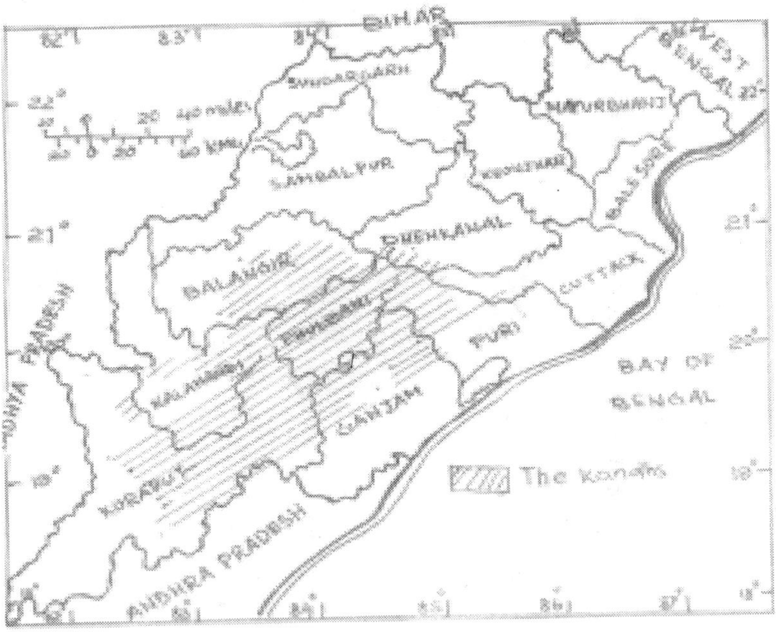

Map 4.3: Concentration of Kandhs in Odisha.

Source: Nabakrushna Chaudhury Center for Development Studies.

Varrier Elwin was the first anthropologist to give his impression about the tribe in the year 1943. Niggemeyer had published a detailed ethnographic account of the Kutia Kandhs, in the year 1964, but as it was written in German language many scholars did not have access to it (Patnaik and Das Patnaik, 1980).

The British officials like Macpherson and Campbell came to know about the community as early as the middle of the 19th century, when they were deputed to the Kandh area for the suppression of the so-called practice of human sacrifice (Known as "Meriah"), which was believed

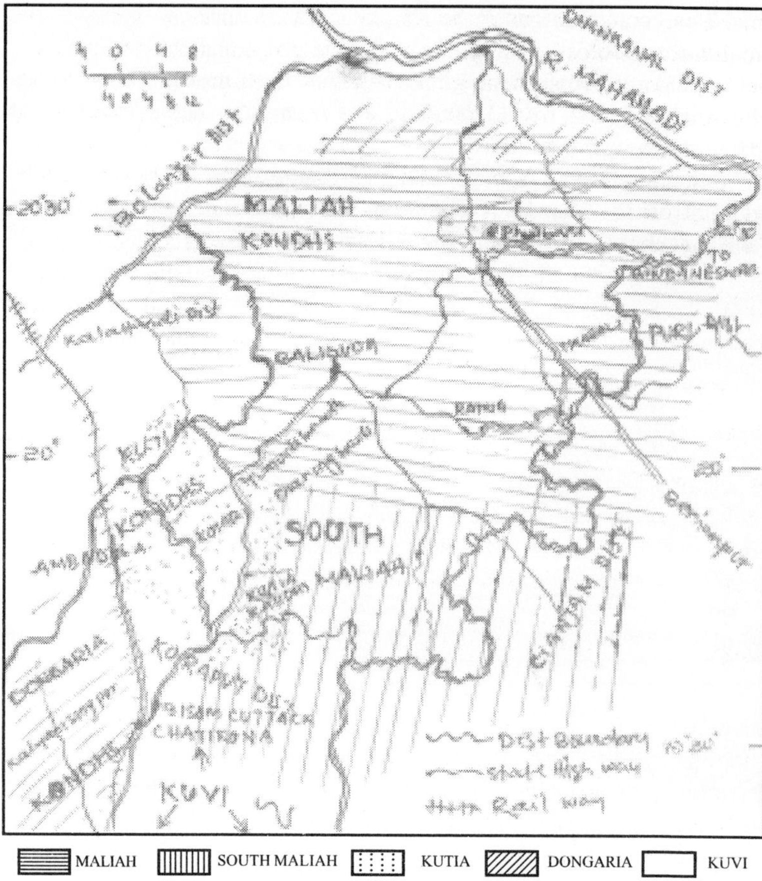

Map 4.4: Concentration of Kandh Sub-groups in Odisha.

Source: Nabakrushna Chaudhury Center for Development Studies.

to yield bumper crop of turmeric. The accounts given by these officials serve as valuable source of information regarding the culture of the Kandhs.

4.2.4 *Economic Life*

The Kandhs, however, born and bred in the midst of rugged hills, dense forests, deep water courses and insalubrious climate, experienced an economic life that was radically different from that of the people of the plains. The economic life of the Kandh and their survival is based on agriculture and forest. Agriculture is the chief occupation of the tribal people of Odisha. Most of the Kandhs claimed to be the original owners of the soil. Referring to the Kandhs, H.H. Risley (1915) reported that Kandhs claimed full rights of property in the soil by virtue of having cleaned the jungle and prepared the land for cultivation. In some villages individual ownership was unknown and the land was cultivated on a system of temporary occupation subject to periodical redistribution under the orders of the headman. Priority of occupation very often formed the origin of the rights. But due to poverty and economic exploitation, they were unable to bring more cultivable land under settled cultivation.

Agriculture

The Kandhs practise both shifting and settled cultivation. The Kutia Kandh and some among the Dongoria Kandh are primarily shifting cultivators. The Dongoria Kandhs practise horticulture also. The Desia and Kuvi Kandhs have taken to plough cultivation.

Shifting Cultivation

Shifting cultivation is known by different names like "Saura Chasa" by the Kutia Kandha and "Horu tasa" by Dongoria and Kuvi Kandhs. But it is popularly known as "Podu chasa" in Koraput Region. In such cultivation plots are clan owned in Northern Odisha. The plots are distributed by the headman of each village in consultation with the village elders. But in south Odisha, the Kandhs by tradition, privately own the shifting lands. During summer, they clean the forest and burn it after the debris dry out. In the ashes thus available, they sow seed after the commencement of the rains. After raising one or two crops, the Kandhs allowed it to remain fallow for few years. In the meantime, the trees would grow sufficiently for a second felling. Then the same process would continue until the land showed signs of exhaustion. They then finally abandoned this land and they cleared a fresh jungle for future crops. Shifting cultivation (Podu) is carried on the hills and hill slopes.

However, it is a rain fed type agriculture with primitive, crude and traditional method of cultivation. The production of land both per acre and per worker is quite low. Availability of plain and flat lands for settled agriculture is quite limited. Good quality of settled land has been alienated since long from them to others due to various socio-economic reasons. Still the plain land agriculture of the Kandhs, where it is practised, suffers from uneconomic holding, tenurial disincentive, crude technology, and low investment etc.

Forest Collection

The Kandhs collect forest produces to supplement their income from agriculture. They collect minor forest produces, house building materials, fuel wood and herbal medicines etc. from the forest. They also go for hunting during their leisure time. But scope of hunting is now quite limited due to large scale deforestation and restrictions imposed on it. They collect various types of fruits, roots, leaves and fibers to supplement their food requirement.

Tribal life mainly moves around the forests. Economically, ecologically, socially and culturally tribal life is inseparable from forest. The agriculture of the Kandhs is to a great extent forest based. The return from agriculture being quite low and unrewarding, and the forest resources fast degrading, the economic life of Kandhs of Koraput region in general and that of the Laxmipur Block in particular is becoming miserable day by day.

Livestock

The Kandhs domesticate cows, buffaloes, goats, pigs and fowls. The cattle are also used for ploughing. Other animals are sold for cash or required for sacrifice in socio-religious activities. The Kandhs generally do not milch their cows. Animal husbandry is not a commercial enterprise for the Kandhs.

Wage Work

Wage earning now-a-days becomes another source of major income of the Kandhs. The Kandhs also work for their own people at a very low wage or in exchange for some food and drink. Cooperative labour exchange happens to be usual practice among them prevailing from a long time.

Trade and Commerce

The Kandhs generally are not interested in trade and commerce. On the contrary, they detested trade and considered it a degrading occupation.

Trade and commerce in the Kandh areas are mostly done by Doms (an SC community), Sundhi (Wine Vendors), Kumuti (moneylenders and traders), and some outside Odia persons.

Cottage Industry

Kandhs also practise cottage industries like rope making, leaf plate making, weaving, spinning, knitting, black smithy, stone carving, wood work, bamboo basketry etc. Such practices depend upon the availability of local resources and skills as well as markets.

4.2.5 *The Social Life*

Most of the Kandh habitations are of small units consisting of 5 to 100 houses. These are scattered too. The village site is usually selected with reference to the geographical situation which is not frequented by the carnival animals, proximity of the village to a source of water and close availability of agricultural fields.

Housing

The traditional houses of Kandhs are "Piri" (straw) thatced mud houses. Now-a-days, gradually the houses are either built or renovated by using bricks, tiles, asbestos sheets but with the traditional pattern by using timber and planks. Most of such houses are being built with Government schemes. The plinth areas of the house are generally 10 ft. × 13 ft. There are two to three steps leading to the door way in height and mostly made of mud and in few cases cement.

Social Institutions

"Kaja-Sahada" or the central street is an important portion of the Kandh village, which enables the people to build houses in order to have a face to face living. In the middle of the village street "Tana Penu" or Earth Goddess is installed. In every village there were bachelor's dormitory separately constructed for both boys and girls. Unmarried boys and girls spend their nights in their respective dormitories. Youth dormitory strengthened the social unity and cohesiveness and solidarity. Its main social function was to impart training to youths in dance and music and the traditional lore of the Kandhs. Youth members were trained to direct their energy for successful adjustment with the people in social, economic, religious and other aspects of life. It provided sleeping accommodation for the unmarried boys and girls and was a store of all musical instruments. It provided a mechanism for initiating the growing generation of the Kandhs into their cultural heritage and the Kandhs dormitory was mainly a sort of matrimonial agency. Pre-marital sexual life is chiefly forbidden in the Kandh society. But "Dhunduni Pachhu" song between boys and girls at the time of match-making before marriage was an interesting part of tribal youths. Unfortunately, such an important social institution is gradually dying down for various reasons.

The Kandhs sometimes live in joint families but mostly nuclear families are found. A son after marriage goes to a separate house to stay. It is the usual practice. The family is patriarchal, where father controls the activities of the family. After his death, entire property of the family is divided into equal parts among the sons. Daughters do not have share over the property.

The Headman

The office of the headman is hereditary. Continuance of the post by a person also depends upon the physical and mental fitness of the person. He is the head of the traditional Panchayat at the village level and presides over the Panchyat meeting.

Family Life — Marriage and Divorce

The parents without a child can adopt a child. Both male and female may go for divorce at their will and can marry for the second time. Widow marriage is allowed among the Kandhs.

4.2.6 *Political Life*

The indigenous tribal communities still have well organized patterns of traditional leadership not only at the village level but also at the "Mutha" level. The "Mutha" consists of a group of adjoining villages and is treated as an administrative-cum-social unit. Each Kandh village is a political unit having its own set of leaders. The headman or "Naik", religious headman "Jani" and "Saunta", the so-called landlord of the village, and other senior members, landlord of the village still have their importance in the Kandh villages. Their posts are hereditary. Next to "Jani" and "Saunta", are "Bismajhi" and "Barika". The "Barika", village messenger, belongs to "Dom" or "Pano" community. Only the post of Barika is remunerative and all other posts are honorary.

Besides, the above traditional leaders, there are socio-religious functionaries like “Bejunis” (female priests) and “Dishari” (Astrologer) who also hold key position in Kandh village.

After the introduction of statutory Panchayats, the traditional leadership is gradually loosing its importance. The PRI members including Ward members, Sarpanch, Samiti members and Zilla Parishad members take part in the Planning and implementing processes at Panchayat, Block and District levels. They are responsible for the implementation of welfare programmes in the rural areas. However, traditional village councils still play an important role in deciding cases like family and social conflicts, deciding dates for socio-religious festivals and community activities etc.

4.2.7 *Household Furniture and Articles*

A careful look at the ‘Kandh’ house gives an indication of the use of simple equipments. These constitute gourd, wood, bamboo and stone articles, besides baskets, earthen pots and iron implements made by “lohars” or “Roholis”. The ‘Roholis’ are a cultural sub-group of the Kandhs. They make agricultural implements like iron shoe shares, spades, axe, arrow heads. The hunting implements like arrow, bow, big sticks are kept in the houses and used as and when necessary. Small clappers, Dung-Dunga, Mouth-organ and flute are some of the musical instruments used by the Kandhs.

Apart from the common materials to be found in a house, sometimes variations are marked in the houses of specialized people.

4.2.8 *Dress and Ornaments*

The Kandhs wear very simple dress that is sometimes not sufficient to protect him/her from extreme climates. Most of them use only loin clothes. The women wear two pieces of clothes, one around the waist up to the knees and another for the upper portion of the body. A male ‘Dongria Kandh’ puts on a cloth called Kodi, 16 feet in length and one foot in width. Some of the sophisticated Kandhs in recent times have started wearing *lungi*, shirts and full pants. On special occasion head-gear is used. Coloured turban is used by the groom during marriage.

Kandh women are very fond of ornaments. They beautify themselves with hair pins, ear rings, nose rings and head necklaces. Wristlets and ear rings are used by the males of the primitive sections of the Kandh community. The males too like to grow long hair and tie these into a knot at their nape in a traditional fashion. Except the Dongria Kandh, other Kandhs tattoo their faces and hands. A knife and an axe are inseparable companion of male Dongria Kandh.

4.2.9 *Food and Drinks*

The staple food of Kandh is Ragi (Eleusine Coracana Gaertn) gruel. Ragi is a major produce of agriculture. It is cultivated in large scale by them. Gradually Kandhs are motivated to grow rice. Now-a-days most of the 'Kandhs' prefer to take rice for dinner and lunch. They cultivate, purchase and even barter rice from non-tribals and to some extent, from the civil supply department stores of State Government. Besides their staple food, the Kandhs consume a variety of edible seasonal products like sweet potato, little millet, vegetables, banana, mango, jackfruit and maize. During the joyful events, rice and meat are the most common items.

The 'Kandh' are very fond of alcohol. They have earned a name for preparation of variety of drinks like 'Pansi Kadu' (Prepared out of fragmented jackfruit juice), "Salap Kadu" (Sagopalm toddy), Irpi Kadu (distilled Mahua Liquor), "Landa" (Ragi-beer) and "Pendum" (Rice-beer). In addition to drinks, they are very fond of taking tobacco that is chewed in the form of powder or smoked.

4.2.10 *Religious Faiths and Festivals*

The Kandhs believe in "Dharti Penu" or Earth Goddess as the Supreme Being. She is all-powerful and is regarded as the highest of all deities. Therefore, she is worshipped in all the ceremonies as a mark of honour and respects.

"Jhakiri", "Sunukudi", and "Jatrakudi" are common places of worship in almost all Kandh villages at different occasions

Gungi Penu, Bhima Penu, Lai Penu and Sita Penu are the deities of stream, hill, forest and wealth respectively. Birna Penu is responsible for rain. Sun is worshipped as 'Dharmu Devata'. They also worship ancestral spirits called the "Dumas". They believe in the existence of "Mahani" (ghost). They also believe in and practise white and black magic.

The Kandhs prefer to have a large number of feasts and festivals round the year. The religious ceremonies and festivals are "Herei Parbu", "Setra Beta", "Bicha Parbu", "Mandiarani", "Pusu Parbu, "Harti Puja", "Sita puja and "Meriah" or "Toki Parbu". Toki Parbu is observed in the month of February-March with pomp and gaiety.

4.2.11 *Health and Hygiene*

The Kandh people have very poor sense of hygiene and sanitation as compared to our modern standard. The poor living condition and lack of awareness about personal hygiene are the factors responsible for their poor health. This results in skin and other infectious diseases. They do not take bath properly and the teeth are not properly cleaned. Many of them wear dirty clothes and use mainly water of the stream and generally they do not prefer to use tube well water even though now-a-days tube-wells are dug in the villages. The Kandhs believe that flowing water is better than any type of stagnant water. Therefore, they suffer from water borne diseases like diarrhea, dysentery and other gastro-intestinal diseases. The diseases like tuberculosis, influenza, cold and cough are also common among the Kandhs. They also suffer from malaria frequently, which is one of the major causes of unnatural and untimely death of the tribals. Most of them believe that the diseases are caused by evil-spirits or "Dumas" and they prefer to go to "Bejunis" and "gurus" rather than to doctors and other health workers for treatment.

4.2.12 *Life Cycle of Kandh*

Below is given a brief analysis about the life cycle of the Kandh Tribe.

Birth

The occasion of birth is rejoiced by every body in Kandh community. Kandhs think that it is a moment when an ancestor takes rebirth and gets back to life. The rebirth of an ancestor is definitely a mark of future prosperity. The joy starts from the moment when a woman gets pregnant. Women play multiple roles as livelihood earners, child bearers as well as child rearers. A woman, right from the conception until the last month before delivery, works in the fields and does other domestic works. She is neither specially cared for nor neglected during pregnancy. However, she tries to keep herself active.

When labour pain begins, some women massage oil of "Mahua" seeds or castor seeds on the abdomen. Such gentle massage continues till child birth. The 'Placenta' is buried behind the house after delivery. After birth, the mother and the child are given a place in 'dapa' for a month. The pollution period is to be observed for one month. During this period, the mother is restricted to move into other rooms and also to move in front of 'Dharani Penu'. She is provided with very light food like hot cooked rice, salt and raggi gruel. At the end of pollution period both the mother and the child are given purificatory bath with turmeric and a paste made of the bark of mango tree.

After the home entry, another religious performance is organized and the child is given a name. When the name is given, the performer offers a sacrifice to satisfy the ancestral spirits. The sacrificial animal may be a pigeon, a fowl, a goat or a buffalo depending upon the economic status of the family concerned.

Marriage

In marriage, the Kandh maintain endogamy. The types of marriages generally observed are arranged marriage, marriage by elopement and marriage by force. In any type of marriage girl's decision is final. The husbands are generally older than wives.

Among the Kandhs, like other tribals, there is the system of bride price in which the boy's side gives some cash, ornament, crops, cloth and cow and liquor etc. to girl's parents. They consider a girl as the daughter of their "Kutumba" (community). Hence, the marriage ceremony takes the shape of a community festival. This bride price varies from place to place. Those who are not able to pay are asked to work in the house of his would be father-in-law until his bride price is thought to be paid. This is known as "Karjami". Both levirate and surrorate type of marriages are prevalent in their society. Polygyny is accepted in all circumstances. Widows are allowed to marry. Some of the advanced sections of the Kandh community in recent time have started imitating to certain extent the Hindu type of marriage.

Death

During deaths, the Kandhs normally practise cremation, but burial is preferred when death is due to infectious diseases. The death rites are meant for the appeasement of the spirit (duma) in the other world. In this performance, mango bark is used as the purificatory material. In normal death, the corpse is not touched by those who are not a relative to the person. The corpse is carried to the cremation ground on a cot (Kateli) or a bamboo mat. On reaching the cremation ground, the corpse is dressed with new clothes brought by the relatives. In each village, the cremation ground is somewhere in the nearby forest. Well to do families may organize a feast for the people who participate in the funeral rites. "Hakki Kadu" (wine for the hunger) is also provided. Those who attended

"Mahani" (cremation ground) will be purified after bathing "Maha eau" which act is performed by the village priests or bejunis. After death, it is believed that the soul of the dead goes to sphere of "Jamarani", the goddess who created the earth. They believe in rebirth.

4.2.13 *Inter-ethnic Relationship*

The ethnic group closest to the Kandh and in constant touch with their socio-economic life is the "Dom" (a Scheduled Caste community). The Doms have settled along with the Kandhs since long. Doms serve Kandh as a barik (the messenger) and assists during trading. Apart from Doms, we come across a local caste Hindu community people known as the "Sundhis". They were wine vendors in tribal areas. Their trading in liquor has considerably reduced in recent times. They have started trading in various other things in Kandh areas. The Sundhis are now found to deal with cooked food items, snacks etc. in the weekly markets. Some of them work also as moneylenders. Other caste of plains, other than "Sundhis" and "Doms" are the "Kaini Jati". They have also inter-ethnic relationship with Kandhs.

Hindu festivals like 'Rath Yatra', 'Dusherra', 'Ganesh Puja' etc. are some of the socio-religious functions which bring Kandhs and other caste Hindus to a common platform.

4.2.14 *Development and Change*

With the march of time and in the era of Planning, some transformation has been noticed among the Kandhs in Odisha. This was because of the development of communication, transport, education, enactment of some protective laws as per the provisions of the Constitution of India. A small number of Kandhs have marginally gained because of various welfare measures undertaken during the plan period. But majority of them living mostly in remote areas, in the hills and forests have not gained much economically and socially even after so many years of planning.

NOTE

1. Data presented for analysis have been copiously drawn from Five Year Perspective Plan under NFFWP (2005-06 to 2009-10) Koraput District (COATS-NFFWP, 2005).

5

TRIBAL EXPLOITATION

5.0 Introduction

In this chapter, an attempt has been made to analyze the causes, agencies and consequences of tribal exploitation in general and that of the Kandhs in particular. At the same time, the Constitutional safeguards meant for the tribals and the developmental programmes in tribal areas have been dealt with. Tribals in India are often characterized as the persons susceptible to exploitation. As stated earlier it is because of their ignorance, illiteracy, simplicity and poverty, they are exploited by moneylenders, traders, wine vendors, government officials and sometimes, by some of the comparatively well-to-do tribals of their own community.

Raghavaiah (1971:11) has pointed out, "in the field of economy, the two are poles asunder. While the tribal is content with his food gathering or pastoral way of life, the non-tribal is advancing to emulate the sophisticated man of the town and city, living very much behind, his tribal brethren. While the tribal still follows his 'Produce to consume' production policy, the non-tribals is taking to intensive cultivation, adopting the 'produce to market' type of cash economy. The tribal is unambitious, simple, honest, unequivocating and straight forward while his non-tribal brother is ambitious, calculating, planning, scheming and patronizing in day-to-day dealings with the tribals. Non-tribals exploit the tribals, but this is not done on a racial basis but as man to man for personal advantage".

The tribals generally have low sense of acquisition, accumulation and mostly lack profit motive in their dealings. At the same time their poverty, ignorance, illiteracy and credulous nature lead them to exploitation easily by various persons or agencies.

5.1 Factors Leading to Tribal Exploitation

A brief analysis of the factors leading to tribal exploitation is given as under:

5.1.1 *Poverty*

The term Poverty was unknown to the tribals for a long time. Their economy was a subsistence economy. Their wants were few, which could be fully satisfied with what they produced and consumed, with the support of natural resources locally available. The concept like poverty and richness are value-loaded and are used mostly in Economic terms. Tribals were happy with their so-called "culture of poverty" and these modern concepts were meaningless to them. It is only after implementation of forest policies, assimilation of modern economy with tribal economy, land tenure and land reforms adopted after independence and measuring of tribal economy in terms of modern axiomatic refinements and large scale deforestation, the tribals found themselves to be poverty-ridden in large numbers and they were treated backward, both socially and economically. In the modern sense of income measurement, the tribals are mostly poverty-ridden. About 90 per cent of them live below the poverty line. The tribals suffer from a vicious circle of poverty. Poverty is considered as the cause and effect of their exploitation.

5.1.2 *Tribal Indebtedness*

The indebtedness among the tribals is another important cause of their exploitation. At the household level, poverty generally leads to indebtedness. The tribals go for borrowing to supplement their food requirements; to meet various socio-religious obligations, to invest in agriculture and to meet other domestic and social obligations. Their drinking habits often compel them to borrow. It is roughly estimated that about 85 per cent of tribal families are affected by indebtedness and 72 per cent of the tribals were indebted to private moneylenders and remaining to meet their credit and consumer requirements from shopkeepers, friends and other sources (Verma, 1990:101). It had been said that the tribals were born in debt, lived in debt and passed on their burden to the progeny (Senapati and Sahu, 1966).

The origin of the problem was mainly due to the introduction of money economy in the tribal areas. Earlier tribal economy was mostly based on barter system. British Government demanded revenue in cash. Non-tribal moneylenders came forward to lend cash to tribals. Money economy gradually substituted barter system. The credulous tribal mind could not fathom the evil designs of the Sahukar (Moneylender) who not only disturbed their economy but also snatched away the smile from the innocent face.

The Sahukar and Moneylenders used to give tribals loan on easy terms for their drinks, marriages, festivals, and agricultural operations. Taking advantage of the illiteracy, ignorance and gullibility of the tribals, the Sahukars and moneylenders used to dictate terms, calculated interest at very high rate and manipulated the accounts in such a way that it became impossible to escape from the debt trap.

The tribals subsequently lost their land, which was mortgaged to obtain loans. The system ultimately degenerated into bonded labour or "Goti" which made the tribal virtually a slave. In the absence of any effective institutional agency of rural finance in the past, they had to fall back upon the moneylenders, traders and others, who could provide loans in times of need. With the implementation of anti-moneylending Acts in tribal areas, moneylending activities by private moneylenders have been checked to some extent. Cooperative Institutions, Regional Rural Banks and SHG groups have started providing loans in tribal areas. But the tribals are yet to take full advantage of such organized credit system.

5.1.3 *Land Alienation*

Land is the main stay of the tribals. Almost all of them are dependent on agriculture and allied activities. Their economy is primarily agro-based. Land is most important tangible asset of a tribal family. However, with the opening up of the tribal areas outsiders in large number entered into tribal territories; the tribal lands started to be alienated to non-tribals. Tribal lands were also alienated due to establishment of various Government as well as private projects. Consequently, a large number of tribal cultivators lost their land and were converted into landless labourers. The incidence of land alienation varies from state to state. According to a sample survey conducted by the Department of Rural Development in 1988, about 30 to 55 per cent of tribal households had been affected by land alienation. It also showed that about 80 per cent of land was alienated to the non-tribals (Verma, 1990:66).

In order to deal with the problem of land alienation in tribal areas particularly lands being transferred from tribals to non-tribals, various laws have been enacted and implemented in the states having tribal concentration to check land alienation. But the Acts/Laws were easily manipulated due to certain loopholes found in them.

In the past, the average tribal family had a fair size of landholding which supported it despite primitive methods of cultivation. It is not so now. Till the first half of the last century, the alienation of land did not create a serious problem for the tribals as the forests were still plentiful; this could save the tribals from food insecurity and provide them opportunity of employment. Problems started with fast degradation of forests in the tribal areas.

Another important cause of Land Alienation in Koraput region was due to construction of public projects like Balimela Dam, Machkund Dam, HAL Project, NALCO etc. and a number of irrigation projects in Koraput region. The acquisition of lands without proper resettlement and economic rehabilitation programmes has uprooted them from their natural habitat and means of livelihood.

Landless tribes living in and around the forest often encroach upon cultivable lands available in the forest. Government declared that all such encroachments in which FIRs had been filed would be regularized and *Patta* (right in the land) would be issued. But delay by forest departments in settling the cases, non-settlement of forest land between the forest and Revenue Department *pattas* could not be issued properly. So, they remained landless. It is expected that "The Scheduled Tribes and other Traditional Forests Dwellers (Recognition of Forest Rights) Act, 2006, if implemented properly, would bring justice to the forest dwellers in general and the tribals in particular." Land alienation to a great extent leads to loss of livelihood and enhancement of poverty. It further lead to indebtedness which ultimately lead to exploitation of severe nature.

5.1.4 *Bonded Labour*

Indebtedness among the tribals has degenerated an evil system of forced labour system known as "Bonded Labour" or "Goti" or "Halia". The indebted tribal persons were unable to repay the loan which was mainly manipulated by the moneylenders and traders and ultimately sold their capital assets and became "landless", "assetless" and even sometimes "homeless". When still the loan could not be fully repaid and tribals had nothing to mortgage and then they ultimately were forced to mortgage their own labour. Many times a lonee was unable to clear up his loan after serving with the Sahukar as "Goti" and the burden was passed on to his successors in the family. With the implementation of the Bonded Labour (Abolition) Act, 1976, the bonded labour system although has been abolished officially, but the practice continues in interior tribal pockets, in a hidden manner.

5.1.5 *Forest and the Tribals*

Since time immemorial, tribals in large number were the traditional habitants of forests. There has been a very close relation between the tribals and forest. As mentioned earlier tribals' socio-economic life, religion and culture — everything is linked with forest.

Forests provide them with prime necessities of life like food, clothing, fuel, fodder, materials to build their houses, edible leaves, tuber, honey, wild gum, meat and fish etc. Their rain coats and umbrellas are made of barks and leaves, mainly of Siali and Sal leaves. They prepare their liquor from mahua flowers, mango juice, jack fruit juice, "salap" (plam) etc. Streams known as "Jhars" in the forest provide them ample water for their use.

Forest, since historical times, provided the main economic base to the tribals. The tribal agriculture practices were mostly forest based. Shifting cultivators and also settled cultivators prepare their land by cleaning the forest. Forest is used for cattle rearing. They collect and sell minor forest products, honey, lacs etc. from forests. They are also getting employment opportunities by Forest Department and Forest Contractors when forest operation activities are undertaken. For bamboo, fibers, rope making material and other MNFP, they depend on forests.

Religious beliefs and practices are closely associated with forests. Special sacrifices are made to forest Gods (Hour Penu) before cutting trees for shifting cultivation and going for hunting etc.

However, the Governments' anxiety to preserve forests treating forest as a source of revenue, clearance of forest for various projects, implementation of forest policies prohibiting forest dwellers to use forests etc., restricted the scope of tribals in the forests and tribals became aliens in their own land. Once the original masters of the forests now became the subjects and were placed under the mercy of forest departments and forest contractors.

Unfortunately, the forest officials and forest contractors have become the other agencies of exploitation of tribals. Tribals are booked under several forest cases and even fines imprisoned. They bribe the pretty forest officials and sometimes to police and excise officials for carrying out various activities for their livelihood in the forest. They are cheated, while selling the minor forest produces to the traders and middlemen. These are some of the ways by which tribals are being exploited in the forest front.

5.1.6 *Problem of Unemployment and Migration*

Traditionally, tribal people were living in a self-sufficient economy though at a subsistence level. They were engaged round the year in cultivation and other activities like hunting, food gathering, picking up minor forest produces etc. As mentioned earlier, with commercialization of forests and forest being treated as a source of State Revenue, tribal rights in forest have been restricted. Carrying out cultivation in the forest, collection of non-timber forest products and hunting have restricted. There happens to be wide scale land alienation. They become virtually landless. Majority of the tribals have become landless labourers. Wage employment opportunities being very limited in interior tribal areas, the tribals faced the problem of unemployment and food insecurity. Consequently, they migrate to other places in search of wage employment. Labour contractors take the advantage of cheap availability of tribal labourers and took them to work even outside the State. They work under inhuman conditions; are underpaid, underfed and physically tortured. There is no end to their exploitation.

5.1.7 *Illiteracy and Ignorance*

Education is key to the socio-economic development of human beings and important tool for empowerment of human beings in general and weaker sections in particular. The literacy rate of the tribals in the district is very low. It is only 18.68 per cent (2001) among the tribals of Koraput as against the general district average of 35.72 per cent and State average of 63.08 per cent. On the other hand, the rural literacy rate of the district is 27.30 per cent constituting 39.16 per cent males and 15.61 per cent females. The literacy rate of rural tribals (figures not available at present) would be still less, i.e. less than 18.68 per cent as estimated at the district average.

5.1.8 *Public Projects and Displacement and Land Alienation*

The tribal areas are rich in natural resources. A number of projects, both major and medium, *viz.* irrigation, energy generation and industrial units have been set-up in the tribal areas. The tribals, due to lack of education and requisite skill are not able to take advantage of the new economic opportunities which have been grabbed by the outsiders migrated to tribal areas. It has not only deprived them of the opportunity in the new ventures but also alienated them from their resource base, i.e. the land and subjected them to exploitation by the middlemen and contractors.

5.1.9 *Social and Cultural Problems*

The tribals are socio-economically disadvantaged groups. They are not only poor, but illiterate, ignorant and credulous in nature. They remained away from the mainstream of civilization and live mostly in hills and forests. They follow taboos of various kinds and stick to their age-old customs and traditions. Poverty, indebtedness and exploitation are parts and parcels of their life. Their exploitation is not only limited to their economy but also extended to social and political fields.

The tribal people believe in malevolent and benevolent spirits. Taking advantage of the belief very often they are cheated by the village priests, 'Gurus'/'Bejunis' and others due to their ignorance. Certainly, the practice is similar to a type of exploitation. Modern political leaders (not all but some of them) have started to take bribes from the poor tribals with a promise to give some benefits under some schemes. But the promises are not fulfilled in all cases.

They observe large number of feasts, festivals and rituals round the year either for better yield of crops or for hunting or to save themselves from malevolent spirits. Marriages, birth and death rites and other rituals are costly affairs in their standard and they usually borrow money during such occasions. Moneylenders, sahukars, traders and intermediaries can easily trap these people during such occasions. Once they are indebted, it is not easy to escape and there is no end to their sufferings. It has been sometimes alleged that innocent tribal girl and women have been subject to sexual exploitation by these people and some other outsiders.

Child labour is widely prevalent in tribal areas. Children after 5 to 6 years of age start helping their parents in various economic activities like cattle rearing, field-work, collecting minor forest products and all other agricultural activities. Senior girls are engaged to take care of small children. This hampers their education. Poverty and ignorance are the factors responsible to engage such small children in household and other economic activities at a time when they are supposed to attend the school for education. This may be treated as a type of social exploitation of small and innocent children even by their parents and sometimes by others outside the family or village.

At the time of marriage payment of "bride price" for getting a girl in marriage is a must among the tribals. If a young man is not able to pay the amount due to his poverty he has to work in his in-laws' house as a labour to compensate the value of the bride price. This may also be indirectly treated as a type of exploitation by his own in-laws, even if it is for few years.

The Kandhs, are too much addicted to liquor. Taking the advantage of their weakness for liquor, the Sundhi sahukars (traditional liquor vendors) and local Doms used to offer them liquor on credit. Once they were too much intoxicated and went beyond their control, these unscrupulous businessmen and traders sometimes took their thumb impression on plain papers. Once it was done, nobody knew to what extent these people would suffer and the amount of wealth including the land that would be alienated.

Dom exploitation in the past was prevalent in almost all villages in Koraput regions.

5.2 Special Note on Dom Exploitation in Kandh Villages of Laxmipur Block

It is alleged that the tribals in Koraput region have been historically exploited by several agencies like moneylenders, sahukars, traders, police, revenue and excise officials and other Government officials, caste-Hindus like Sundhi (wine vendors), Kumutis and Doms. A special reference needs to be made about the role of "Doms" in exploiting the Kandhs in Laxmipur Area of Koraput District.

The "Doms" in Koraput region and "Panos" in Bolangir and Kandhmala region are defamed as the exploiters in tribal areas of Odisha. They both belong to SC community. They act as moneylenders, petty traders, liquor vendors, contractors, and middle-men in trading activities and in course of their operation they exploit the poor and innocent tribes in various ways. In Koraput areas, the Doms also work as "Barik" or messengers to the headman of the village. So he has also an important social function to play.

Scheduled Caste people are treated as untouchables by the tribal people. So, sometimes they try to ill-treat the tribals by intentionally touching the tribal women, using their "Chuan" (Water Stream used for drinking water), wells and sometimes forcibly entering into tribal huts etc.

The Doms have co-settled with tribals in Koraput region since long. A scholar states about the role of Doms while writing on Dongaria Kandhs as follows:

> "The Doms are immigrants from the plains of the districts — Bolangir and Kalahandi. They have permanently settled in Niyamagiri hills by engaging in petty trade and business with the Dongaria Kandhs and exploiting them at the cost of their isolation, credulous nature and ignorance. In spite of that both the groups are dependable and have developed symbiotic relationship from the past not known in the history" (Das Patnaik, 1984).

Rout (1964-65) also made a study on Dom exploitation in Kandh villages of Koraput District. The study made an attempt to trace a few instances of exploitations in the Kandh villages of Kumbhikota and Laxmipur areas of Koraput District. A total of 86 exploitation cases were collected. Table 5.1 gives a quantitative picture of such cases of exploitation.

Table 5.1: Types of Exploitation of the Kandhs by both Governmental and Non-governmental Agencies

Sl.No.	*Types of Exploitation*	*No. of Cases*	*Percentage*
1.	Stealing and forcibly taking away crops, cattle and other valuables	45	52.3
2.	Cheating by Forest Department and by Police people	15	17.4
3.	Cheating in barter and business	14	16.3
4.	Land encroachment	9	10.5
5.	Exploitation by mining people	2	2.3
6.	Rape and seduction	1	1.2
	TOTAL	**86**	**100.0**

Source: Adibasi, 1964-65: 21-28.

Deducting seventeen cases (serial no. 2 and 5) of exploitation by Government agencies the scholar stated that the rest sixty-nine cases were done by Doms. To put it in more concrete terms about 20 per cent of exploitation cases were related to Government Agencies, while in 80 per cent cases the Doms were found to be the culprits.

In both Laxmipur and Kumbhikota areas, Doms were found to be the chief exploiters. However, people around Laxmipur, the Block headquarters, were a little advanced, they are not easily cheated by Doms, but, in Kumbhikota, on the other hand, they fall a prey to exploitation, as the Kandhs mostly inhabit interior rocky terrains. Doms not only exploit the Kandhs of their own village, but extend their grip to the neighboring villages also.

Rout (*ibid.*), in his research study has pointed out various kinds of Dom exploitation in the Kandh villages. They were as follows:

(i) Land encroachment by Dom Sahukars on mortgage, by force, or by any other unfair means.
(ii) Cheating in barter and marketing.
(iii) Demanding crop after harvest, groups of Doms numbering ten to twenty move to the threshing floor of the Kandhs and demand a major share of the harvest.
(iv) Stealing crops, cattle and other valuables.
(v) Highway Robbery — means forcibly taking away things in broad day light.
(vi) Rape and seduction.

5.3 Nature and Extent of Exploitation

As stated earlier, concentration of tribals mainly the Kandhs is the highest in Laxmipur Block out of 14 blocks of Koraput district. They constitute nearly 85 per cent of the total tribal population of the block. Their economy mainly revolves round agriculture, NTFP collection and wage labour. Their socio-economic life is mostly characterized by poverty, hunger, underdevelopment, illiteracy, ill health, malnutrition and food insecurity. The reasons are manifold. Uneconomic and undulating landholdings, low productivity of the land, lack of resources to invest in agriculture and in trade, illiteracy and ignorance and above all, their exploitation are the major causes of their poverty and deprivation. They are socio-economically exploited.

An attempt has been made in the following paragraphs to trace the extent of exploitation in Kandh villages of Laxmipur Block as well as the causes thereof. The field investigation has brought into light the present practices of exploitation of Kandhs in the sample villages.

5.3.1 *Land Transfer*

The sample villages under study are predominantly inhabited by Kandhs. Other than Kandhs a few families of Doms, Shundis and other caste

Hindus and Christians are found in these and near-by villages; but they are in minority. Since long, most of the valuable plots of paddy land prepared by Kandhs near the stream bed or closer to some water sources had been alienated to non-tribal sahukars, traders, wine vendors etc. The major cause of such land alienation was indebtedness.

After the enactment of Acts like "The Orissa (Scheduled Areas) Transfer of Immovable Property (by Scheduled Tribes) Regulation, 1956 (Regulation 2 of 1956) and its Amendment Regulation of 2000, transfer of land from tribals to non-tribals has almost been checked.

As per rule, land owned by the tribals can neither be sold nor can be mortgaged to the non-tribals. An unintentional consequence of this state of things resulted in the fact that some of the well-to-do tribals belonging to their community have got an opportunity to purchase lands from the tribals at a throw away price. It is because there is no bar in transferring land from tribals to tribals. As a result, the gap between rich and poor within the tribal community is growing day-by-day. Comparatively better off tribals have started exploiting their brethren. We may call them as "tribal exploiters" (See case study no. 9).

Land Alienation for Establishment of Aditya Alumina Company

Recently, for the establishment of Aditya Alumina Company Ltd. at Kansariguda by HINDALCO Industries Ltd. Group, several acres of lands of the village Biriguda and Rajan Panasaguda of Odiapentha Panchayat in Laxmipur Block have been acquired with the intervention of the state Government. A total amount of 439.45 acres of private land from Koraput district have been acquired for this purpose. Out of this, 111.96 acres of private land has been acquired from Rajan Panasguda (sample village of Odiapentha Panchyat), out of which 103.42 acres belong to the tribal families. Compensation has been paid at the rate of ₹ 3,42,000 per acre, it is revealed.

Out of 20 sample households taken in the study from the village Rajan Panasguda, only 9 sample households lost 20.50 acres of land to the company. As the families did not receive compensation during the period of data collection the anticipated amount of money to be received towards compensation has not been included in income calculation.

The case of land encroached families who have lost land for the purpose has not yet been decided. It is also revealed that, all the sample families had encroached more than 45 acres (approximately) of Government land mainly in the foothills of Kodinga Mali, Melka horu

(Hill), Hechi horu and Godka horu (local name of the hills which is acquired by the company as Government land) situated in west and western-south part of the village Rajan Panasguda (Left side of Koraput-Rayagada Railway line).

It is interesting to note that the Kandh families are interested to surrender their lands to the industry because of cash compensation and the promises made by the authorities for providing job in the industry and it is found that the company executives created an environment as if they were acquiring lands from these villages by showing mercy to the tribals.

The tribals of this area are depending on forest and its adjoining valleys (mentioned as above) for their livelihood. They have been depending on these natural resources for their food requirement, cattle rearing, collection of minor forest products and other necessities of their livelihood. However, they have no legal records of rights over such lands and hence are not entitled to receive any kind of compensation. The Government also claimed that there was no forest in the mines area. Hence, there is no question of dependence of the people on forest land. Company promises to provide alternative sources of livelihood through NGO interventions, plantation in the waste land, providing educational facilities etc. But it practically did very little in the affected villages of Rajan Panasaguda and Biriguda. The same company also acquired 800 acres of private land and 900 acres of Government land from Rayagada district.

Another important information reported during field study is that in most cases utilization of such compensation money is not made productively by the tribals. They spend this money mostly for purchasing fashionable consumer durables like motor cycle, radio, TV, C.D. etc. So a sustainable livelihood of these affected people in future is doubtful.

5.3.2 *Exploitation: Causes and Consequence*

Indebtedness

When the Kandhs borrow in cash or kind from non-tribals like Sundhi, Kumuti, Doms and other Sahukars, they borrow with a contract that the borrowers have to repay the loan mostly in terms of grains when the next harvest is over. The rate of interest for such loan is generally kept very high. This is sometimes even one hundred per cent or goes up to 200 to 300 per cent per annum. In case of crop failure or any other natural calamity in the ensuing year and the debtor fails to repay his loan amount the creditors demand more amount at a compound interest rate towards his principal. Table 5.2 shows the extent of exploitation through moneylanding by various agencies like tribal, non-tribal and SC, Sahukars or moneylenders.

Land Alienation

In long run, the debt burden becomes so heavy that the Kandhs are forced to surrender land to the creditor. Money and crops are also sometimes lent to the Kandhs against the mortgage of land. In the past, as it was reported during field study, on the occasion of non-payment of loan amount, the land was ultimately surrendered to the creditors. Thus, land alienation happens due to non-payment of the loan amount.

Under acute hardship and/or to meet socio-economic obligations a Kandh usually sells a piece of land. As, they cannot sell it to other non-tribals due to legal restriction, they are bound to sell it to some of their own relatives and kinsmen. Many times they sell the land at a throw away price.

Bonded Labour

Indebtedness among the tribals in the study area ultimately leads to a degenerated system of labour which is known as "Bonded Labour", locally known as "Goti" or "Halia". The poor tribals borrow money from the moneylenders to meet their economic, social and religious needs. As they have no other assets they mortgage their own labour in lieu of the loan taken. In spite of legislative measures adopted since 1976 to abolish this evil system, it is found that the system still continues in the area in one form or the other. The said labour gets nominal wage ranging between ₹ 2000 and ₹ 7500 per annum, with some other marginal benefits like clothes, medicines, a lunch etc. Bonded labour or Goti which was quite a common feature in rural tribal areas is not openly found, but the system is still in a hidden form or in a separate name (see case study no. 10).

Liquor Culture

The tribals in general and the Kandhs in particular have a liquor culture of their own. They need it during all ceremonial occasions and rituals. The Kandhs are very much addicted to liquor. In the past Sundhis and Doms were generally liquor vendors but now-a-days some of the tribals are also found distilling and selling liquor. Too much being addicted to liquor and procuring loan for obtaining liquor is another cause of their being exploited.

Migration

Non-availability of employment in the native area, expectation to get higher wages outside and attraction of city life etc. induce the tribals to migrate outside. They are easily captured by the labour agents and allured with various attractive promises, which are rarely fulfilled. The irony of the fact is that, none of them goes after registering their names either in the Panchayat or Block headquarters or in any labour office. Illtreatment received from the employees, longer hours of work in a day, poor and unhealthy camp environment, low-payment from the contractor etc., as it was reported during field study, are the common complaints generally made by the migrant labourers.

It is also found that out of the money they earn, they buy many consumer durables like a pair of goggles, a pair of jeans, boots, a transistor or radio set, a camera, a bottle of Indian made foreign liquor besides some clothes for their family members and toys for their children. This extravagance actually costs them dearly and they lose more than what they gain. The money left is not enough for survival till the next harvest and they again fall into the trap of the moneylenders. Sometimes, the migrant labourers return home with empty hand after being severely exploited and tortured at the work site.

5.4 Extent of Exploitation

The field study in both roadside and remote groups of villages reveals that the Kandhs are still victims of various types of exploitation. Nevertheless, it is not easy to find out such cases of exploitation and prepare a quantitative schedule for the present study. Vested interest local political power structure created obstacles to go deep into the problem in the study area and victims of exploitation feared to open up in the matter. However, based on the available information after creating close intimacy with the respondents and others in the field an attempt has been made to find out the extent of exploitation. Table 5.2 gives the details of such findings.

It is found that, total number of cases of exploitation by SC is highest in the sample villages and it is 311 cases, followed by non-tribal traders, moneylenders and sahukars which are 280 cases in total. In

Table 5.2: No. of Cases of Kandh Exploitation Revealed, Agencies and Types of Exploitation in Sample Villages of Laxmipur Block, During the Year 2009-10

Sl.No.	*Agencies & Types of Exploitation*	*No. of Cases*					
		Road-side Villages	*%age*	*Remote Villages*	*%age*	*Total*	*%age*
1.	**Tribal to Tribals**						
(a)	Moneylending (with high rate of interest)	4	5.33	21	18.10	25	13.09
(b)	Liquor vending	18	24.00	08	6.90	26	13.61
(c)	Land mortgaging and land acquiring	15	20.00	17	14.66	32	16.75
(d)	Cheating in trade and barter	6	8.00	16	13.79	22	11.52
(e)	Bribe to PRI members	32	42.67	54	46.55	86	45.03
	Total	**75**	**100.00**	**116**	**100.00**	**191**	**100.00**
2.	**Non-Tribal traders, moneylenders and Sahukar's (Except SC)**						
(a)	Cheating in trade and barter	75	66.37	104	62.27	179	63.93
(b)	Moneylending (with high rate of interest)	6	5.31	10	5.99	16	5.71
(c)	Liquor vending	12	10.62	18	10.78	30	10.72
(d)	Cheating and bribe taking of Govt. officials (forest police, excise and revenue personnel	20	17.70	35	20.96	55	19.64
(e)	Land mortgaging and land acquiring	00	00	00	00	00	00
	Total	**113**	**100.00**	**167**	**100.00**	**280**	**100.00**
3.	**SC Exploitation**						
(a)	Higgiling	48	37.80	39	21.19	87	27.98
(b)	Forcibly or tactfully taking away cattle etc.	2	1.57	5	2.72	7	2.25
(c)	Moneylending (with high rate of interest)	17	13.39	23	12.50	40	12.86
(d)	Trade and barter (including weight and measure)	52	40.94	100	54.35	152	48.87
(e)	Highway robbery	0	0.00	0	0.00	0	0.00
(f)	Harassing Kandh women	0	0.00	0	0.00	0	0.00
(g)	Liquor vending	8	6.30	17	9.24	25	8.04
	Total	**127**	**100.00**	**184**	**100.00**	**311**	**100.00**

Note. Information collected basing only from the answers of the respondents and no judicial probe has been undertaken to confirm the facts.
Source: Field study.

addition, 191 cases of tribal to tribal exploitation are also recorded from the field study.

Out of the total 191 cases of tribal to tribal exploitation, 86 cases (45.03%) are in the form of bribe given to elected PRI members like, Sarpanch, Samiti and Zilla Parishad members; 32 cases (16.75%) are found to be land mortgaging and land encroachment by well-to-do tribal followed by 26 cases (13.61%) through liquor vending, 25 cases (13.09%) through moneylending and high rate of interest and 22 cases (11.52%) as cheating in trade and barter. We may call such agents as "tribal exploiters".

However, cases of cheating are more. Out of a total of 280 cases of exploitation and cheating by non-tribal traders, (except SCs) in 179 cases (63.93%) they are cheated. Similarly, out of 311 cases of exploitation by SC, 152 cases (48.87%) are found cheating practices in trade and barter (including weights and measurements).

Out of 280 cases of exploitation by non-tribal traders, money-lenders and sahukars (except SCs), 55 cases (19.64%) are found in the form of bribe given to Government officials like forest, police, excise and revenue personnel etc. Further, 30 cases (10.72%) relate to cheating by liquor vendors and 16 cases (5.71%) to moneylending at high rate of interest.

Similarly, out of 311 cases of SC exploitation, 87 cases (27.98%) are in the form of haggling (snatching the tribal commodities in the corn fields, villages, nearby hats etc.). 40 cases (12.86%) relate to moneylending at high rate of interest; 25 cases (8.04%) are cheating by SC liquor vendors and only 07 cases (2.25%) are found to be in the form of forcibly or tactfully taking away cattle and/or other domestic animals.

Cases like highway robbery, sexual harassment of the Kandh women by SC people and land encroachment by non-tribals and SC people are not found during 2009-10 in the sample villages.

5.5 Types of Exploitation — A Brief Analysis

5.5.1 *Cheating in Barter, Trade and Marketing*

Kandhs are not experts in marketing skill till today. Whenever a Kandh wants to sell his crops or cattle he often takes the help of a Dom or other outside agent and these middlemen sell their goods and cattle on behalf of Kandhs. They are unscrupulously cheated by such middlemen and traders. They rarely get the actual market price for their commodity.

Haggling

Haggling is very common practice by outside traders in nearby hats and weekly markets. If a Kandh brings some agricultural product, seasonal fruits or any forest produces for sale in the market, first it is snatched away by outside traders and then the price is fixed which is at the mercy of the traders. They never get the price prevailing in the market at the time and they are exploited in the broad day light. This type of exploitation is done by non-tribal middleman and traders. Although such cases are included in cheating in trade and barter by non-tribal traders (except SC), such cases were reported in case of SC exploitation (see Table 5.2).

Weights and Measures

Traders coming from outside very often cheat the tribal producers and collectors through manipulation of weights and measures. This mostly happens when things are transacted through indigenous units of measurement or even transacted through metric measures by various tricks.

After the harvest, the Doms, Sundhis, Kumuttis and petty traders visit Kandha villages with clothes, utensils, bamboo products, dried fish, potato, onion and other fashionable and eatables and exchange these things for crops. They allure the tribals to buy their goods and sell these goods at very high prices. The credulous Kandh cannot realize the extent to which he has been exploited. Cheating through trade and barter has been found by almost all agencies of exploitation, i.e. tribals to tribal, non-tribal traders and the SCs. It is the highest in case of non-tribal traders except SCs, i.e. 63.93 per cent followed by SCs 48.87 per cent and by tribals 11.52 per cent (see Table 5.2).

5.5.2 *Forcibly Demanding Crops after Harvest*

At the harvesting season, in the past, groups of Doms numbering ten to twenty were going to the threshing floor of the Kandhs and demanding a major share of the harvest (Rout, 1964-65). The Kandhs are very much afraid of the Doms. They, out of fear, surrendered a part of their produce to the Doms.

Now-a-days such practices of forcibly snatching away crops have considerably been reduced. They pretend themselves to be their good friends, protectors, well-wishers and service providers and ask politely to give a part of their produce. The helpless Kandhs don't resist giving a part of their produce.

5.5.3 *Stealing Crops, Cattle and Other Valuables*

Very often, cattle of the Kandhs are found missing either in the cow sheds or in the forest. Local Doms generally steal cattle and sell them in distant places or slaughter for meat in the forest (Rout, 1964-65).

Livestocks are also stolen away after giving prior notice to the owners. The Doms may demand some money, crops or a cow from a Kandha as gift. The Doms do not hesitate to forcibly taking away things from Kandhs in broad day light, which is termed as "highway robbery".

However, such practices have been reduced now a days considerably but are not totally abolished. Out of various types of Dom exploitation in Kandh villages, a total number of 7 cases (2.25%) were reported as forcibly or tactfully taking away cattle, but cases of stealing were not detected.

5.5.4 *Sexual Harassment*

Sometimes local Doms forcibly take away Kandh girls and exploit them sexually. This leads to serious social problem in Kandh society, often resulting in ostracisation of the aggrieved family. This is another reason why the tribals are very much afraid of the Doms. The innocent tribal girls and women are also sometimes subjected to sexual exploitation by the local contractors, drivers and by some dishonest Government officials. Many times the incidences are suppressed by the people or cases are settled through village councils. Of course, these are now rare cases. No such case was reported during the field survey in the sample villages, may be due to mind set of hiding.

5.6 Agencies of Exploitation

The tribals still continue to be victims of exploitation of various types. The nature, causes and types of exploitation are manifold. Our field investigation reveals that Kandhs of the sample villages have been more or less exploited by various agencies. The type and nature of exploitation has also been changed to certain extent with the passage of time. An analysis of the agencies of exploitation presently existing in the sample Kandh villages is made as under.

5.6.1 *Tribal to Tribal Exploitation*

It was brought to the notice of the investigator during field survey that some of the well-to-do tribals in the sample villages and nearby villages belonging to the same Kandh community are semi-educated, politically empowered or elected in any capacity in any tire of Panchayati Raj system. These people have acquired comparatively good communicating skills, i.e. they can speak Odia clearly. This section of the Kandhs is aware of the rules and regulations (i.e. aware of ignorance of rules and regulations by the mass who can be cheated). Unfortunately, emerging Kandh elites involve in cheating and exploiting their own kinsmen (see Case Study No. 3).

There are also some cases of moneylending by Kandh sahukars at a high rate of compound interest (even more than 200%) against mortgage of land of the lonee Kandhs, selling liquor in the villages and cheating through it. Now-a-days there are instances of cheating and taking commission by comparatively enlightened and politically empowered Kandhs with a promise to help their own community members (see Case Study No. 9).

There are also instances of the Kandhs being exploited by their own community members who are politically powerful in recent times for getting special benefits like old age pension, Indira Awas Yojana, Job Card, Madhu Babu Pension etc. Concentration of political power in the hands of a few tribals leads to concentration of economic power and *vice versa*.

Social exploitation by some of the tribals to their own community members was also found during the field study. Case study No. 4 reveals about "Karjami" as a kind of social exploitation. During marriage, birth and death rites, exploiting tendency of comparatively well to do tribals to their own brothers is seen in the tribal villages. Blind belief prevalent among the Kandhs also creates problem for themselves (see Case Study No. 8). It transpires from Table 5.2 that cases of exploitation of tribals by tribals is 45.03 per cent. Cases of bribes have been taken by tribal PRI members with promises to provide certain benefits. There are also instances of moneylending, land mortgaging and cheating in trade etc.

5.6.2 *Moneylenders and Sahukars*

Indebtedness is an important characteristic feature in the life cycle of the Kandhs as well as that of the other tribals. Poor economic conditions and social extravagance combined with their customs and traditions compel them to borrow from different sources. They are often exploited by moneylenders, traders and sahukars belonging to both non-tribal and tribal communities. The poor tribals pay very high rate of interest (see Case Study No. 3). From the field investigation it was revealed that exploitation through moneylending were 13.09 per cent in case of tribals to tribals, 5.71 per cent in case of non-tribals and 12.86 per cent by the SCs in their respective spheres (see Table 5.2).

5.6.3 *Traders*

As stated earlier, in the remote sample villages due to poor communication facility and fear of haggling, the Kandhs generally prefer to sell their agricultural goods and other commodities to traders and intermediaries who go to their villages to purchase. They are forced to sell their goods at a price lower than the prevailing market price. They are also cheated on weights and measures. (Case Study No. 1 and 5) As it would be seen from Table 5.2 tribals were cheated and exploited in 63.93 per cent cases by non-tribal traders, 48.87 per cent in case of SC traders and 11.52 per cent in case of tribal traders.

Though, tribal economy is progressively being monetized still in interior tribal villages most of the transactions are done through barter. Barter system opens the door of exploitation to the tribals by the traders.

5.6.4 *Elected Representatives*

The posts of PRI members in tribal areas have been reserved for the tribals with the passing of PESA Act. As mentioned earlier some of the (not all) elected representatives have started exploiting their own tribal brothers in several ways. The field investigation revealed that there were 32 cases (42.67%) in roadside villages and 54 cases in remote villages (46.55%) in which PRI members had accepted bribes with promises to provide certain benefits to the tribal beneficiaries. (See Table 5.2 and also Case Study No. 3).

5.6.5 *Liquor Vendors*

As mentioned earlier, the tribals do have a liquor culture. In pleasures and pains, during festivals and rituals, the tribals in general and Kandhs in particular, consume liquor. Most of them are also addicted to liquor. The local Sundhis and SC people were traditional liquor vendors in the past. Even today, they sell country liquor and in both the groups of sample villages; tribal liquor vendors are found in less numbers. The tribals are frequently exploited by the liquor vendors and the Kandhs of the sample villages are no exception to it. In 13.61 per cent of liquor vending cases by tribals to tribals, 10.72 per cent cases by non-tribal and 8.04 per cent by SC vendors, the tribal Kandhs have faced exploitation (see Table 5.2).

5.6.6 *Government Officials*

Some of the unscrupulous police, excise, revenue and forest officials have been alleged to be the exploiters of the simple tribals since long. Unfortunately, in recent times some dishonest officials-in-charge of implementing developmental and welfare programmes do not hesitate to exploit the tribals whenever an opportunity arises. Most of them charge as percentage of the funds allotted for implementation of the schemes and programmes in their areas (see Case Study No. 7). Also Table 5.2 shows that there were about 20 per cent cases in which sample tribal respondents had faced exploitative incidences by various Government officials.

5.6.7 *Voluntary Organizations*

Many Voluntary Organizations too have exploited the name of tribals and tribals themselves by using funds received in the name of tribal development to pursue their own agenda. Black listing of NGOs by various funding agencies, including CARPET is a mere tip of the iceberg (Vaid, 2004).

All efforts by Voluntary Organizations have been directed towards solving the problems without targeting the causes that create problems.

5.6.8 *Doms*

Doms belong to SC category who is co-settlers with the tribals. They seem to be the major exploiting agency in Kandh areas of the Laxmipur locality. The nature of their exploitation has been stated earlier. Another trader group "Relly" who belongs to SC community, also exploits the tribals in trade and barter. Relly people are the main group of hagglers found in Laxmipur and nearby Kakirigumma hat areas. As the people of study villages mainly depend on Laxmipur and Kakirigumma weekly hats they are often subjected to exploitation by such people.

However, Dom exploitation in these study villages and in the locality has been considerably reduced in recent time and the practice of "Highway Robbery", stealing cattle and crops, demanding crop after harvest, have also come down to a great extent. Nevertheless, such practices have not totally been abolished. These local intermediaries and traders have also become politically powerful. They are to a certain extent treated as king makers who generally finance the tribal leaders to win the Panchayat elections. Ultimately, these people manage to get the job works on contract basis in the villages with political support. Naturally, quality of work suffers and sometimes the fund is also misappropriated. However, these are really cases of corruption, but indirectly it, more or less, leads to exploitation of the poor tribals as they are deprived of the full benefit of the Government welfare measures through the funds meant for the purpose. In Table 5.2, it can be seen that there were in total 311 cases of SC exploitation in the sample villages of Laxmipur block during the period under study. It included haggling, forcibly or tactfully taking away animals, moneylending, trade and barter and liquor vending. No instance of highway robbery and ill-treating Kandh women was reported during the period of investigation.

5.7 Case Studies

In addition to the information collected through household surveys and interviews, some case studies were conducted on various aspects of exploitation in the sample Kandh villages of Laxmipur block. Here follows some case studies of selected persons who have suffered from exploitation of various types:

CASE STUDY – 1

NAME	:	Sri Fakir Muska
AGE	:	25 Years
FATHER	:	Tili Muska
CASTE	:	ST-Kandh (Converted Christian)
VILLAGE	:	Kanapadi
G.P.	:	Toyaput
BLOCK	:	Laxmipur

Sri Fakir Muska is a Kandh of Kanapadi village of Toyaput G.P. He belongs to the BPL family. The BPL card is in the name of his father. Every month he used to receive 25 kgs. of rice. His grand father who is already dead was an Antyodaya Card Holder. So Fakir although staying separately, still he is using his father's BPL Card bearing No. 762151 (issued on May, 2002).

It has been stated by Fakir Muska that he and his friend Siku Muska, aged about 26 of village Kanapadi jointly received a 50 kg. bag of rice by submitting their genuine BPL Cards to the dealer Sri Mahandia, a Dom belonging to the village Sorisapadar. After receiving the bag and before distributing the rice equally, i.e. 25 kgs. each, he and his friend Siku somehow decided to weigh the bag again and see whether it contained actually 50 kg. Then they found that the weight of the rice bag was 46 kg instead of 50 kgs. Thus there was 4 kg. less in a bag of 50 kg. When again they approached to the dealer he argued that he had received the bag as it was. Now they realized that they had been cheated and exploited even by the dealers appointed by the Government. Poor and simple tribals could not generate enough courage to go against the dealer and complain to the higher authorities.

This is also happening in case of kerosene. It is given to the customers @ ₹ 12 per liter by the dealer, while the Government fixed rate is ₹ 10.50 per liter. Further, the quantity of kerosene is approximately 900 ml. although the cardholders pay for one liter. The kerosene is being distributed to the villagers of this village by another dealer named Sri Bindhyahani Bisoi of village Dumuripadar of Toyaput G.P. He is a Sundhi Sahukar. He and his ancestors had been exploiting the tribals since time immemorial through distilling and selling liquor, moneylending and trading etc. With the passage of time and circumstances such traditional Sahukars and traders have also changed the mode of their business and have managed to take dealership of PDS materials and some of them have taken to the activities like petty contract works etc.

It was because Sri Fakir Muska and his friend Siku Muska were found to be little intelligent, they went for cross-checking the PDS articles received and found that they had been exploited. But innumerable ignorant and credulous poor tribals living in interior high lands and villages are subject to exploitation of various kinds by both private and public agencies like this.

CASE STUDY – 2

NAME	:	Sri Makar Muska
AGE	:	27 Years
FATHER	:	Late Lingu Muska
VILLAGE	:	Kanapadi
G.P.	:	Toyaput
BLOCK	:	Laxmipur

Sri Makar Muska, a tribal Kandh is a marginal farmer and NTFP collector. Last year he decided to cultivate Kandul (arhar) and as initially he did not have money for investment, he borrowed ₹ 300 from Sri Rajendra Khosla belonging to Balipeta village under Balipeta Panchayat of Narayanpatna Panchayat Samiti. Sri Khosla is a scheduled caste person. He borrowed the money in the month of July. The loan was taken with the oral agreement to repay the principal with interest in the form of the Kandul (arhar), i.e. 15 "Manas" of Kandul (Approximately one Mana = 31/2 kgs.) after the harvest and it would be at ₹ 20 per Mana during the month of Pausa (January). Sri Muska paid the same as per the agreement when the local prevailing rate of Kandul (Arhar) ₹ 50 per Mana. So, he paid an excess amount of ₹ 450 for 6 Months towards interest. The rate of interest came to 300 per cent per annum.

Even if Regional Rural Banks and other Cooperative Banks are operating in Laxmipur areas including the branches of some nationalized Banks, still the tribals go to the local moneylenders with whom they have contact since long past. They borrow in cash and repay in kind without realizing the excess amount paid towards interest. One of the reasons for such happening is that they get the loan easily and immediately from Local Sahukar. Tribals generally do not like to take loans from Banks which involves a lot of paper works and other procedural formalities.

CASE STUDY – 3

NAME	:	Sri Makar Muska
AGE	:	27 Years
FATHER	:	Late Lingu Muska
VILLAGE	:	Kanapadi
G.P.	:	Toyaput
BLOCK	:	Laxmipur

This is another story of sufferings and exploitation narrated by Makar Muska of Kanapadi village. He is dwelling in a poorly built mud walled thatched house. He became an applicant for Indira Awas house. He approached the local Sarpanch, who is a man belonging to the Kandh community. He had to pay bribe to the Sarpanch for an Indira Awas house. He paid an amount of ₹ 2000 to be shared by both the Sarpanch and the Secretary of the G.P. The Secretary of the G.P. was Sri Gupta Hikoka who also belongs to the Kandh community of Dumuripadar village. He was promised to be sanctioned an Indira Awas House in his name. Sri Makar Muska is a poor man. He did not have any savings. Hence, he borrowed ₹ 2000 by pledging + total of gold (approximately 6 gm.) to Gupta Bisoi (Sundhi by caste) of Dumuripadar village @ ₹ 3 interest per cent per month (36% per annum). Later on, when he could not repay the loan in time and interest amount increased to ₹ 900, Makar Muska had to mortgage 3 small prices of low-lying paddy[1] land (approximately 25 cents or 1/4th of an acre) to Sri Abhi Muska of Kanapadi and paid the interest amount to Gupta Bisoi.

When Sri Makar Muska could realize that very high rate of interest was being charged by Gupta Bisoi; he again brought a hand loan from Tili Muska of Kanapadi village and released the Gold. But in order to pay back the loan of Tili Muska he further mortgaged the same Gold with Nidi Muska of Kanapadi village. When Nidi Muska was in need of money and demanded his money back the gold was sold for ₹ 5,500 and the loan amount was cleared. From the rest ₹ 3,500 he had to purchase gold worth of ₹ 3,000 for his wife as she had earlier lost + tola of gold on account of above transactions. The rest amount of ₹ 500 was spent by Makar Muska on liquor and merry-making.

Sri Muska is yet to receive (at the time of field study) a house under Indira Awas Yojana although two years have been passed since he applied for the benefit, but he is being caught in the loan trap. One loan leads to another and in the process he has to lose his gold and land etc. Elected representatives belonging to same tribal community thus have started exploiting their own people. Sri Muska's case is a concrete example.

CASE STUDY – 4

NAME	:	Sri Hikoka Besu
AGE	:	34+ Years
CASTE	:	ST (Kandh)
VILLAGE	:	Dumuripadar
G.P.	:	Toyaput
BLOCK	:	Laxmipur

Hikoka Besu came to Keutaguda village (a small Railway Station on the Koraput-Rayagada Railway Line) as a migrant labourer (case of migrant labourers are rampant in the area). Besu, fell in love with Pulaka Laxmi aged about 28 years. She is the daughter of Pulaka Lingna of Tandipur in Kolnara Block of Rayagada district. Tandipur is adjacent to Keutaguda. Both Besu and Laxmi fled away to Dumuripadar and got married as per their traditional custom. But when the parents of Laxmi and the villagers of Tandipur demanded bride price as per the tribal custom, Besu mortgaged his small plot of low-lying paddy land (about 20 cents, i.e. 1/5th of an acre), sold all his cattle, 4 in number (2 cows and 2 calves) and also borrowed ₹ 4,000 from his sister. A total sum of ₹ 8,000 was given as bride price by Besu.

Besides the payment of this cash amount of ₹ 8,000, Besu was asked to give one tola gold to Laxmi as an item of bride price. As he could not arrange extra amount of money to purchase gold he finally accepted KARJAMI which means he has to work in his father-in-law's house till his would be in-laws are satisfied that he had worked enough equal to the value of the gold. Besu served as "Karjami" and lost his independence to work. Presently he is working as an attached labourer in his father-in-law's house. He is now staying there. He is of course, treated as a member of the family. Besu does not know when the period of "Karjami" would be over. There is no exact stipulated time for "Karjami". It depends upon the mercy of in-law's house. Besu, is now having no low-lying paddy land of his own. Of course, he possesses 1+acres of dry dongor land at Dumuripadar which is lying fallow. His house at Dumuripadar is also partially damaged due to lack of maintenance. Besu is blessed with a son in April, 2008. Social exploitation of this type is still in practice among the Kandh society.

CASE STUDY – 5

NAME	:	Smt. Hema Kuldipiya (pseudonym)
FATHER	:	Sri Jhandu Kuldipiya
AGE	:	46+ Years
CASTE	:	SC (Relly)
VILLAGE	:	Laxmipur
P.S.	:	Laxmipur
BLOCK	:	Laxmipur

Smt. Hema Kuldipiya, generally trades in commodities like vegetables, brooms, ginger and other Minor Forest Products at Laxmipur market near Ambedkar Chowk at Laxmipur. During interview, she confessed that tribals living near block headquarters or State highways were not so simple now-a-days as they were years back. It is very difficult to purchase different products at a lower price from them as they are now aware of the prevailing market price and they generally charge us the same price at which commodities are sold to other customers. So, it becomes difficult in her part to carry-on the business with the hope of getting a high profit as she was getting in past.

She admitted that she had to manipulate in weight and measurement. As per her version she can manipulate 2 to 3 kgs. of commodities while purchasing 10 kgs. of any commodity through tricks in her hands and legs.

She also confessed that haggling was a common practice while purchasing goods. They generally preferred to purchase commodities from the tribals (especially from Kandhs) as Kandhs are comparatively simple and innocent. The traders get good amount of profit through haggling while purchasing commodities from the Kandhs.

CASE STUDY – 6

This case study shows exploitation of Kandh tribals as migrant labourers.

NAME : Sri Sahab Muska
AGE : 22 Years

NAME : Sri Kishor Muska
AGE : 22 Years

NAME : Sri Taila Muska
AGE : 40 Years

NAME : Sri Asbi Muska
AGE : 30 Years

NAME : Sri Madhaba Muska
AGE : 22 Years

NAME : Sri Santosh Hikoka
AGE : 18 Years

NAME : Sri Jilla Muska
AGE : 19 Years

NAME : Sri Ramachandra Muska
AGE : 23 Years

And

NAME : Sri Dhobulu Muska
AGE : 30 Years

All the above persons belong to Kanapadi village. They were tempted and persuaded by Sukuri Miniyaka, belonging to Kandh community of the nearby village Chingna, of Balipeta Gram Panchayat of Narayanpatna

Block, and decided to go to Bangalore as migrant labourers. Sukuru told them that they would get @ ₹ 1500 per month with free fooding, boarding and medical care if necessary. Sukuru Miniyaka took these 11 persons of Kanapadi village to Balugaon of Khurda district by Hirakud Express train on 27 October, 2007. Sukuru paid all the expenses of these people up to Balugaon.

Sachi Pradhan, the main broker at Balugaon received these people and Sukuru returned from Balugaon after receiving his commission. Sachi Pradhan took these persons to Bangalore by train. These people worked for about 5 months in Bangalore. During their work, they were compelled to work from morning 8 am to evening 8 pm with a lunch break from 2 pm to 3 pm; they were engaged intra sporting industrial raw materials. In every week each labourer was receiving ₹ 50 as a token money towards wages from the contractor. They asked for their wages for many a time but did not get it. So, they decided to return to their village and the contractor only gave ₹ 1500 per person to go back to their villages and asked them to return from their village as early as possible.

These people returned to their village with empty hand because ₹ 1500 was almost spent in the return journey. Poverty, lack of employment opportunity, credulous nature and ignorance among the tribals lead them to migrate to distance places and ultimately they are compelled to do hard and overwork with subsistence wages.

CASE STUDY – 7

NAME	:	Sri Pada Muska
FATHER	:	Sri Dharma Muska
AGE	:	62 Years
CASTE	:	ST (Kandha)
VILLAGE	:	Kanapadi
BLOCK	:	Laxmipur

Sri Pada Muska of Kanapadi village like 10 other senior members of the Kandha community of the same village spent already ₹ 400 to apply for old age pension. It is for the 2nd time that Pada is applying for this. Last year though he had applied but his application was rejected. The reason is not yet known to him. He belongs to BPL family, the total annual earning of the family is less than ₹ 10,000.

After a detailed discussion with Sri Pada Muska it was revealed that he spent the amount in the following manner to apply for the old age pension.

(i)	For xeroxing of Photo Identity card and form etc.	₹ 13
(ii)	Paid to the Medical Incharge, UGPHC, Laxmipur for obtaining an old age certificate	₹ 50
(iii)	Paid to the Revenue Inspector to receive the income certificate	₹ 100
(iv)	To & fro expenses to go to RI office	₹ 40
(v)	Paid to the Sarpanch to recommend his name to receive old age pension	₹ 150
(vi)	Other Misc. Expenses (Approx.)	₹ 50
	Total	**₹ 403**

Other 10 persons of the same village spent money in the similar manner while applying for old age pension. None of them have yet received the benefit (by the time of field study).

It is an irony that the Medical Officer-in-Charge, the RI and the elected Sarpanch, all belong to the ST community. None of them hesitated to receive money from such poor tribals for providing the service, which they should do as a part of their duty. It seems as if everyone is eagerly waiting to exploit the poor and innocent tribals (even functionaries belonging to their own community) once an opportunity is available.

CASE STUDY – 8

Name	:	Smt. Salme Miniaka
Age	:	60 Yrs
Husband	:	Late Denka Miniaka
Caste	:	Kandh (ST)
Village	:	Bandikar
Panchayat	:	Burja
Block	:	Laxmipur

Smt. Salme Miniaka and her daughter Gatte Miniaka, aged about 35 years, of Bandikar village are ex-communicated and are compelled to stay at a distance place outside the village. As per Kandh custom if somebody is ex-communicated by the community, then nobody keeps any relationship (neither social nor economic), with them. They are not allowed to use common places like Bherna Munda (common place to gossip), common water sources like well, tube-well, common bath place in the stream etc. and nobody dare share even fire with them.

Smt. Salme, it is alleged knows witchcraft or black magic locally known as "PANGANA". The villagers alleged that she is responsible for the death of Balumunda Miniaka, Ranju Miniaka and Gida Miniaka of Bandikar village. All of them died during the last two years.

Both the mother and daughter are now leading a miserable life in the village after being ex-communicated. Gatte, the daughter is over-aged. It would be very difficult in her part to get a groom for marriage. This type of blind belief among the Kandhs leads to severe social, economic and psychological sufferings and tensions similar to that of exploitation of the persons victimized.

CASE STUDY – 9

Name	:	Nidi Miniyaka
Age	:	35 Yrs
Father	:	Sukuru Miniyaka
Caste	:	Kandh (ST)
Village	:	Minapai
Panchayat	:	Kuttinga
Block	:	Laxmipur

Sri Sukuru Miniyaka, father of Nidi Miniyaka, had mortgaged 5 acres of land to Purna Miniyaka of same village for a loan of ₹ 60 only as long as 15 years back. Somehow due to financial difficulties he could not repay the loan. But now when Nidi wants to get back his land, Purna is demanding 1 Tula (about 12 gm) of gold and ₹ 11,000 cash for releasing mortgaged land. But as per the condition at the time of agreement (verbal), there would be no interest to be paid for the loan and the creditor would not pay any share on the produce of the land to debtor. So, Nidi is liable to pay only ₹ 60 to free his land from bondage. Now the fresh condition imposed by the creditor (interestingly he is a Kandh) has led to several round of quarrels between two families. The matter is supposed to be taken to the village council (the traditional) or panchayat for deission.

CASE STUDY – 10

Name	:	Krushna Miniyaka
Age	:	58 Yrs
Caste	:	Kandh (ST)
Village	:	Champi
Panchayat	:	Kuttinga
Block	:	Laxmipur

Krushna Miniyaka borrowed ₹ 2000 from local Sahukar belonging to general caste of the village Upper Chami in order to purchase a pair of bullocks. The agreement (verbal) was that Krushna's son Santosh aged about 16 years, would work as bonded labourer (Goti) for one year in Sahukar's house. With the legal restrictions imposed after implementation of Bonded Labour Act in tribal areas, both the parties agreed that they would not make it public that Santosh worked as bonded labour (Goti). When asked by outsiders it would be reported that he is a daily labourer. But as per the old practice Santosh became a full-time servant of the Sahukar for one year. In addition to the advance received, it was agreed that he would be offered some clothes on different occasions, food and medicines, if he fell ill.

Jilla Koleka (50 yrs.), Ani Saunta (12 yrs.), Sukha Disari (55 yrs.), Durjya Disari (50 yrs.) and Selia Hikoka (45 yrs.) are some of the tribals found to be working as Goti or Hallia at Champi. They took advance from local Sahukars in order to meet their urgent socio-economic needs and pledged their labour towards repayment of their loan. Such practice of bonded labour (Goti) still continues (though un-officially or secretly) in the interior tribal pockets of Koraput district.

It may be mentioned here that the above persons do not come under sample households of the scholar. But the scholar out of his own interest gathered such information, when he came to know that the practice of "Goti" is widely prevalent in the village concerned where non-tribal Sahukars (moneylenders and traders as well as big landowners) are dominating in the rural economy.

NOTE

1. Low-lying paddy land means the permanently cultivable land, particularly in valleys, as contrasted with shifting cultivation fields (dongor land) on hill slopes.

6

A PROFILE OF SAMPLE VILLAGES AND ISSUES OF EXPLOITATION

6.0 Introduction

Laxmipur Block of Koraput District has been purposively chosen for an in-depth study. Out of 13 Gram Panchayats in Laxmipur Block, one village from each Panchayat having maximum concentration of Kandh population has been selected for present investigation. Again 20 Kandh households from each village were selected randomly. However, only in Kanapadi village of Toyaput G.P. 24 households were taken in the sample. In all, 264 Kandh households from different villages were taken for a detailed study.

6.1 A Profile of the Sample Block Laxmipur

6.1.1 *Location and Boundary*

Laxmipur Block is situated between 18°47' to 19°08' N latitude and 83°11' to 83°26' E longitude and has a geographical area of 310.33 sq.kms. The Block headquarters is situated at a distance of 58 kms. from State highway towards north-east of the district headquarters, Koraput. It extends in the west up to Dasamantpur Panchayat Samiti, in the east up to Narayanpatna Panchayat Samiti, in the south up to Koraput Panchayat Samiti and in the north up to Rayagada and Kasipur Panchayat Samitis.

6.1.2 *Physiography and Soil Type*

The Block is situated in a section of Eastern Ghats' high land, which consists of a series of mountains and high hills. It is situated at a varying altitude of 600 to 1000 meters above MSL. Laxmipur Block is covered under Eastern Ghat high zone (NIAEM, 2001).

Different types of soils are found in the Block and can be categorized into low, medium and high fertile soil. The soil of the Block is mostly red, mixed red and yellow. As per the soil testing reports available, the soils are acidic and poor in fertility status. They are highly eroded, rich in iron and aluminium and usually deficient in Bronze and Zinc. Soil acidity and iron toxicity are problems of the Block (Strategic Research and Extension Plan of Koraput District, 2001).

6.1.3 *Formation of the Block*

Laxmipur Block started functioning on 1st June, 1960 and was declared and started working as phase-II Block from 1st January, 1975. As mentioned earlier, it has 13 Gram Panchayats, 100 revenue villages with 75 hamlets.

6.1.4 *Demography*

According to 2001 census, the total population of the Block is 55,268 out of which 37,951 (68.66%) are Scheduled Tribes (STs), consisting of 18,745 males and 19,206 females. It may be mentioned here that the STs constitute 49.62 per cent of the total population of the district. Table 6.1 depicts clearly Gram Panchayat-wise distribution of households and population of Laxmipur Block.

Table 6.1 reveals that out of the total population of 55,268 (27,452 males and 27,816 females) persons, 7,383 (13.35%) persons belong to SC category. So out of the total population 45,334 (82.01%) belongs to SC and ST category in the Block. Although the Block average of tribal population comes to 68.66 per cent, eight Gram Panchayats (out of 13), i.e. Champi, Burja, Goudaguda, Kutinga, Odiapentha, Pipalpadar, Toyaput and Tunpar have an average population more than it. Out of the rest, Gram Panchayats (GPs) like Kusumguda and Panchada have a tribal population more than 60 per cent and Bhitargada, Kakiriguma and Laxmipur have a tribal population of 54.04 per cent, 49.64 per cent and 46.73 per cent respectively. On the other hand, GPs like Burja, Kakiriguma, Laxmipur, Panchada and Pipalpadar have SC population higher than the Block average of 13.35 per cent.

The density of population (i.e. number of persons living per square km.) in the Block is 178, as compared to district average of 134 and state average of 236.

Table 6.1: Gram Panchayat-wise Distribution of Households and Population in Laxmipur Block of Koraput District (2001)

G.P.	*No. of H.H.*	*Population*			*SC*			*ST*		
		M	*F*	*T*	*M*	*F*	*T*	*M*	*F*	*T*
Bhitargada	1149	2153	2290	4443	247	235	482 (10.84)	1142	1259	2401 (54.04)
Burja	980	2170	2081	4251	340	334	674 (15.85)	1694	1638	3332 (78.38)
Champi	660	1462	1431	2893	144	126	270 (9.33)	1126	1098	2224 (76.87)
Goudaguda	1108	2101	2124	4225	176	156	332 (7.85)	1527	1564	3091 (73.15)
Kakiriguma	1016	2044	1991	4035	310	313	623 (15.43)	1005	998	2003 (49.64)
Kusumguda	654	1391	1387	2778	193	189	382 (13.75)	846	824	1670 (60.11)
Kutinga	1023	2140	2137	4277	263	271	534 (12.48)	1842	1835	3677 (85.97)
Laxmipur	1499	3125	3116	6241	630	675	1305 (20.91)	1416	1501	2917 (46.73)
Odyapentha	1082	2105	2247	4352	267	286	553 (12.70)	1611	1731	3342 (76.79)
Panchada	1395	2693	2685	5378	432	441	873 (16.23)	1782	1781	3563 (66.25)
Pipalpadar	1308	2637	2788	5425	461	469	930 (17.14)	2155	2297	4452 (82.06)
Toyaput	925	1909	1890	3799	30	32	62 (1.63)	1554	1513	3067 (80.73)
Tunpar	801	1522	1649	3171	186	177	363 (11.44)	1045	1167	2212 (69.75)
Grand Total	**13600**	**27452**	**27816**	**55268 (100%)**	**3679**	**3704**	**7383 (13.35%)**	**18745**	**19206**	**37951 (68.66%)**

Note: Figures in brackets indicate percentages to respective totals.
Source: Census, 2001.

6.1.5 *Workers and Non-workers*

Out of the total workers in the Block, 56.14 per cent are main workers (who worked for 183 or more days during the year) and 46.86 per cent are marginal workers (who worked for less than 183 days during the year) (COATS-2005). The non-workers showing mostly dependency ratio in the Block are 29,743 (53.81%) out of the total population of 55,268.

Table 6.2 shows the distribution of workers from total population as per the 2001 census.

Table 6.2: Sex-wise Distribution of Main, Marginal and Non-workers in Laxmipur Block (2001 Census)

	Total Number of Persons	*Male*	*Female*
Main Worker	14,330	11,080	3,250
Marginal Worker	11,195	4,020	7,175
Total	**25,525**	**15,100**	**10,425**
Non-worker	29,743	12,352	17,391
Grand Total	**55,268**	**27,452**	**27,816**

Source: COATS-NFFWP, 2005.

About 90 per cent of people in the concerned Block live purely in rural areas. The rest of the population lives in semi-urban areas. Communication facility in the Block is poor. Only 28 villages are connected with at least district roads (Zilla Sadaks) which means only 33.33 per cent villages are having all weather communication. Low level of literacy, poor communication facility and poverty indicate the general backwardness of the Block.

6.1.6 *Main and Subsidiary Occupation*

Agriculture and wage work are the main sources of occupation of the people in Laxmipur Block. People practise both settled and shifting cultivation. They also collect minor forest products like fuel wood, charcoal, bamboos etc. in order to support their meager earnings from agriculture. Yield per hectare of land is only 19.01 qtls. of food grains against the District average of 23.29 qtls (DDA, Jeypore, 2007-08).

6.1.7 *Extent of Poverty and Composite Development Index*

Total number of ration cards issued by the Department of Civil Supplies,

Odisha in Laxmipur Block is 15,268 (Data collected from the concerned Department), out of which 10,040 BPL, 3,396 Antyodaya, 101 are Annapurna cards and 1731 APL Ration Cards. The families having BPL Cards are poor families, Antyodaya card holders as very poor families and Annapurna card holders as the poorest of the poor households. Therefore, 88.66 per cent of the total ration card households in the Block are either poor (65.75%) or very poor (22.06%) or poorest of the poor (0.66%).

Majority of the population is tribals (68.66%) having maximum concentration of Kandhs (more than 85 per cent of the total tribal population). Hence, it is evident that majority of the Kandhs are poor in the Block.

The composite Development Index developed on the basis of twelve socio-economic and infrastructure development indices, put Laxmipur Block at number 12 among the 14 Blocks of the district in terms of level of development (COATS-NFFWP, 2005, p. 3.194).

6.1.8 *Agriculture*

Agriculture practised in Koraput region in general and of Laxmipur Block in particular is predominantly rain fed. Average rainfall of this Block is 800 to 900 mm and it is limited between June to September. High intensity rainfall spread over a relatively short period does not support multiple cropping. Further, the absence of water catchments and storage mechanism results in much of water falling on the farmland flowing out unharvested. Net area sown in the Block is 8,327 hectares.

Shifting cultivation in the hill slopes by slash and burn method is still prevailing in some parts of this Block. The cropping practice followed by farmers in Podu land is mixed one. Major crops grown are niger, raggi, paddy, maize, millet, arhar and turmeric.

Lack of adequate irrigation facilities is a major problem in this region. However, construction of check dams, percolation tanks and lift irrigation schemes prove to be useful in providing irrigation to some of the settled agricultural fields.

6.1.9 *Literacy Rate*

The overall literacy rate of the Block is only 27.71 per cent that consists of 39.29 per cent of males and 16.28 per cent females as per 2001 census.

There are 76 primary schools, 33 upper primary, 6 high schools, 5 Sevasharm schools and one college imparting mostly general education in the Block.

6.2 Laxmipur Block — At a Glance

1.	Date of Formation of the Block	:	01/01/1960
2.	Geographical Area	:	310.33 sq.km.
3.	No. of GPs	:	13
4.	No. of Revenue Village	:	100
5.	No. of Hamlets	:	75
6.	No. of Wards	:	150
7.	No. of Households	:	13,600
8.	Total Population	:	55,268 (2001 Census)
9.	ST Population	:	37,951 (68.66%)
10.	SC Population	:	7,383 (13.35%)

Public Institutions

1.	Hospitals	:	4 nos. 2 Nos. of P.H.C. (1. Laxmipur, 2. Kakiriguma)
		:	2 nos. of Dispensary (1. Kutinga, 2. Keskapadi)
2.	Veterinary Hospitals	:	2 nos. (Laxmipur & Kakiriguma)
3.	Police Stations	:	2 nos. (Laxmipur & Kakiriguma)
4.	Sub-Post office	:	2 nos. (Laxmipur & Kakiriguma)
5.	Telephone Exchange	:	3 nos. (Laxmipur, Champi & Kakiriguma)
6.	Public Sector Banks	:	3 nos. (KCCB at Laxmipur, IOB at Laxmipur & KPGB at Kakiriguma)
7.	College	:	1 at Laxmipur
8.	High schools	:	6 nos. (3 T.R.W. High schools)
9.	Upper Primary Schools	:	33 nos.
10.	No. of Primary Schools	:	76 nos.
11.	No. of Sevashram Schools	:	5 nos.
12.	No. of Primary Schools Hostels	:	13 nos.

Agriculture

1.	Total Geographical Area	:	28,620 Hect.

2.	Total Cultivate Land	:	17,670 Hect.
	(a) Kharif	:	13,413 Hect.
	(b) Rabi	:	4,257 Hect.
3.	Paddy Land-I	:	570 Hect.
	Paddy Land-II	:	595 Hect.
	Paddy Land-III	:	975 Hect.
	Low Land	:	1,065 Hect.
	Medium Land	:	1,225 Hect.
4.	No. of Agricultural Families	:	12,700 nos.
5.	No. of watersheds	:	16 nos. (*Source:* A.C.A. & IWDP-VI)
	(a) Treatable area	:	8,000 Hect.
	(b) Villages covered	:	22 nos.
6.	Main or Principal Crops	:	Niger, Raggi, Paddy, Maize, Millet & Arhar.
7.	Average Rainfall	:	800 to 900 mm.
8.	No. of MIP	:	1 (156.03 Hect. in Kharif) 17.08 Hect. in Rabi
9.	No. of L.I. Points	:	19 (301 Hect. in Ayacut area)
10.	No. of Diversion weir	:	260 (5,600 Hect. in Ayacut area)
11.	Other Sources (Tanks & Ponds)	:	1,231 Hect.
12.	No. of Pani Panchayat formed to maintain and protect the irrigation sources	:	146 nos.

Drinking Water

(a)	No. of Tube Wells running	:	522
(b)	Sanitary Wells running	:	68

(*Source:* Laxmipur Block Office, Koraput District.)

6.3 The Sample Villages[1]

As mentioned earlier, 13 villages from 13 GPs were selected for an in-depth study. These are grouped under two categories, namely — Road Side villages and remote/interior villages. Those villages either adjacent or within 100 meters to State highways/Zilla Sadaks are considered as roadside villages. On the other hand, villages away from the state highway/Zilla Sadaks are regarded as interior/remote villages. This has been done in order to find out and compare if there is any significant difference in the field of economic pursuits, socio-cultural life and nature and extent of exploitation etc. among the road-side and remote villages.

6.3.1 *Road-side Villages*

Out of the 13 villages, six were detected as road-side villages. They are Mandalaguda of Pipalapadar G.P. (21 kms. from Block H.Q.), Minapai of Kuntinga G.P. (10 kms. from Block H.Q.), Bandikar of Burja G.P. (3 kms. from Block H.Q.), Rajanpanasaguda of Odiapentha G.P. (8 kms. from Block H.Q.), Kanjariguda of Tunpar G.P. (26 kms. from Block H.Q.) and Upper Champi of Champi Panchayat (13 kms. from Block H.Q.).

6.3.2 *Remote Villages*

The remote villages with respective Gram Panchayats and distance from Block H.Q. are as follows:

Name of the Village	*Name of the Panchayat*	*Distance from Block HQ*
Marbaiguda	Laxmipur	6 kms.
Kanapadi	Toyaput	12 kms.
Kakiriguma (Maliguda)	Kakiriguma	19 kms.
Tala Champi	Kusumguda	16 kms.
Lachamani	Goudaguda	23 kms.
Charada	Bhitargada	26 kms.
Panchada (Jhodikhanda)	Panchada	28 kms.

6.4 The Sample Households

The Kandh families may be classified into nuclear, joint and extended ones. Nuclear family consists of parents with two or three children. Joint family includes parents, grand parents and children. Extended family consists of parents, grand parents, uncle, aunts, sisters, children etc.

On the basis of household survey conducted, the distribution of Kandh households by type of family size is shown in Table 6.3.

Table 6.3: Distribution of Total Sample Kandh Households by the Type of Family

Types of Family	*Total No. of Households*	*Percentage*
Nuclear	181	68.56
Joint Family	54	20.46
Extended	29	10.98
Total	**264**	**100.00**

Source: Field data.

Table 6.4 reveals that out of 264 families surveyed 181 families (68.56%) are nuclear families. There are 54 families (20.46%) who live in a joint family set up. The extended families consist of only 10.98 per cent of the total household surveyed. Hence, a majority (68.56%) of Kandh families are nuclear in character.

6.4.1 *Family Size*

The size of family is a crucial factor in determining the well-being of each and every family. It influences the income expenditure and socio-economic conditions of the family. Table 6.4 shows the distribution of Kandh households by the family size.

Table 6.4: Distribution of Total Sample Kandh Households by the Family Size

Family size	*Total No. of Households*	*Percentage*
02 to 04	127	48.11
04 to 06	98	37.12
06 to 08	33	12.49
08 and Above	6	2.28
Total	**264**	**100.00**

Source: Same as Table 6.3.

Table 6.4 reveals that 48.11 per cent of Kandh families fall under the norm small family (micro family) size with 2 to 3 members; 37.27 per cent of family has the size between 4 and 6 members; 12.49 per cent has a family size of 7 to 8 members and only 2.28 per cent has family size of more than 8 members. It is revealed during survey that most the persons among the ST Kandhs have gone for family planning measures.

6.4.2 *Demographic Features*

Total population of the sample households in both road-side and remote villages is 1,216. Table 6.5 shows the age and sex distribution of population in the sample households of the villages taken under study.

Table 6.5: Age and Sex Distribution of the Sample Households of Laxmipur Block in Koraput District

Age group	*Road-side Villages (No. of HHs-120)*			*Remote Villages (No. of HHs-144)*			*Grand Total (No. of HHs-264)*		
	Male	*Female*	*Total*	*Male*	*Female*	*Total*	*Male*	*Female*	*Total*
0 — 6 years	51	55	106 (18.62)	52	52	104 (16.07)	103	107	210 (17.27)
7 — 14 years	41	57	98 (17.22)	45	62	107 (16.53)	86	119	205 (16.86)
15—59 years	168	160	328 (57.64)	198	204	402 (62.13)	366	364	730 (60.03)
60 and above years	23	14	37 (6.52)	17	17	34 (5.27)	40	31	71 (5.84)
Total	**283**	**286**	**569 (100%)**	**312**	**335**	**647 (100%)**	**595**	**621**	**1216 (100%)**

Note: Figures in orackets indicate percentages to respective totals.
Source: Same as Table 6.3.

Taking the sample population of all the 13 villages into consideration (both Road-side and Remote) it is seen that there are more number of females than males (i.e. 595 males and 621 females). The sex ratio, 1044 females per 1000 males, is favourable in the sample villages. This is, more or less the demographic characteristics of tribal population of India.

Nearly 60.03 per cent of the total population is within the age group of 15-59 years, 17.27 per cent of the total population is within 0-6 years, 16.86 per cent of the total population is within 7-14 years and only 5.84 per cent of the total population is within the age group of 60 and above. The demographic characteristics of the two types of tribal villages (i.e. Road-side and Remote villages) are more or less, similar to that of the total population. The dependency ratio (taking child population and old people) comes to 39.97 per cent although a part of the child population and old persons are found to be engaged in one form of economic activities or the other.

6.4.3 *Level of Education*

The educational status of the sample population belonging to the Kandh community of Laxmipur Block is presented in Table 6.6. Although absolute number of literates according to their status of education is given in the table, literacy rate is analyzed on percentage basis.

Table 6.6: Educational Status of the Sample Households

Class	*Road-side Villages (120HHs)*			*Remote Village (144HHs)*			*Grand Total*		
	Male	*Female*	*Total*	*Male*	*Female*	*Total*	*Male*	*Female*	*Total*
Read up to Class-III	21	20	41	27	14	41	48	34	82 (39.04)
Read up to Class-V	27	7	34	19	4	23	46	11	57 (27.15)
Read up to Class-IX	19	10	29	22	5	27	41	15	56 (26.67)
Read up to Class-X	3	1	4	2	2	4	5	3	8 (3.80)
Read up to +2	3	1	4	1	0	1	4	1	5 (2.39)
Read up to +3	0	0	0	0	0	0	0	0	0 (0)
Any Technical Experience	1	0	1	1	0	1	2	0	2 (0.95)
Total	**74**	**39**	**113**	**72**	**25**	**97**	**146**	**64**	**210 (100)**

Note: 1. Population in the age group of 0-6 years has been excluded while calculating the rate of literacy.

2. Figures in brackets indicate percentages to respective totals.

Source: Same as Table 6.3.

Literacy rate of the road-side sample villages comes to be 24.40 per cent as against 17.86 per cent in remote interior villages. Male literacy rate is higher than female literacy rate. Male literacy rate is 31.89 per cent and female literacy is 16.88 per cent in road-side villages as against 27.69 per cent and 8.83 per cent respectively in interior villages. Only one person each from road-side and remote villages is having some technical education.

Taking the total sample population into account, the literacy rate comes to 20.87 per cent, which consists of 29.67 per cent of males and 12.45 per cent females. This is against the overall literacy rate of 27.71 per cent in the Block that consist of 39.29 per cent of males and 16.28 per cent of females (2001). The literacy rates of sample Kandh population and that of overall Block population are far behind the district average of 36.20 per cent and the State average of 63.61 per cent. Out of total literates in both the groups of villages, 39.04 per cent of them reported to have read up to class-III and 27.15 per cent up to class-V and 25.67 per cent up to class-IX. Only 6.19 per cent of the population has read up to class-X and +2 standards.

Road-side villages have shown better literacy rate than that of remote villages, but difference is not very much significant.

The Kandhs give very little importance to education. Of course, some of them are gradually becoming conscious about the benefits of education. However, their poverty compels them to engage their children in one form of economic activities or the other than sending their children to schools. Through formal interview and discussion, it was found that there was a feeling among the Kandhs that, after education their children would become alienated from their families as they would migrate to the towns for taking employment. Moreover, they believe that the so-called educated children are reluctant to take up their traditional occupation either in the fields or forests. Going to school is a matter of willingness of their children, most of them do not mind if the child is unwilling to go to school. A cursory look during field study showed that the drop-out rate was quite high among the tribal children. The low literacy among the Kandhs is considered to be the root cause of their socio-economic backwardness.

6.4.4 *Other Socio-Economic Indicators*

Housing

Habitation and housing condition is considered as an indicator of socio-economic status of the household/community concerned.

Since historical times Kandh houses are found to be mud walled and straw (Piri) thatched low roofed houses. Houses in rows, i.e. two rows of houses facing each other across a street or tract/open space are connected to each other. Nevertheless, now a days it is noticed that some of tribals have remodelled their houses and they live in small but *pucca* houses built under Government schemes. Others still have low roof Piri thatched houses.

Distribution of sample households on the basis of their mode of construction is depicted in Table 6.7.

Thatched houses are made of "Chandi/Piri" (types of straws/grass used for thatching) with mud walls, semi-*pucca* houses are cement floored with brick walls, either cemented or plastered with mud and *pucca* houses are fully cemented houses with cement roofing. About 79.93 per cent of the Kandh houses are found to be semi-*pucca* houses.

The Kandh settlements are small; each settlement having houses between 20 and 50. It is not because of modernity or development that there has been a shift in tribal house pattern, but it is mostly due to non-availability of forest produces required for construction of thatched houses in recent time. The plinth area of a Kandh house generally varies from 10ft. × 13ft. × to 12ft. × 15ft. Most of the houses have three rooms (nearly 53%). Only 2 per cent of houses are found among the sample households with four or more rooms. Majority of tribal households do not have windows. Windows are available only in 11.36 per cent of houses (i.e. 30 out of 264) and latrine facility is available only in 9 households out of 264 (3.4%). It is revealed that, there is a proposal to electrify the houses of poor tribal under "Biju Gramya Jyoti Yojana". Majority of the Kandhs do not have separate kitchen. In some cases, rooms are found to be used for cooking purpose. Pets like goats, sheep, cock, pigeon etc. do not have separate place to live and they are kept inside the living room.

Table 6.7: Distribution of Sample Households on the Basis of their Mode of Construction of Houses

House Particulars	*Roadside Villages*	*Remote Villages*	*Total*	*Percentage*
(a) Piri Thatched Mud House/Huts	19	29	48	18.18
(b) Semi-Pucca Houses	99	112	211	79.93
(c) Pucca	2	3	5	1.89
Total	**120**	**144**	**264**	**100**

Source: Same as Table 6.3.

Most of the sample households (96.59%) are self-owned. On account of their independent mentality and availability of Anabadi land as well as low-cost required for construction of their traditional type house they do have durable houses. In Kandh families sons after their marriage prefer to construct their own houses and live separately.

Health and Sanitation

Health is an important determinant of the status of human resource. It determines the mortality rate and is an important aspect of human development index. Generally, the tribals are not much concerned about their health in the initial stage of the disease. They seek medical treatment only in the last stage. Even today most of them believe diseases are caused due to bad effects of the evil spirits locally known of "Dumas" (ghost) and "Mahane" (evil spirits). Now-a-days, of course, gradually they have started to visit doctors to cure their diseases, still they seek the help of local "Gunia/Dissari" for getting relief from several diseases. About 92 per cent of sample families, it was ravealed, have first consulted local "Gunia/Dissari" during last year in connection with various diseases.

It was interesting to note that almost all respondents opined positively for accepting family planning measurers. Nevertheless, acceptance of family planning measures with number of living children differs. About 33.33 per cent respondents (88 out of 264) replied that after four children they would prefer to adopt family planning measures, 36.36 per cent of the respondents (96 out of 264) preferred to have the same after three children, 26.51 per cent after two children, and 4.16 per cent (11 out of 264) preferred to go for it after one child. It is also found during the field study that 51.89 per cent families (either male or female) have adopted family planning measurers.

During the field survey, it was observed that a majority of the Kandh houses from outside appeared to be clean. But in reality they do not take much care of the neatness of their houses inside and also personal cleanliness. They are living mostly in unhygienic condition, for which they suffer from diseases of various types.

Major ailments from which the tribal Kandhs suffer are fever, general weakness, malnutrition, skin infection, T.B., body pain etc. It is also noticed that skin infection and dysentery are very common among the tribal people. It is mainly due to unsafe drinking water and unhygienic practices in taking their food. Despite availability of tube-wells in most of the villages now-a-days and spring based water facility in some of the villages they still do prefer to drink water from the hill streams/ "Chuan" etc. In addition, generally they drink any type of water available at their work-site.

Clean environment is also essential for the well-being of any community. The tribals usually do not have any arrangement for waste disposal and these are deposited nearer to their houses. Cow shed and pigsty are generally much closer to their living houses creating an ugly or dirty environment especially in the rainy season.

Health status and life expectancy are closely related to each other. High life expectancy is an important indicator of human development. A conventional estimate in the study villages showed that the life expectancy of the Kandhs is very low, i.e. below 50 years.

Social Awareness

Mass media is considered as an important means of creating social awareness among people. Due to illiteracy, Kandhs seldom use news papers and also due to non-availability of electricity or any other sources of energy electronic mass-media is far from their reach. From among the sample, only 10 per cent of households do have only radio. Further, lack of communication is another hurdle in their development. Extension officials, N.G.O. functionaries etc. are engaged in creating social awareness among rural and tribal people. But communication becomes ineffective to a great extent, as such people do not know "Kuvi" dialect used by the Kandh people. Ultimately, the sources of social awareness to a considerable extent are work-site, gossiping near "Verna Munda" (generally situated in the middle of the Kandh villages) etc.

Decision Making

Ability to take decision is also considered as one of the major indicators of the levels of socio-economic advancement of any society. It was reported during field study that the traditional functionaries like "Jani" (head-man for rituals), "Sauntas" (traditional land distributor and head-man in a Kandh village) and other leaders of traditional Panchayats and presently the PRI elected members take decisions regarding many social and economic affairs and Kandhs generally do not disobey such decisions even if, some of them adversely affect their socio-economic conditions. Although the statutory Panchayati Raj Institutions are taking decisions regarding socio-economic welfare activities in rural tribal areas, the decisions taken in traditional village Panchayats relating to internal community affairs and family as well as clan level conflict resolutions are still binding on the members of the community.

Status of Women

The social structure of Kandhs centers around the family. Women members occupy an important position in tribal households. The women enjoy more or less, equal social status with their men counterparts and are the cornerstones of the Kandh socio-economic life. They bear heavy responsibilities in the fields of preparation of food and feeding the family members, marketing, agricultural activities, forest collection including fuel wood collection and food gathering etc. Women are the custodian of cash, and are mostly controller of the household budget in tribal families. Even they work more number of hours in a day than their male counterparts. During the field study, it is observed that women responded many of the questions asked clearly which depicts their dominance in the family.

6.4.5 *Tribal Economy — A Brief Analysis*

A brief analysis of some important aspects of the Kandh (Tribal) Economy is made as under:

(A) *Markets*

(i) Product Market

Generally, the Kandhs are lacking adequate skill of marketing in both buying and selling of final products. They purchase a limited number of consumer goods for their daily use. Barter system still prevails in Kandh villages, although their economy is progressively being monetized. Again group behaviour in marketing plays an important role among the tribals. If by any means, the trader is able to convince a group of Kandh about the quality and price etc. of the product (either in selling or in purchasing) others will follow the process and the trader is able to get a good amount of profit through the transaction. The tribals are cheated and exploited in the marketing process by non-tribal traders and businessmen.

(ii) Factor Market

Factor market may be defined as the purchase and sale of factors which are used in the production process. In economics the factors of production constitute land, labour, capital and organization. A brief account of the above factors of production and their contribution in the production process of the Kandhs is given in the following paragraphs:

Land

Traditionally, in the Kandh communities the land was communally owned. In the slash and burn agriculture (podu), each family within Kandh group used to be allocated a patch of land by the headman of the village according to its needs and ability to cultivate. Ownership rights remained undisputed and Kandh family enjoyed the operational rights so long as it remained as a member of the clan organization. However, settled agricultural paddy lands were privately owned. As there was plenty of forest and Dongar land available and population was less, landlessness problem was almost unknown among the Kandhs. Due to massive deforestation for several reasons and restrictions imposed on the use of forests, the extent of Podu cultivation became limited. Yield from agriculture could not support their basic food needs. Gradually, most of them found themselves to be landless, when population went on increasing and forest area decreased. Table 6.8 indicates the landholding position of sample Kandh households.

Table 6.8: Distribution of Land among the Sample Kandh Households in Laxmipur Block

Landholdings with Patta (ROR)	*Number of Households*	*Percentage (per cent)*	*Total Land Holdings with ROR (in acres)*	*Total Encroached Land*
Less than 1 acre	42	15.91	22.52	11.45
1 to 2 acres	78	29.54	123.05	211.90
2 to 5 acres	52	19.70	175.24	167.50
5 to 10 acres	24	9.10	205.75	123.80
Total	**196**	**74.25**	**526.56**	**514.65**
Landless	68	25.75	00	130.60
Total	**264**	**100**	**526.56**	**645.25**

Source: Same as Table 6.3.

It is observed that out of the 264 sample households, 196 (74.25%) households possess some land (with ROR — Record of Right) and rest 68 (25.75%) families are landless. Average land per landholding household (with ROR) comes to 2068 acres and average landholding for all sample households (with ROR) comes to 1.99 acres. On the other hand, average landholding per household of encroached land comes to 2.44 acres. However, the extent of land owned by these Kandh families is very less. It is interesting to note that as many as 90.90 per cent sample households are either landless, marginal or small landholders having land less than 5 acres each. Most of the fertile lands in the Kandh villages are found to be fragmented into very small pieces. Good amount of low-lying paddy lands have been alienated from the tribals since long.

It is found that most of the tribals encroached Government lands like, forest land, *anabadi* land etc. Landless households (those not having own *Patta* land) encroached 130.60 acres and even households possessing some land encroached 514.65 acres of Government land. Most of these lands are used for shifting cultivation. By the fact itself, it depicts the dependence of tribals on forest land.

Labour

Landless people and marginal as well as small farmers constitute the labour force those who work as wage labour. It is noticed that Kandhs in the study area supply cheap labour to the non-tribal landowners and others. There are wage differences between male and female labourers. The male labourers are paid higher wages than the women labourers. In Government works and even in NREGA works going on in the locality, they are unable to get the minimum wage declared by the Government. It is found in the study villages that the payment of wages is manipulated in various ways. The locally fixed wage rate varies from ₹ 20 to ₹ 30. In Some places in addition to such fixed wages, a day time food (mostly gruel) is given to the labourers.

In agricultural operation labour (mostly family labour and hired labour) is the most important input. The tribals also go for non-farm wage works whenever and wherever available.

Capital

Capital in our present purpose refers to input which is utilized for further production. In agricultural sector, main items of capital of the tribal Kandhs include seed (either home supplied or purchase) and some amount manure or fertilizers. Modern agricultural inputs like chemicals, fertilizers, pesticides, pump sets etc. are seldom used by the Kandh farmers. Being poor, they are unable to invest in such type of capital inputs. They are not very much aware of the incentives provided by the Government and other agencies. In other non-agricultural operations, they operate with indigenous tools available locally. Therefore, they still stick to their traditional practices in economic pursuits.

Entrepreneurship

Entrepreneurship combines and co-ordinates all other factors of production in the channel of production. It involves risk, decision-making, innovation and above all, a temperament for profit making and financial prosperity.

But the tribals in general and the Kandhs in particular do not have the temperament for profit making. By nature they want to be contented with the fulfilment of their limited wants. They are adverse to any change and hence, less innovative. They lack entrepreneurial qualities mostly due to lack of education, awareness and above all, the profit motive.

(B) *Employment Pattern*

The main source of livelihood in the sample villages is found to be agriculture supplemented by wage work mostly in case of road-side villages. In remote villages it is agriculture and NTFP collection including food gathering. They cultivate both foothill plain lands and hill slopes (basically known as 'Horu Tasa'). Table 6.9 shows sex-wise engagement of the persons in both Road-side and Remote villages with their respective percentages. Adult male and female workers engaged in various economic activities have been taken into account in the present study.

Table 6.9 shows that in the sample, 58.96 per cent of the total workers was engaged in cultivation of land for their living. Next in importance comes forest collection. About 23.94 per cent of the total labour force was engaged in NTFP collection (including food gathering) and 17.1 per cent of workers, majority of whom are landless, was engaged in the gainful activities like agricultural labourers and non-farm wage works and a few of them worked as watchman, peon and Anganwadi cook etc.

It is also found that a good majority of the workers (77.75%) in road-side villages have reported to be engaged in agriculture, although most of them must be disguisedly employed. On the contrary, in remote villages 43.78 per cent workforce is engaged in agriculture. In remote villages, a considerable number of workers (i.e. 40.79%) go for non-timber forest collection like fire-wood, bamboo, seasonal fruits, brooms, rope, food etc. It is because there are some forest growths available in remote village areas, while road-side village areas are mostly denuded of forest cover.

(C) *Cropping Pattern*

The cropping pattern of the sample households is shown in Fig. 6.1. Important crops raised by the Kandh farmers include paddy, raggi and other millets. The share of vegetables in total production is only 5 per cent.

Fig. 6.1 shows that cultivation of paddy (rice) constitutes 35 per cent of the total agriculture produce. It is followed by raggi (25%). These two constitute their main food items. About 18 per cent of the produce constitutes spices like turmeric, mustard and chilly etc. These are sold in the local *hats* or to the traders traditionally associated with them since historical times. Other agricultural produces sold in the

Table 6.9: Sex-wise Engagement of the Persons in Various Economic Activities both in Road-side and Remote Sample Villages

Primary Occupation	*Road Side Villages*			*Per cent*	*Remote Villages*			*Per cent*	*Grand Total*			*Per cent*
	M	*F*	*T*		*M*	*F*	*T*		*M*	*F*	*T*	
Cultivation	120	135	255	77.75	87	89	176	43.78	207	224	431	58.96
Agricultural Labourers	10	7	17	5.18	15	11	26	6.47	25	19	44	6.02
NTFP collection including food gathering	4	7	11	3.35	80	84	164	40.79	84	91	175	23.94
Non-farm wage works	24	18	42	12.81	7	10	17	4.23	31	28	59	8.07
Other works	2	1	3	0.91	10	9	19	4.73	12	10	22	3.01
Total	**160**	**168**	**328**	**100**	**199**	**203**	**402**	**100**	**359**	**372**	**731**	**100**

Source: Same as Table 6.3.

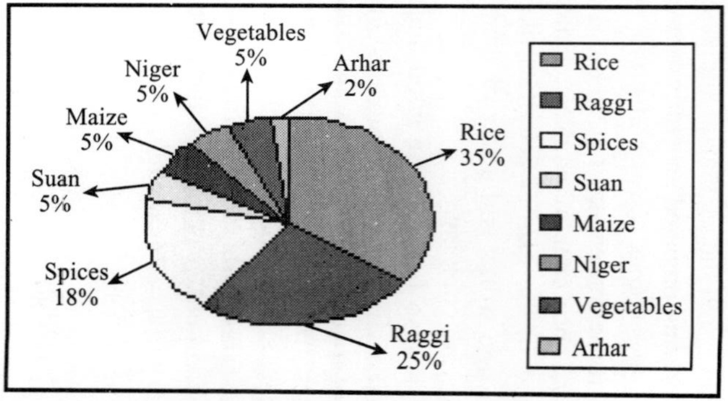

Fig. 6.1: Cropping Pattern of the Sample Households.

Source: Computed from field data.

market or weekly *hats*, are the items like vegetables, arhar etc. However, a major portion of the agricultural product is consumed at home and fewer amounts are sold in the market.

(D) *NTFP Collection*

NTFP collection from forests is considered to be the 2nd best possible source of livelihood of the Kandhs of the study area. They mainly go for collection of fire-wood. It constitutes 60-70 per cent of their total non-timber forest collection. The other forest products collected are brooms, thatching grass, *siali* leaves, fodder grasses etc. and these are mainly used for self-consumption and little surplus, whatever, is sold.

Seasonal fruits, leaves, roots etc. are also collected but these are used mainly for their self-consumption. They also collect other products like sal seeds, mahua flower, mahua seeds, honey, lac, turmeric etc. This shows that the tribals depend on forest to a considerable extent although forest is fast degrading in Koraput district.

(E) *Animal Husbandry*

The Kandhs keep cattle, pigs, goats, sheep and poultry birds, but these are mostly kept for domestic use. Animal husbandry as a commercial venture has not gained any ground among the Kandhs. The people also do not milch their cows. Cattle population is either used in cultivation of land or sold in the market when there is a demand for it to be given in the bride price. There is a demand for animals and birds during their festival days either for sacrifice or for feast.

(F) *Wage Labour*

Landless persons and almost all the marginal and small farmers go for wage works (both agricultural and non-agricultural) whenever and wherever available in the locality. In recent times, the NREGS of the Government has given an opportunity for wage labour. However, exchange labour system mostly prevails in Kandh villages during various agricultural operations on the basis of mutual reciprocation. However, when they work in farms of non-tribal persons either in the village or outside, they get wages for it.

(G) *Business and Trade*

Tribals are usually averted to business and trade. Trading and business activities are carried on by non-tribals, mostly Telugu Kumutis, Sundhi (traditional liquor vendors) and Doms in Kandh areas of Koraput district. However, the Kandhs have gradually started doing pretty trades in recent times. SHG movements have instilled sense of business habits among the Kandhs in recent years.

6.4.6 *Income of the Sample Households from Various Sources*

Agriculture and forests are found to be the main sources of livelihood of the Kandhs followed by wage labour. The other activities like livestock rearing, business and trade and services etc. contribute marginally to their economy.

Table 6.10 shows the total income earned by the sample households in both road-side and remote villages from various sources.

Table 6.10: Income Received by the Sample Households (in Road-side and Remote Villages) during the Year 2009-10 from Different Sources

Sl. No.	*Source of Income*	*Income from Various Sources (in ₹)*			*Percentage*
		Road-side Villages (120 HHs)	*Remote Villages (144 HHs)*	*Total (264 HHs)*	
1.	Agriculture	5,91,178	7,27,380	13,18,558	30.62
2.	NTFP Collection (including food gathering)	77,608	9,96,037	10,73,645	24.93
3.	Income from Wage Labourer	4,49,350	5,70,218	10,19,568	23.68
4.	Income from Business (including SHG)	80,450	1,66,300	2,46,750	5.73
5.	Income from Animal Husbandry	1,43,960	1,56,265	3,00,225	6.97
6.	Other Income	3,19,300	28,270	3,47,570	8.07
	Total	**16,61,846**	**26,44,470**	**43,06,316**	**100.00**

Source: Same as Table 6.3.

The total income of the sample households in the road-side villages from various sources is ₹ 16,61,846 and that of remote villages is ₹ 26,44,470 and the combined total income of these two groups of sample villages is ₹ 43,06,316 during the period from April 2009 to March 2010. From these it is estimated that the average annual per household income in road-side villages comes to ₹ 13,848.72 and that of remote villages is ₹ 18,364.38. With this amount of total income, the per capita annual income in road-side villages is estimated to be

₹ 2,920.64 and that of remote villages it is ₹ 4,087.28. The combined annual per capita income of all the households is estimated to be ₹ 3541.37 and per capita monthly income comes to ₹ 295.11.

As it has been shown earlier 58.96 per cent of the total workforce was engaged in cultivation only and it earned 30.62 per cent of the total income. On the other hand, 23.94 per cent of the total workers were engaged in forest collection including food gathering and earned 23.93 per cent of total income. But it is interesting to note that 14.09 per cent of labour (6.02% agricultural labour plus 8.07% non-farm wage labour) was engaged in wage labour and it contributed 23.68 per cent to the total income.

Planning Commission of India defined the poverty line as the per capita monthly private consumption level of ₹ 325.79 for rural area and ₹ 528.49 for urban area in Odisha, the all India average being ₹ 356.30 and ₹ 538.60 respectively for rural and urban areas (*Orissa Agricultural Statistics 2006-07*, Directorate of Agriculture and Food Production, Orissa, p. 77). However, the base of the estimate was the year 2004-05. As stated earlier, the Report of the Expert Group set up by Planning Commission of India under the Chairmanship of Suresh Tendulkar in November-2009, suggested a monthly per capita expenditure of 407.78 in rural areas and ₹ 497.31 for urban areas (for 2004-05) in Odisha as the standard estimate of poverty line. In our study, per capita monthly income in road-side villages is ₹ 243.38 and in remote area it is ₹ 340.60. The combined average income in both the areas per month comes to ₹ 295.11. This level of income is far below the per capita monthly expenditure level required to determine poverty line as estimated both by the Planning Commission and Tendulkar Committee.

6.4.7 *Consumption Expenditure in Sample Kandh Families*

Level of expenditure and pattern of expenditure of a community give a picture of the economic status of its members. Tendulkar Report on Poverty estimation in November, 2009 recommended 365 days average expenditure pattern to estimate new poverty line in India. Unfortunately, the Kandhs do not keep any account of what they purchase or consume. A few consumer durables and intoxicants like liquor, tobacco, dry fish, matchbox, kerosene, rice, medicine are purchased by them. Still an attempt has been made to collect the amount spent by them (both in terms of self-consumption of goods and services as well as purchased) through personal interview, which they told from their memory.

Table 6.11 shows the expenditure pattern and amount spent by both the groups of villages in the study area.

Table 6.11: Expenditure Made by Sample Households of both Road-side and Remote Villages of Laxmipur Block during 2009-10

Sl. No.	*Type of Expenditure*	*Roadside Villages (120 HHs)*	*Remote Village (144 HHs)*	*Total Expenditure of all Sample (264 HHs)*
1.	Fooding	9,32,685 (50.54)	12,32,361 (51.08)	21,65,046 (50.85)
2.	Clothing	4,90,820 (26.60)	6,19,480 (25.67)	11,10,300 (26.08)
3.	House Construction and Repair	40,850 (2.21)	57,500 (2.38)	98,350 (2.31)
4.	Festival and Rituals	80,502 (4.37)	1,36,512 (5.66)	2,17,014 (5.10)
5.	Education	17,950 (0.97)	19,020 (0.79)	36,970 (0.87)
6.	Intoxicants	1,01,903 (5.53)	1,75,099 (7.26)	2,77,002 (6.50)
7.	Other Consumer Durables	77,716 (4.21)	84,947 (3.52)	1,62,663 (3.82)
8.	Health Care	61,886 (3.35)	59,360 (2.46)	1,21,246 (2.84)
9.	Transport	41,000 (2.22)	28,500 (1.18)	69,500 (1.63)
	Total	**18,45,312 (100.00)**	**24,12,779 (100.00)**	**42,58,091 (100.00)**

Note: Figures in brackets indicate percentages to respective figure.
Source: Same as Table 6.3.

As it is seen from the Table 6.11 in the total budget of household expenditure of the sample Kandh families a little more than half (50.85%) of the expenditure is made on food. Next in importance comes clothing. It occupies 26.08 per cent of the total annual expenditure of the sample households. The expenditure for education is much negligible in both the groups of villages, which are the only 0.97 per cent and 0.79 per cent in road-side and remote villages respectively. It is only 0.87 per cent in all the households taken together. Less than 3 per cent of the total expenditure (i.e. 2.84%) is made on health care. Intoxicants including liquor claimed 6.50 per cent of the total expenditure, which is more than the expenditure made in festivals (i.e. 5.10%).

Per household annual expenditure in road-side group of villages is estimated to be ₹ 15,377.60 and for remote villages it is calculated to be

₹ 16,755.40. Again per capita annual expenditure for road-side group of villages is estimated as ₹ 3,243.07 and for remote group of villages it is ₹ 3,729.17 and combined annual per capita expenditure comes to ₹ 3,501.71. Therefore, per capita monthly expenditure (combined) is estimated to be only ₹ 291.80. It is far below the poverty line set by new Expert Committee (Nov. 2009) which is ₹ 407.78 for rural areas of Odisha.

Taking the total annual income over expenditure into account, we find an average surplus of ₹ 182.67 per family. On the other hand, we have seen that all these Kandh families live below the poverty line. This marginal surplus of expenditure over income does not indicate any level of well-being of these people. They still lead a subsistence life. They are very poor indeed. Therefore, during emergency they have to go for debt even today. Indebtedness is a common feature of the poor tribal economy.

6.4.8 *Indebtedness*

Acute poverty and unfulfilled wants, most of which are basic in character, compel the tribal families to incur loans. They also go for borrowing to meet their socio-religious needs and festivals.

About 19.16 per cent households from road-side sample villages (23 out of 120 HHs) are found to be indebted and the outstanding loan amount of all the households of road-side villages is ₹ 48,500. Average per household loan of indebted families comes to ₹ 2,108.70. On the other hand, 58 households in remote villages (40.27%) are found to be indebted and the total outstanding loan amount is ₹ 1,21,000. The average per family loan of indebted households thus comes to ₹ 2,086.20. Taking all the indebted families of both the groups of villages it is estimated that the average amount of loan made by the sample indebted families is ₹ 2,092.59.

Sources of Loan

The study reveals that for the indebted sample households, 35 per cent of the loan amount was brought from friends and relatives, 28 per cent from village moneylenders and traders, 15 per cent from banks and other institutions (excepting SHGs). Similarly, 8 per cent of loan amount was brought from other sources like NGOs, and grains banks etc. Newly emerging SHGs have also supported these tribals in providing 14 per cent of their loan requirements.

Rate of Interest

In the time of emergency, poor Kandhs agree to pay any amount of rate of interest to incur a loan. Even the amount of grains is paid for crop loans only for a period of three to four months. In other words, the rate of interest becomes 100 per cent for a lending period of three to four months. The loans brought from moneylenders and traders generally carry such exorbitant rates of interest.

6.4.9 *Bonded Labour*

In the past when institutional loans through banks and cooperative societies were not available to the rural tribals they had to heavily rely upon local moneylenders and traders. The tribals being illiterate could not understand the way the principal and the rate of interest on loans were calculated. The unscrupulous moneylenders could easily cheat and exploit the tribals and in the process they lost their lands and other assets. When no tangible assets were there with the tribals to mortgage, they mortgaged themselves and worked as bonded labourer (or Goti). There were instances that a person could not repay the loan to the sahukar during his life time, and after his death his son was asked to work as Goti with the *Sahukar*.

With the implementation of Bonded Labour System (Abolition) Act of 1976, it is presumed that the system has been officially stopped or reduced to a considerable extent. But the system has not fully stopped in the Kandh areas of Laxmipur Block. It is still found here and there though mostly in a hidden form. It was reaveled during the field study (also see Case Study No. 10 on page 117 as an instance).

Concluding Remarks

From the above analysis, we may infer that the Kandhs in Laxmipur Block lead a poor life. On an average they are found to be below the poverty line. They still lack the basic infrastructural facilities. Till today interior tribal villages and even most of the road-side villages do not have electricity facility. They lack sanitation facilities. Their health care programmes are very poor. The communication network is also poor.

A majority of the Kandhs live in unclean surroundings; the average member of a family consists of 4 to 5 persons. Sex-ratio is in favour of females. About 60.03 per cent of the population is within the age group of 15-59 years as a result of which the dependency ratio comes to 39.07 per cent. Of course, some children below the age 15 years and some senior persons above 60 years are found to be engaged in some gainful activities. Literacy rate is found to be very low among the Kandhs. It is found to be 20.87 per cent (29.6% of males and 12.45% of females). Participation of women in primary occupation is almost equal with their male counterparts. About 83.9 per cent of total working population depends mainly upon cultivation and NTFP collections. Important crops they cultivate are rice and raggi, along with some minor millets and oil seeds. Their marketing skill is quite poor. They are often cheated in product and factor markets. Average per capita monthly income of the sample Kandh respondents was ₹ 295.11 and their average monthly expenditure was ₹ 291.80. The per household loan burden of indebted family is ₹ 2,092.59. They borrow at an exorbitant rate of interest from the local moneylenders and traders.

Therefore, poverty combined with low level of literacy, ignorance lead them to be exploited by moneylenders, traders and *Sahukars*. They arc even-being exploited by some of the Government officials and PRI members also.

NOTE

1. Location of the villages mentioned above for detailed study are shown in the Laxmipur Block Map (Map 4.1).

7

PROTECTION, FAILURE AND REACTION

7.1 Introduction

Communities which are known as STs mostly lived in primitive conditions in pre-independent India. They were isolated from the so-called mainstream life. The British Government in India also kept them in isolation with the policy of 'non-interference'. They were among other weaker sections of Indian society, more vulnerable to economic exploitation. Justifiably, one of our national goals, as was articulated during the national movement and is enshrined in the constitution, is the establishment of egalitarian society. This entails equity and justice for all sections of the society without any discrimination. Therefore, the Constitution of India provides for a number of safeguards for the weaker sections in general and Scheduled Tribes (STs) and Scheduled Castes (SCs) in particular (see Goswami, 2003). In addition to these safeguards, there are laws to bring them at par with the rest of the society.

Apart from the efforts of national leaders and even before the commencement of the Constitution, the government was concerned with the protection of the tribals against exploitation. The Government of India Act, 1935 made special provisions for tribal areas. The Governor was given a special responsibility in respect of these areas. No Act of the Federal or of the Provincial legislature applied to such areas unless the Government so desired.

At the time of the framing of the Constitution of India, the need to have special provisions for the tribals was felt on the three main grounds. These were:

(i) distinct and different tribal social customs, organizations and beliefs;
(ii) the fear of exploitation by the people of plains; and

(iii) the need to make suitable financial provisions so that tribal people could run their affairs through the local councils.

The various safeguards in favour of Scheduled Tribes, as Danda (1981) comments (see Vidyarthi, 1981) may be broadly divided into two parts, *viz.*:

1. Protection, and
2. Development.

The first one refers to the Government's respect for customary laws of the tribes including their rights over lands and forests. This is what A.K. Danda (1981) means 'protection'. The second one refers to special provisions to improve the socio-economic life of the tribal people. These include the policy of favoured treatment in matters of opportunities and the policy of providing political reservations for overcoming their historically accumulated backwardness. This is covered by the concept of 'development' as suggested by Danda (1981).

Protection of interests of Scheduled Tribes is very essential for their development. The protective provisions are contained in Articles 15(4), 16(4), 19(5), 23, 29, 46, 164, 330, 332, 334, 335 and 338, 339(1), 371(A), 371(B), 371(C), Fifth Schedule and Sixth Schedule. Articles 15(4), 16(4) and 19(5) are exception to the fundamental rights of equality and freedom guaranteed under Part III of the Constitution. Provisions relating to development of Scheduled Tribes are contained mainly in Articles 275(1) and 339(2).

It needs to be mentioned that the tribes enjoy all such privileges and safeguards meant for all citizens of the country, for STs are also the citizens. In addition to general provisions of safeguards there are specific provisions for both ST and SC groups and for STs alone. A few provisions are discussed.

7.2 Constitutional Safeguards

The Constitution of India has provided a number of safeguards for the protection and development of Scheduled Tribes. Article 15(4) vests suitable authority in the state for making special provision for advancement of any socially and educationally backward classes of citizens. Article 46 prescribes that the state shall promote with special care the educational and economic interest of weaker sections of people and in particular, of the Scheduled Castes and Scheduled Tribes and shall protect them from social injustice and all forms of exploitations.

Article 275 relates to the special provisions providing grant-in-aid by the Union Government to the states for the welfare of the Scheduled Tribes and up-gradation of administration in the scheduled areas. Article 332 provides for reservation of seats for Scheduled Castes and Scheduled Tribes in the Legislative Assemblies of the States.

The Fifth Schedule of the Constitution contains provisions relating the administration and control of Scheduled areas and Scheduled Tribe in Fifth Schedule Areas. The eight states (i.e. Andhra Pradesh, Bihar, Gujarat, Himachal Pradesh, Madhya Pradesh, Maharashtra, Odisha and Rajasthan) having Scheduled Areas come under Fifth Schedule areas.[1] They are required to constitute Tribes Advisory Council, which must be consulted on all policy matters relating to the Welfare and Development of Scheduled Tribes. The Governors of the States have been bestowed with special powers and responsibilities in the administration of such areas. Reservation in seats and special representation in Parliament and State Legislature have been ensured under Article 334 and reservation of services under Article 335 of the Constitution.

After Independence and during plan periods a lot of welfare measures and economic development schemes and projects have been implemented in tribal areas.

7.3 Tribal Welfare Measures in Pre-Independence Period

During the British rule the approach to the administration of tribal areas was marked by the intention of leaving the tribal areas isolated as far as possible. The intention was translated into strategic move of designing such areas excluded or partially excluded. As a result, these tribal areas received least attention and were left to the whims and caprices of the local Zamindars and Petty Officials, who exploited the tribal to the maximum possible extent. This naturally resulted in further alienation and isolation of the tribal communities from the mainstream of economic development and civilization.

7.4 Tribal Development in Post-Independence Period

After Independence, and particularly after the promulgation of the Constitution, there has been a number of safeguards and schemes for protection and development of Scheduled Tribes. In furtherance of the objectives of saving tribals from exploitation and to promote their socio-economic development, Pandit Jawaharlal Nehru, the first Prime

Minister of India, in consultation with Verrier Elwin, his Advisor in Tribal Affairs, had enunciated five guiding principles for tribal development, popularly known as "Tribal Panchsheel". These are:

- Tribal people should develop along the line of their own genius and we should avoid imposing anything on them. We should try to encourage in every possible way to develop their traditional art and culture.
- Tribal rights in land and forest should be protected.
- We should try to train and build up a team of their own people to do the work of administration and development. Some technical personnel from outside will, no doubt, be needed especially in the beginning, but we should avoid introducing too many outsiders into tribal territory.
- We should not overadminister these areas and we should work through their own social and cultural institutions.
- We should judge the results not by statistics or the amount of money spent, but by the quality of human character that is evolved. (Nehru 1959, in Elwin 1959, xiii, also see Government of India Report, 1960: 13).

Though guidelines of tribal development were recorded in 1959 in the *Philosophy for NEFA* (Elwin, 1959/1988), the national government showed its commitment right from First Five Year Plan launched in 1952.

During the First Five Year Plan, the plan outlay was of the order of ₹ 2,356 crores, out of which a lump sum of ₹ 39 crores was earmarked for the various schemes 'for the Backward classes including Scheduled Tribes, Scheduled Castes, ex-criminal tribes and other backward classes. During this Plan the expenditure on tribals was 17.47 crores out of the total expenditure of ₹ 1,960 crores, while the tribal population was 2.25 crores out of the total population; the percentage expenditure on the development of tribals was only 0.83 per cent of the total as against the tribal population which was 6.61 per cent of the total population.

It is to be mentioned that tribal development was visualized as a part of the general development but with special treatment to tribals. Because of general nature, the aim of First Five Year Plan was to bring about the overall change of the tribes and tribal areas through Community Development Programmes (CDP). Steps were also taken to meet the special needs of tribal people with respect to their culture, traditions, social and psychological problems. Voluntary organizations were also encouraged to work in tribal areas. The welfare measures were primarily meant to eradicate poverty, spread education and provide health benefits.

During the Second Plan, Special Multipurpose Tribal Development (SMPT) Blocks were established in order to bring about rapid improvement in economic and social standards of the tribals. Initially, the limited number of programmes introduced in most of these blocks did not really reflect the nature of specific needs of the tribals. The programme was further intensified in the Third Plan and more number of such blocks were opened. But it was felt that in spite of the SMPT blocks programmes, the tribals could not get their due share in the general development programme. Hence, it was considered necessary to evolve a new strategy for their socio-economic development and the concept of Tribal Sub-Plan (TSP) was introduced during the Fifth Five Year Plan with twin objectives of accelerating socio-economic development of the tribals and their protection against various forms of exploitation. Areas having more than 50 per cent tribal concentration was identified and during the Fifth Plan, 21 Integrated Tribal Development Agencies (ITDAs) were formed comprising 118 blocks out of 314 blocks in Odisha. In addition to these, six micro projects were formed for development of primitive tribal groups, meant for the Bonda, Lanjia Soura, Dongaria Kandh, Kutia Kandh, Juang and Paudi Bhuiyan. At present 17 numbers of such micro projects are functioning in the State for the welfare of 13 particularly vulnerable Primitive Tribal Groups (PTGs).

During the Sixth Plan period, the areas with population of 10,000 or more of which more than 50 per cent of the population are tribals have been covered under "Modified Area Development Approach" (MADA). In the Seventh Plan this has been further relaxed so as to cover smaller areas with total population of 5000 and with more than 50 per cent tribal concentration under the "Cluster Approach". Again Dispersed Tribal Development Programme (DTDP) is being implemented by the Odisha Scheduled Caste and Scheduled Tribes Development Finance Cooperation for the benefit of families living outside the above special project areas.

An area specific approach for development named Orissa Tribal Development Project (OTDP) was launched in 1988-89 in Kashipur block of Rayagada district jointly by the International Fund for Agricultural Development (IFAD), Government of India and the State Government for all-round development of tribal areas.

The funding for the Tribal Sub-Plan was to come from the Annual Plans of the State and Central Ministries, special Central Assistance to

Tribal Sub-Plan, grants and institutional finance. It is required that the State should provide a percentage of its annual plan, which is not less than the percentage of tribal population of the State. Similarly, each of the Central Ministries are also required to earmark 8.08 per cent of their annual plans for the tribal sub plan and take up the projects, programmes and activities for the development of tribal communities.

But it has been observed that "though most of the State Governments have been earmarking funds for the TSP in proportion to the tribal population, in large number of cases, this earmarking is only notional. Actual utilization is often far less than the allocation. Diversion of TSP funds for other sectors is quite common" (National Commission for SCs and STs, 1998-99). The position of Central Ministries is not much different.

The VIIIth Plan Working Group for STs reveals that the overall performance of the efforts made during the plan period has not been very much encouraging. It reports, "After the adoption of TSP strategy, Central and State Governments have enacted protective laws to check exploitation of tribals by non-tribals especially the moneylenders and private traders. But in actual implementation this has not received priority. There are still instances reported by the States of tribal land passing into the hands of non-tribals despite the existence of these laws" (Vaid, 2004).

The Ninth Five Year Plan focused on social justice and empowerment strategy which also applied to tribal population. The Tenth Five Year Plan (2002-2007) was formulated mainly to consolidate the schemes in order to achieve what could not be achieved in previous plans. It is clear from the Mid-Term Appraisal of the Ninth Five Year Plan (1997-2002).

It is to be mentioned that for realization of plan objectives, programmes and schemes were implemented through Autonomous District Councils of VIth Schedule Areas, Development Councils/ Agencies within tribal sub-plan framework in Vth Schedule areas and through State government in states like Arunachal Pradesh, Nagaland where neither provisions of Vth nor VIth Schedules are applied. In Odisha tribal areas are covered under the provisions of Vth Schedule.

7.5 The Important Protective Laws

Some of the important protective laws or Regulations to protect the tribals from exploitation and pave the way for their socio-economic upliftment are stated as under:

- The Orissa (Scheduled Areas) Transfer of Immovable Property (by Scheduled Tribes) Regulation, 1956 (Regulation 2 of 1956) and its Amendment Regulation, 2000.

Under this provision any transfer of immovable property by a member of Scheduled Tribe shall be null and void unless made in favour of another member of Scheduled Tribe or with previous permission in writing of competent authority. Regulation 2 of 1956 has been further amended in 2000, to empower the Gram Panchayat and Gram Sabha in prevention of land alienation in the Scheduled Areas as per the Panchayat (Extension to Scheduled Areas) Act, 1966. This Amendment Regulation, 2000 has made provision for total prohibition of transfer of tribal land in Scheduled Areas from members of STs to others, if the land remaining after transfer will be reduced to two acres in case of irrigated land and five acres in case of unirrigated land. It also provided for restoration of land transferred from a member of the Scheduled Tribe to others without permission from the competent authority.

- Orissa Money Lenders Regulation, 1967 (Regulation 2 of 1968) is in operation with a view to regulating and monitoring moneylending activities in the Scheduled Areas of the State.
- Orissa Debt Relief Act, 1980, is in force with a view to providing relief to small farmers, rural artisans and agricultural labourers.
- Bonded Labour System (Abolition) Act, 1976 — As per this Act, the bonded labour system has been officially abolished since 1976. The liberated bonded labourers are rehabilitated with employment opportunities including self-employment.
- National Forest Policy, 1988 stipulated that all the agencies responsible to forest management should ensure that the tribal people are closely associated with the generation, plantation, development and harnessing of forests so as to provide them gainful employment. It has also recognized that the protection of rights of tribal in forest is the key to ameliorate their conditions.
- Scheduled Tribes and other Traditional Forest Dwellers (Recognition of Forest Rights) Act, 2006. The Act seeks to provide rights over land in their occupation to Forest Dwelling Scheduled Tribes and other traditional forest dwellers who have been residing there for generations but whose rights could not be recorded.

- The National Tribal Policy (which is at the draft stage) aims at facilitating translation of constitutional safeguards into reality with simultaneous socio-economic development. It encompasses various issues relating to protection of rights of tribal communities side by side with socio-economic development.

7.6 Failure in Objective Realization

Despite constitutional safeguards, favourable policy and protective regulations, the tribes still epitomize poverty and backwardness in human development indicators. To put it straight, planning and implementation of various projects and schemes for socio-economic development of tribals, achievement in realizing the objectives is far behind. There has not yet been perceptible improvement in the socio-economic condition of tribals in general, though there has been some changes in their economic pursuits. It has been estimated that about more than 90 per cent of the tribal families still live below the poverty line and the number is ever increasing (Orissa Development Report, 2002). Sample studies further showed that in interior tribal highlands about 100 per cent of the tribal families lived below poverty line (Samal, 1992). Due to this stark poverty marked by lack of employment opportunities, tribals still are facing food insecurity and they are compelled to consume mango kernel, tamarind seed powder and available roots, leaves and fruits to satisfy their hunger. It has led to migration of tribal labour force to distant places in search of employment and they are very often subject to exploitation of inhuman nature.

Institutional credit facilities have been provided in rural tribal areas through cooperative banks mostly by LAMPS and Regional Rural Bank. It is alleged that legal measures to curb the activities of the money-lenders and traders have failed in most of the cases to have impact on the severity of the problem due to ineffective enforcement machinery and lack of proper alternative sources of credit for meeting tribal consumption as well as production needs. The problem of tribal indebtedness often is aggravated and compounded with the government's subsidy-cum-loan schemes, which further lead the tribals into deep indebtedness (Tenth Five Year Plan, Vol. II, p. 458).

7.7 The Tribal Unrest

A general situation that is evident when tribes contacted external forces during colonial period and development forces after Independence is reflection of deprivation, poverty, and marginalization, and so on. How much they gained or gain from such contacts is a debatable matter. But what they lose is their rights over natural resources — land, forest and water. Tribals are more concerned with their loss than their gain, and so the loss weighs more against the gain. The situation of deprivation, marginalization and exclusion in the process of state sponsored development is what can be conceptualized as structural violence following Galtung's conception (1969, 1971 and 1990). The violence on the other hand causes counter-violence having different manifestations such as unrest, protests, uprisings, revolution, insurgency, rebellion and any of the type.

Needless to say, one course out of the failures in realizing development goals is unrest of different intensities. In the following paragraphs tribal unrest over loss of resources is discussed in brief with passing reference to Colonial period.

Tribal unrest and sometimes armed revolts among the tribal communities of India is not a recent phenomenon. During British period, a number of known and recorded cases of tribal unrest took place. Raghavaiah (1971: 261-266) pointed out that, nearly, 80 cases of revolts recorded from 1778 to 1947 among the Indian tribes. After 1947, the country has been witnessing continuous armed insurgency in many tribal areas. There are instances like Bastar tribal movement, the Naxalite insurgency in Naxalbari of West Bengal, Andhra Pradesh, Utter Pradesh, Chhattisgarh and Odisha. The country has also been witnessing continuous armed insurgency in north-east regions.

What is evident is that behind armed struggles, the causes were interference, starting from the British period, in their traditional cultures and life ways. The interference reflects in the form of exploitation of the tribals by non-tribal traders and moneylenders, restriction of access to forests through implementation of forest policy, and finally in the loss of tribal agricultural land to the non-tribals. These are perhaps the most crucial factors which adversely affected the economic life of the tribal communities (Reddy, 1987:6).

Following Reddy, it can be stated that tribal struggle for identity means two things in India. First and foremost is their struggle against alienating their basic resources, land and forest resources to the non-tribals and secondly for preservation of their cultures. The first one has led them to armed struggle against their exploiters and their supporter, and also to protest movements against the non-tribal immigrations into tribal area. They even protest creation of biosphere reserves, wild-life sanctuaries, establishment of industries and irrigation and hydro electric projects in their midst which largely benefit the non-tribals. Coupled with the objective of keeping hold on their traditional resources, the second aspiration of preservation of their traditional culture has forced them to take to the course of political movements seeking separate states for themselves (*ibid.*: 14).

7.7.1 *The Kandh Uprisings in Odisha*

Gopinath Mohanty observes in his article to the souvenir published at the Second All India Tribal Welfare Conference at Bhubaneswar as follows:

> "And the country can't forget their contribution to the cause of independence. All the *adivasis*, to whichever race they might belong, have a strong urge for freedom and a natural sense of justice and at times, in periodical upheavals under the British Rules, they have amply exhibited it. It is the Kandhs who first took up arms against the British in the Ganjam and Nayagarh 'malias' in 1817 which then spread all over coastal Orissa and over several other areas and was headed by Bakshi Jagabandhu, Bidyadhara Mohapatra Bhramarabara Ray, the ex-commander of Raja of Puri. This was followed in the eighteen hundred and thirties by the rebellion of Dora Bisoi, the Kandha in the eighteen hundred and fifties by the rebellion of the famous Chakra Bisoyi, a Kandha of Bisipada, in Phulbani, who moved like a storm over the land of his conquest, baffled the British, defecated the troops sent against him, in many battles and was never caught. At the time of first war of national Independence, called by the British the 'Sepoy Mutiny', Surendra Sai, a Gond chief and a scion of the royal line of Sambalpur, waged a glorious battle against the British for which he is accepted as a natural hero".

During British rule, initially the rebellions of the Kandhs in Odisha were directed against the British. It continued for about 20 years, i.e. from 1837 to 1856 in which the majority of the Kandh population of Ghumusar, China-ki-medi, Kalahandi and Patna actively participated. The Savars and some local militia clans also joined them. The Kandhs lived in vast hill tracks which stretched from the Presidency of Madras to that of Bengal covering central provinces. They were virtually independent in their mountainous habitats. The Kandhs fought with *tangis* — a sort of battle axe, bows and arrows and even swords. The British rulers in the name of suppression of so-called human sacrifice (mariah) alleged to be prevalent in Kandh areas entered into these areas. As it was deep-rooted socio-religious system among the Kandhs, they retaliated with armed struggle. The British created the Mariah agency comprising all Kandh areas to be administered by an agent who was directly responsible to the central government. Capt. S.C. Macpherson was the first agent and he took over the charge of the agency in December, 1845. Initially British authorities tried to persuade the Kandhs to give it up. When the persuasion efforts failed, the British authorities decided to use force. Nevertheless, due to topography of the area and indomitable spirit of the Kandhs, the war against them continued for a number of years.

Chakra Bisoi, a Kandh tribal from the village Tarabadi of Ghumsar played a leading role in the fight against the British. He aroused the Kandhs against the British not only for their interference in the socio-religious practices of the tribals but also for causing them undue sufferings. Instead of offering protection to the tribals from the exploitation by *zamindars* and *sahukars* (moneylenders), the British authorities themselves exacted various taxes such as plough tax, house tax etc. Thus, the common man was hard pressed by the burden of taxes and other oppressive measures of British agents. They joined the revolt. This movement continued till 1956-57 (Verma, 1990:49-51).

7.7.2 *The Kandh Revolution in Kalahandi*

During the reign of twenty seventh Nagavansi ruler of former princely state of Kalahandi Fateh Narayan Deo, the Kandhs of Madanpur-Rampur Zamindari rebelled for some time but it was easily quelled by the skilful management of their affairs. Chakara Bisoi took shelter in the banks of Tel river hiding alternatively in Madanpur Zamindari and then at Janasingha. The British commissioner of Nagpur called upon the Raja of Madanpur to handover Chakara Bisoi to him. The Raja of Madanpur declared that, he was ignorant of Chakara Bisoi's presence in his estate. Meanwhile another Kandh head Rendo Majhi had taken the charge of the rebel in 1853. It was told that he was arrested during a Mariah Sacrifice.

In the report of Lt. Elliot in 1857, it was stated that Chakara Bisoi and his associates were encouraged by the Raja of Madanpur. The Raja was removed from the management of the estate and detained under the surveillance of his chief Udit Pratap Deo, the Raja of Kalahandi. Udit Pratap Deo ruled for 23 years and died in 1881. He had adopted Raghu Keshari Deo as his son but he was a minor of 4 years at that time. So, the administration was conducted by the eldest Rani, Asha Kumari Devi. For improvement of agriculture in the state, Udit Pratap Deo brought Kultha cultivators to Kalahandi from Sambalpur. The Kulthas exploited the poor and simple minded Kandhs and deprived them of the best of their lands. It was during the weak rule of Asha Kumari Devi that the great Kandh rebellion took place in May 1882 from Asurgarh Narla region.

During July-August 1932, there was Kandh uprising against the British in Narayanpatna area, but was suppressed in September of the same year by armed reserve police.

The British Government, however, started to introduce several measures for the welfare of the tribal people, such as, opening of schools and construction of roads in the heart of Kandh territories. However, these measures could not redress all the grievances of the tribals. Consequently, discontentment and disillusionment among the tribals continued for a long time and there were several sporadic rising in the hill tracks till independence.

After independence undoubtedly special provisions were made for tribal development and to protect them from exploitation but the discontentment among the tribals continued due to:

- Inadequate implementation of constitutional safeguards;
- Lack of participation to tribals in development process;
- Lack of accountability;
- Lack of tribal leadership;
- Land alienation and displacement without adequate rehabilitation;
- Exploitation in forestry and other economic activities; and
- Socio-cultural factors (Verma, 1990: 170).

Such factors lead to discontent among the tribal surface repeatedly in one form or another, *viz.* either demand for a separate state or the demand for better deal of development. This situation is susceptible to exploitation by anti-national forces.

7.7.3 *Kandhmal Issue*

Kandhmal in Odisha has become infamous after the chain of incidents that have taken place. Kandhmal is the home of communal conflicts since early nineties of the last century. After split of the old district "Boudha-Phulabani" into two separate districts, the conflict looked like communal in which about 40 people lost their lives and the district was renamed as Kandhmala to cool down the agitated Kandh Tribal population and restore peace in the district. The District looked normal for quite a long time from outside but the hatred remained as if looking for a spark only to erupt. Violence started from 25th August 2008 as a spontaneous reaction to the killing of Swami Lakshmanananda Saraswati on 23rd August, 2008 along with four other devotees. On 9th Sept., 2008, the Maoists, who worked underground made an official press release and claimed the responsibility of killing of Swami Laxmanananda Saraswati.

It was believed by the masses that the provoked Hindu fanatics with the killing of the Swami and his followers have massacred the Christians. In reality the riot is not only because of the clash between the people belonging two religious faiths; the most significant reason is the clash between the "Kandh" (ST) and "Pano" (SC) community most of whom are converted Christians. There was a continuous clash between these two communities over several issues. The Kandh Section belongs to Scheduled Tribe community and the Panos to the Scheduled Caste. About 80 per cent of Panos of Kandhmal have been converted to Christianity. As per the prevailing law, if SC people are converted to Christianity, they will not get reservation facility. On the other hand, if ST people convert, they will have the reservation facilities. The Pano community, therefore, wanted to be given the ST status to make use of the reservation which was opposed severely by Kandh community.

In pursuance of the Presidential Order 2002, "Kui" tribe is one of the 18 Kandha or Kandh group of tribes in the state. Panos on the plea that they speak "Kui claim tribal status and have tried to take the advantage of reservation facilities. After Kandhmal riots, specially appointed vigilance officials have taken note of 593 cases of such fake tribal certificates" (*Telegraph*, 10th Jan., 2009).

Christian missionaries started their work of conversion and converted almost all the people belonging to the Pano community. In 1961, Christian population was 19,128 and in 2001 it was increased to 1,17,757. This must have provoked Swami Lakshmanananda and the VHP.

On 24th Dec., 2007, a structure set up to hold Christmas celebrations in Brahmanigaon was attacked and destroyed. The structure was nothing more than the pandal encroaching the main road of the town. That was enough to start an ugly argument, which ended in the Hindu damaging the Pandal and injuring two Christians. After that, a rumour that prominent VHP leader Swami Laxmanananda Saraswati had been attacked by a Christian mob at Daringbadi, led to a wildfire of violence across Kandhmal.

At the same time, trouble was also brewing in the area between the Kandh tribals and the Dalit Panos. The mutual hatred had been simmering for the past 20 years with seven Kandhs and nine Dalits being killed in clashes since 1994.

In the late 1960s of last century establishment of an *ashram* in Chakapad, by Laxmanananda Saraswati, among others, have been propagating an anti-Christian campaign in Kandhmal.

Election campaigns at the interval of few years fed on and spread religious hatred. Christians say religious intolerance has seeped into the bureaucratic and judicial system as well and it is that which explains the administrations indifference to the anti-Christian violence in Kandhmal (ND TV, dated 7th Jan., 2008).

Killing of Graham Staines, an Australian missionary and his two sons, ten year old Philip and six-year-old Timothy on the night of 22nd January, 1999 has also turned the issue to be an international concern.

Therefore, the matter is not too simple to describe the incident as just ethnic or communal clashes. It is combined effect of Ethnic, Communal, Political and Extremist forces. It is the failure of civil society over some of the crucial issues of the humanity.

7.7.4 *Chasi Muliya Adibasi Sangha*

Narayanpatna and Bandhugaon based Chasi Muliya Adibasi Sangha (CMAS) is the end result of pent-up emotions and discontentment of native Kandh tribes arising out of long years of suppression, usurpation of their land by non-tribals, cruel action and exploitation by money-lenders, liquor-vendors and police, callous and negligent attitude of revenue and development officials. The recent outburst was mainly the inspiration from catalysts like Com. Gananath Patra and others which raised the emotions of tribals and forced them to confront with the police and other non-tribals which ultimately proved genocidal to the tribal people themselves.

It was prior to 1975, the Andhra Orissa Border Regional Committee (AOBRC) was constituted by Andhra Pradesh State Committee with Com. V. Ramalingachary, Gananath Patro, and Viswam as its active members. The AOBRC took steps to reorganize the leftist movement in

East Godavari and Srikakulam Districts and also took steps to give a shape to the movement in Koraput and Ganjam Districts of Odisha. The Emergency was declared within a short period after the AOBRC began its work. Yet it continued to work under severe repression. Com. V. Ramalingachary left the Party citing Political differences. Com. Gananath Patro took up the responsibility of forming the Odisha state committee and spreading of party activities in the state. Due to consistent efforts, the people movement in the AOBRC area took a concrete shape by 1982 and lead to many Adivasi uprisings. In the process of these struggles, the Agency Girijan Sangham, Ryatu Cooli Sangham (AP) and Chasi Muliya Adivasi Sangham (Orissa) came into existence (interview with Com. S. Jhansi, 2009).

The CMAS popularly known as 'Sangham Party' was active and gained its momentum in Narayanpatna and Bandhugaon Blocks of Koraput District a few years ago. Both these blocks are having more than 90 per cent tribals belonging to the Kandh community. In course of time there was a fraction and both these Blocks were guided by two different groups of leaders of the Sanghas. The mode of their activities became different and sometimes it led to clash among them. The CMAS of Narayanpatna is with the CPI-ML organization led by Com. Gananath Patro and CMAS of Bandhugaon area is led by the CPI-ML activists based in Andhra Pradesh. The CPI-ML (New Democracy) is also active in these two blocks (Online Edition, *India's National Newspaper*, Monday, 7th Sept., 2009).

However, initially, the movement in these two Blocks was headed by Mrs. Kondagiri Paidamma with main objectives of safeguarding the tribal rights over land, water and forest. It was mostly in democratic manner. But after arrival of leftist leaders like Com. Srikanta Mohanty and S. Jhansi from Vijayanagaram, N. Bhaskar Rao (Locally known as Vasu) from Parvatipuram and Gananath Patro from Balasore, the momentum took a sharp turn. In the meantime there was a clash between "Kandhs" (Local S.Ts) and "Doms" (Local S.Cs) in Tala Gumandi village of Narayanpatna Block over water for irrigating cultivatable land. The Kandhs were supported by CMAS. The tribal with support from outside leaders dominated over the local Scheduled Caste people, who were few in number. In course of time, being inspired by the leftist leaders, "Kandhs" also targeted local Sundhis (traditional liquor traders), Kumutis (the intermediary and traders) living in the area since long. One of the main reasons of split between the Sanghas of Narayanpatna and Bandhugaon Blocks was on the issue of lemon grass plantation and lemon grass plants. Cultivators of Andhra Pradesh established a number of lemon grass plants in Bandhugaon Block and to feed these plants they cultivated lemon grass mainly in the lands of the tribals which they took on lease. It is alleged that CMAS was initially collecting money from these lemon grass plants to meet their day-to-day expenditures. But when Com. Gananath Patro started opposing such plants and plantation and laid emphasis on traditional cultivation like rice, raggi etc. in place of lemon grass there was a split and there were two separate Sanghas in the two blocks. Of course, on the plea of fighting in a non-violent manner, Bandhugaon CMAS was guided by leaders like Mrs. Paidamma, Mr. Srikanta Mohanty, Miss. S. Jhansi, Mr. Vasa and local Kandh leaders like Arjuna Kendurka.

On the other hand, with the objective of developing indigenous cultivation in place of lemon grass Narayanpatna CMAS was continuing agitation under the leadership of Com. Patro and local leaders like Nachika Linga and Wadeka Singhana.

It is also alleged from various quarters that the Maoists supported both these groups. Long standing land problems, inactive Government machinery in solving such problems and overall poverty of the tribals and their exploitation provided a good scope for leftist activists to spread their activities. The Government machinery failed again and again to take serious note of the basic problems of the tribals and to solve them at the right moment.

Both the CMAS have been leading a tribal movement propagating to prevent exploitation, restoration of tribal lands illegally alienated, stop manufacturing and selling of the liquor and prevent mining activities by the multinational companies in the region. They say that they do not believe the Government and they do have their own strategies to solve their problems. Nachika Linga, the president of CMAS of Narayanpatna opined and categorically said, "I want all the tribals, Dalits and poor to earn their bread and to cover their bodies with cloths and I don't believe in parliamentary path. Parliament and Assembly halls are nothing but like pits in river beds".

The CMAS is claiming to have undertaken various activities among the poor and tribal people for last 15 years with the following objectives[2]:

- to create awareness among the tribals about their real situations in which they are living;
- to oppose and stop the production and sale of liquor and other intoxicants to tribal which have damaging effects on their health and economy;

- to resist any further land-alienation in tribal areas and restore already alienated land to the tribal people;
- to distribute the available "Anabadi" and other forest lands viable for house construction and agriculture among the landless and poor people;
- to assert and implement rights of tribals on forest like collecting and selling of forest products;
- to ensure the payment of wages fixed for the daily labourers and to completely uproot all the related corrupt practices and manipulations;
- to stop the corrupt practices of percentage (P.C.) payments in all the developmental and welfare works;
- to see that the services in the fields of health and education really improve in tribal and rural areas;
- to see that various programmes meant for the welfare of the BPL/APL families including NREGS are sincerely implemented without any corruption;
- to oppose the programmes like mining, water bodies and power plants which would cause land alienation and go against the basic human rights, especially to save, protect and conserve Maliparvat, Deomali hills which carry Bauxite.

7.7.5 *Unrest in Narayanpatna*

Forceful occupation of lands under the possession of non-tribals (mostly traders, moneylenders and liquor vendors), supposed to be taken away from the local tribals (either legally or illegally, by the "Chasi Mulia Adivasi Sangh" in Narayanpatna and Bandhugaon blocks) and frontal attack on distillation and sale of liquor were the two main strategies and objectives of unrest and uprisings in recent years. Sri Nachika Linga, a tribal youth belonging to Bhaliaput village of Narayanpatna block, presently leading the movement of Chasi Mulia Adivasi Sangha as its president expressed that he along with his family members had bitter experience of exploitation as "Goti" (bonded labour) by the local non-tribal Shundhi Sahukar. Sri Linga had a brief political career of being elected as a ward member and then holding the post of Naib Sarpanch. The leftist leader of repute like Com. Ganatha Patro is the friend, philosopher and guide to Sri Linga. He is accepted as the advisor of CMAS. At a point of time when the agitation took a serious turn, Sri Linga was arrested and imprisoned in Koraput Jail and then released. Again there was a clash between the tribals and non-tribals in which

Sri Linga was assaulted. This provoked the tribals and resulted in severe violence in entire Podapadara village in which lived Sri Kantha Parida and his family, the ex-Sahukar to whom Sri Linga and his family members served as "Goti". The dwellings belonging mostly to non-tribals in the villages like Podapadara, Borigi and Kumbhari etc. of Narayanpatna block were destroyed. The affected persons lost their houses, belongings, cattle etc. and took shelter in various places at district headquarters, of course, with help from district administration. It is reported that about 2000 acres of agricultural land were occupied by force from the non-tribal landholders of Narayanpatna block and distributed among landless tribals and Dalits by the Sangh leaders (*Swabhiman*, Jan. 2010: p. 11).

A number of rallies, public meetings and gatherings were organized in Narayanpatna as well as in other places by the CMAS to highlight various local problems, the most important among them being the land and liquor issues. The situation went out of control when the tribals, under the leadership of Sri Linga and Com. Patro, became violent and attacked and forced the non-tribal inhabitants to leave their homes and hearths and go out of the area. "Hundreds of non-tribal families were forced to flee from their homes as violence flared despite the deployment of paramilitary troops in certain pockets" (*India News*, 3rd Dec., 2009). Normal life of the people of the locality was disturbed due to frequent road blockades by felling roadside trees on the roads either by the members of CMAS or by the Naxals. Sometimes police personnel and civilians lost their lives due to landmine explosions. Government offices were attacked, official papers were burnt and furniture were either damaged or taken away. Development activities in both the blocks of Narayanpatna and Bandhugaon mostly came to a standstill. Extension officials developed a fear complex and became reluctant to work. On the other hand, Santi Committees were formed in several places outside Narayanpatna and they protested against the Chasi Mulia Adibasi Sangha and did not allow the Sangha members to enter into their areas in order to spread their activities.

Ghinua Bahini

The Chasi Mulia Adivasi Sangha formed a local youth paramilitary force like organization known as "Ghinua Bahini" or "Lal Bahini" as narrated by Com. Gananath Patro in an informal interview with him by the scholar with his guide and some other academicians from Koraput. "Ghinua, is a character in a story written long back by an eminent Oriya writer Late Bhagabati Charan Panigrahi. Ghinua was an expert hunter who was killing man eaters (tigers). Situation compelled him to revolt against Govinda Sardar who was a wealthy man and at the same time an exploiter of the poor. Ghinua killed Govinda Sardar and surrendered himself before the police, saying that he found no difference between a man-eater and Govinda Sardar. Ghinua Bahini formed by Chasi Mulia Adivasi Sangha is name after this character of Bhagabati Charan Panigrahi", said Com.Patro.

Members of the Ghinua Bahini are dressed with red color uniform (so they are also named as Lal Bahini) and are equipped with traditional weapons like bow arrow, axes, *bhala* etc. Their duty is to guard the villages and keep an eye on the outsiders entering into their locality.

The Unfortunate Incident of Police Firing

The situation took an unfortunate turn on 20th Nov., 2009 when hundreds of the members of Chasi Mulia Adivasi Sangha along with Ghinua Bahini gathered before Narayanpatna police station and protested against the harassment being made to the people in the villages by police and paramilitary forces during search operation. On the plea that the protesters became violent and wild, attacked the police station, and tried to snatch arms and ammunitions, the police opened fire and killed two tribal leaders. Many of the protesters were injured also. However, some of the civil society organizations and enlightened citizens expressed their doubts about whether the situation really warranted to go for a firing by the police at that point of time. After this incidence, police force became more active. The main leader of the Sangha Sri Nachika Linga was absconded and Police declared him as "fugitive". Many of the tribal leaders went underground. Finally, Com. Gananath Patro, advisor of the Sangha was arrested and kept in Koraput jail.

NOTES

1. According to the provisions of Fifth Schedule and President's order there are 10 States at present having Scheduled Areas. These are: Andhra Pradesh, Chhattisgarh, Gujarat, Himachal Pradesh, Jharkhand, Madhya Pradesh, Maharashtra, Odisha, Rajasthan and Telangana.
2. Manifesto of CMAS, Narayanpatna based on pamphlets distributed by their members to the scholar during his visit to Bhaliaput of Narayanpatna

8

SUMMARY AND CONCLUSIONS

In the present study, an attempt has been made to enquire into the contemporary socio-economic conditions of Kandhs living in Koraput district and to see to what extent they have been able to raise their living standard and are saved from exploitations of various types. In spite of various Constitutional safeguards and ameliorative measures undertaken by the government and non-governmental agencies, the tribal problems relating to their poverty, unemployment and food insecurity etc. remained intricate and to some extent insoluble. The Kandhs are backward, rather very backward, tribe. They have mostly remained away from the main-stream of civilization. In the midst of hills and forests they lead a life of poverty, exclusion and deprivation. Traditional method of agriculture and dependence on forest collection are two principal pillars of their economy. They are mainly shifting cultivators. The primary method of their agriculture is not only a toilsome affair, but it is the most unreliable source of livelihood, as the harvest, mainly depends on timely rain and favourable climatic conditions. The land they cultivate is less fertile. Constant crop failures or the scanty crops harvested from shifting cultivation lands hardly feed a Kandh family for five to six months. They have less amount of low-lying paddy land. They supplement their food requirements through collection of wild and edible forest products. Hence, they lead a life of starvation, poverty and food insecurity. Poverty, food insecurity, indebtedness, illiteracy, ignorance, fatalistic attitude, liquor culture etc. lead these people to be exploited in the hands of comparative powerful agencies.

While going to analyze the living conditions of the Kandhs of Koraput district with samples of Laxmipur Block, an attempt was made to know the nature and extent of exploitations still prevailing in the tribal communities in general and that of Kandhs in particular. Laxmipur Block is taken as a sample in the study, taking one village each from

13 Panchayats of Laxmipur Block. In order to have a comparative study in the socio-economic status of tribals living in road-side villages and interior villages, six numbers of road-side villages and seven numbers of remote villages were selected for present study. Twenty numbers of Kandh households from each village (24 from Kanapadi) were randomly selected. A total of 264 Kandh households were selected for an in-depth study of socio-economic conditions of the Kandhs and to know the extent of exploitation still prevailing. The study further intended to examine how far poverty is the cause and effect of the exploitation of the tribals. It was further intended to know the impact of exploitation on socio-economic lives of Kandhs. Present study is undertaken with certain hypothesis that the Kandhs still suffer from exploitation in the hands of non-tribal *Sahukar*, moneylenders, traders, SC people and by the persons belonging to their own community. Even some of the PRI members and Government officials were no exception to it. Secondly, it was assumed that the degree of exploitation had declined in the tribal areas after implementation of various anti-exploitative Acts due to Constitutional safeguards.

The field investigations in the sample villages brought to light the fact that the Kandhs were still very poor in their living. They were mostly illiterate and ignorant. They still followed primitive technologies in their economic enterprises. Agricultural productivity in the hilly and shifting land is very poor. The sample study revealed that nearly 91 per cent of the families are either landless or small or marginal farmers. Interestingly, 15.91 per cent of landholders had land less than 1 acre each and about 30 per cent farmers had land up to 2 acres. This shows the extent of uneconomic landholdings from which the Kandhs of study area suffer. So, they encroached upon forest lands for shifting cultivation.

Agriculture hardly supported a family for five to six months in a year. Social extravagance and low income led to indebtedness during emergency. This indebtedness opened the doors of exploitation of various types. Since time immemorial it has been the main reason of land alienation and bonded labour (or GOTI) and resultant exploitation. However, with the implementation of Anti Land Alienation Act and Bonded Labour Act, the practice of alienation of land from tribals to non-tribals and bonded labour system had almost officially stopped. However, data gathered revealed through survey, discussion and case studies in the study area clearly proved that these exploitative practices were not fully eradicated. These practices continued in a hidden manner. An unintentional consequence of these restrictions was found to be that lands were transferred from the poor needy tribals to some of the well-to-do tribals of their own community. There was no bar in the transfer of land from tribals to tribals.

Acquisition of land for public purpose with government support went on. Land alienation due to establishment of Aditya Alumina Company Ltd., for example, was going on in the study area with direct state intervention. As stated earlier, poor agricultural practices coupled with small landholdings, lack of irrigation facility and poor quality of land were the major causes of poverty among the Kandhs. During the lean season off-firm employment opportunities in these areas were found to be inadequate. Employment opportunities created by forest department, block, Panchayats, and other Government and voluntary organizations are not sufficient to meet the people's demand. The Kandhs being hill and forest dwellers, their dependence on forest for livelihood is too much. Forest provides them food, fodder, firewood, housing materials, agricultural inputs, medicines and drinks etc. With large scale of deforestation due to various reasons, forest area is reduced to a great extent and availability of edible fruits, roots, tubers etc. had come down. Forest was no more able to support the tribal economy to the extent that it was doing in the past. Collection of forest produces had become mostly unremunerative when compared with the time spent for collection of such produces. Most of the tribals found continuing the collection because of non-availability of alternative source of livelihood in lean seasons.

The Kandhs were found both socially and economically very backward. Literacy rate was very low among them. It was only 20.87 per cent in the Sample study villages which consists of 26.67 per cent of males and 12.45 per cent of females. It was quite low when compared with the state level overall literacy rate (i.e. 63.61%) and national average of 64.85 per cent. Their monthly average income was estimated at ₹ 295.11 and expenditure at only ₹ 291.80. With these average levels of monthly income and expenditure they remained far below the poverty line which was set by new expert committee, on November 2009 and which was estimated to be ₹ 407.78 in rural areas of Odisha. Hence, the sample Kandh families were found to be very poor. Though their income is marginally higher than their expenditure, this did not show that they were economically better off. They lived in a subsistence economy. During emergency, they resorted to borrowings. It was found from the sample survey that nearly 31 per cent of families were indebted. About 63 per cent of loan was taken from non-banking sectors like friends and relatives, moneylenders and traders. Sometimes, the rate of interest on loans incurred from these indigenous sources varied from 100 per cent to 300 per cent per annum. They mostly utilized these borrowed amounts to meet their bare necessities of life like food, clothing and shelter and to fulfil conventional necessities like expenses on socio-religious function, which included feasting and drinking.

An analysis of their housing pattern showed that their living rooms varied from a minimum of one room to a maximum of three rooms. A large majority of sample households did not have electricity and latrine facility and drainage system. Kandh houses appeared to be clean from outside but really these were not hygienic. Often, pets were kept either inside the house or much closer to their house creating an unhealthy environment especially in rainy season. They took very little care for their personal health and sanitation.

Their fatalistic attitude towards health and sanitation, and no interest in education along with low level of income were found contributing to their backwardness. They suffered from vicious Circle of poverty. "They are poor because they are poor".

It was also found that status of women in Kandh society was comparatively high. They took part in decision making in family affairs. Family economy was mostly controlled by women. Awareness level of women was generally low. As mentioned above, the literacy rate of sample Kandh women was as low as 12.45 per cent. Gradually tribal women were empowered after the passing of PESA Act and spread of SHG movement in tribal areas.

Land disputes were found to be major problems in Kandh inhabited areas. Poverty and indebtedness among them often led to land alienation and subsequent litigations.

As a result, several uprisings and conflicts occurred in Kandh dominated areas. Recent agitations by Chasi Mulia Adivasi Sangh in Narayanpatna and Bandhugaon blocks with support of leftist forces were the examples in the matter.

As mentioned earlier, the poverty, lack of profit motive in economic dealings and lack in awareness and entrepreneurial skills and above all their simplicity were the reasons for which Kandhs were exploited in the hands of various agencies. The exploitation still continue in various names and shapes and mostly in a hidden manner in tribal pockets inhabited by the Kandh. Neither the creditor nor *Sahukar* nor the loanee openly confessed the facts as there are anti-exploitative legislations and Acts found in force.

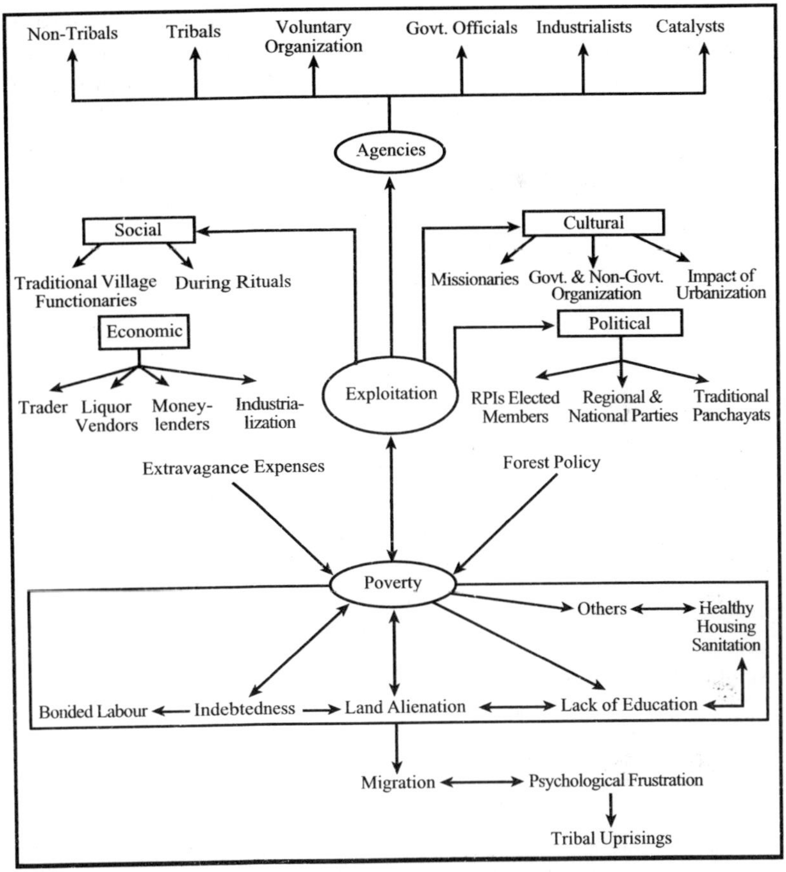

Fig. 8.1: Retrospect Effect: Poverty, Exploitation, Causes, Types and Agencies.

Fig. 8.1 shows the cause and effect relationship between poverty and exploitation. Despite implementation of various Acts, policies, and programmes for tribal development, no perceptible improvement was found in them. Poverty and exploitation acted as cause and effect to each other. The general notion that, "Tribals are exploited by non-tribals" is always not true. There have now emerged tribal money-lenders and *Sahukars* who do not hesitate to grab the lands of other tribals and to whom we may call as "tribal exploiters". Due to enactment of different protective laws in general and after implementation of PESA Act, 1996, in particular, the situation in tribal areas are gradually changing. Semi-educated youths and people from comparatively well to do tribal families are occupying political powers. It is interesting to find that some of them were after gaining political leadership did not even hesitate to exploit their own people whenever such opportunities were available. On the other hand, exploitation by non-tribal moneylenders and traders had come down to certain extent, but it was not totally stopped. It was also found that about 33 per cent of total households had given bribe of one kind or the other either in the form of cash or kind to the elected members (most of them are tribals) to receive some benefits from the Government programmes. But these benefits were not always easily available. Many times they were cheated. This amounted to exploitation of tribals in the hands of politically and economically powerful tribals. Land alienation from tribal to tribals was also a matter of concern. Such well-to-do tribals were taking a major share of the benefit schemes meant for development of tribal areas and tribal people. As a result of all these inequality among the tribals is creeping-up.

The age-old traditional type of exploitation by the "Doms" in the Kandh village had come down to a considerable extent but it was not totally stopped. However, they were found changing their strategies of exploitation and adopting various fraudulent means to cheat the Kandh people while doing business transactions with them. Some of them continued to act as moneylenders or creditors charging high rate of interest from Kandhs.

Lack of awareness on the part of Kandhs about the developmental programmes resulted in their poor implementation or no implementation. They were found either cheated or exploited in the process of plan implementation. For most of the officials, tribal development was considered an act of either charity or a matter of preparing statistics. Corruption in a more or lesser degree, was alleged to exist in the implementation stage of most of the government programmes. Taking the poverty and other social backwardness of tribals into account, we may simply say that corruption is the other name of exploitation. Full benefits of development programmes never reached the needy tribals. A document published by Government of India in the Ministry of Home Affairs (1977) lamented, "We can not have development at this rate". It further stated, "In the name of tribal development, we have spent a lot of money during last several plans. But when accounting was made at the end of last period of the safeguards to the tribals in the constitution, it was found that actual benefits trickling down to the tribals have not been consistent with the promise we have made. Expenditure has not resulted in the benefits that should have accrued to this population. Unfortunately, the developmental programme for the tribal areas did not yield the desired results. . . . More than 75 per cent of the total benefits have not reached the tribals . . .". The fact is more or less true at present also.

Exploitation relating to social and cultural life of the Kandhs was also rampant in these areas. There had been several unrest and tensions between converted Christians and Hindu communities in the tribal areas. The constant clashes between the two communities and at the end the killing of Swami Laxmanananda Saraswati in Kandhmala District in recent past was a case to the point. Poor tribals and non-tribals, of both the communities, had undergone several sufferings in the process. The Kandhs were found being exploited in trade and barter due to their ignorance and unawareness. It was found that they were cheated by the traders through weight and measure and not paid prevailing market prices for their goods or services rendered. They were loosers in bargain and exploited in the process of haggling. The Kandhs were often found to be exploited by local liquor vendors. It was easy to exploit them as the Kandhs were addicted to liquor to a great extent. Sometimes, the government officials belonging to revenue, exercise, police and forest department, did not hesitate to exploit the Kandhs.

Poverty and unemployment also led to migration. It was found that migrant labourers in search of employment went to near-by towns, districts and states. The result of migration was more or less the same, i.e. low payment, over-work, ill-treatment and harassment. Instances of migrations and the pathetic plight of tribal migrant labourers have been narrated in the body of the present study.

The state of poverty and exploitation of the Kandhs led to discontentment, psychological frustration and tribal uprisings. The seed is already sown by Chasi Mulia Adivasi Sangh of Narayanpatana and Bandhugaon blocks of Koraput district. All the efforts by government and non-governmental agencies directed towards solving the problems of tribals further baffled the situation. Hence, on the basis of the study undertaken and analysis made we may infer that the Kandhs of Koraput are by and large very poor in their living. They mostly live below the poverty line. They still suffer from social maladies like illiteracy, ill health and ignorance. They had been historically suffering from exploitation of various types in the hands of various agencies. Constitutional safeguards and anti-exploitative rules and regulations are not able to save the tribals from exploitations totally, though the extent or degree of exploitations has come down. Some new types of exploiters have also emerged with the passage of time.

Suggestions/Recommendations

After the discussions and analysis so far made, it is now evident that poverty and exploitation are acting upon each other with cause and effect relationship in the tribal socio-economic life. This is very much true among the Kandhs of Koraput district. The benefits of plan programmes and schemes meant for tribal welfare have not reached the beneficiaries to the full extent. A majority of tribals including the Kandhs have still remained backward both socially and economically. Illiteracy, ignorance, simplicity and above all poverty of the Kandhs are still leading to exploitation of various types either in an open manner or in a hidden manner. Here follows few humble suggestions for raising the socio-economic conditions of tribals in general and that of Kandhs in particular which will ultimately help them to escape the trap of exploitation.

- Education should be given priority in tribal areas. It is the key to all socio-economic development. It will enrich their knowledge, enhance the level of awareness and empower them to take effective part in their own development and that of their area and community. Hence, the officials in Education Department and village level community members should together see that educational institutions function effectively and efficiently. Special attention should be given to bring more and more girls (and also the boys) to schools and retain them to complete their education.
- The ongoing developmental plans and schemes should be effectively and sincerely implemented in tribal areas in general and that of Kandh concentrated areas of Koraput in particular. It is better to implement the welfare programmes through socio-cultural institutions of tribals so that it will pave the way for their sustainable development. Credit needs of the Kandhs including consumption credits must be timely and easily available by institutional credit organizations. Employment guarantee programmes should be implemented sincerely. The grain banks must be opened in villages having no grain banks and these should function effectively. These will save the poor tribals from the problem of food insecurity. To be more specific, assured employment facilities need to be provided to the rural tribals through schemes like NREGS, Swarna Jayanti Grama

Swarojagar Yojana and other economic benefit schemes. This will give them employment security and help to stop migration.

- Anti-exploitative Acts and Rules should be strictly implemented in tribal areas in general and that of Kandh concentrated areas of Koraput in particular. There should be intensive awareness campaigns to educate the tribals about various rules, regulations and schemes. They must be empowered enough so that they take part in planning and implementation of various programmes at grass-root level.
- Tribals who have attended the higher levels of development both socially and economically should be identified and excluded from availing special assistances meant for backward tribals because of whom limited resources could be effectively utilized for betterment of the needy tribals.
- Tribal culture and traditions having positive values should be protected, preserved and linked to their development.
- Local specific priorities of the tribals must be identified, policies reoriented and programmes redesigned.
- An honest and corruption free administration is the prime necessity in the present context to save the tribals from exploitation and to see that socio-economic development schemes are properly and effectively implemented in the tribal areas. As mentioned above, steps should be taken to empower the tribal PRI members through awareness campaigns and training programmes.

Needless to say, transparency and accountability should be included as crucial component in tribal administration and implementation of programmes in tribal areas.

Tribals' right on land and forest should be properly reorganized as it has been one of the important aspects of "Tribal Panchsheel"of Pandit Jawaharlal Nehru. Of course, the PESA Act and Scheduled Tribe and other Forest Dwellers (Reorganization of Forest Right) Act, 2006, are the policies which take care of all these aspects and hence, need to be implemented sincerely with letter and spirit.

To conclude, more awareness has to be created among the people in rural areas for taking active part in the planning and executing stages of the poverty eradication and infrastructure development schemes implemented at village level. This is what the 73rd Amendment to the Constitution applicable to Scheduled Areas aims at. Government

Officials, Welfare extension Officers, NGOs and public representatives must join their hands to see that coordinated efforts are directed towards all-round development of tribals in general and that of the Koraput region in particular. Such suggestions are not new, but they are repeated as the situation still warrants.

BIBLIOGRAPHY

Abdul, Aziz (1983). *The Rural Poor: Problems and Prospects*, New Delhi: Ashish Publishing House.

Addae-Korankye, Alex (2014). "Causes of Poverty in Africa: A Review of Literature", *American International Journal of Social Science*, Vol. 3, No. 7, December 2014, pp. 147-153.

Agro Economic Research Centre (1973). *Santal Rural Economy: A Study Based on Village Survey in Santal Praganas*, Santiniketan.

Ahseshaiah, Malcolm S. (1990). "The Right to Work", *Bulletin of Madras Development Seminar Series*, 29(7): 339-44.

Aiyappan, A. (1965). "Development of Tribal Areas", *The Economic Weekly*, June 12, 1965, pp. 949-50.

Anuradha, K. and Jagannath Dash (2019). "Participation of South Odishan Tribes in Naxal Movements: A Contextual Analysis", in M.C. Behera (ed.), *Shifting Perspectives in Tribal Studies — From An Anthropological Approach to Interdisciplinarity and Consilience*, Singapore: Springer.

Bailey, F.G. (1960). *Tribe, Caste and Nation: A Study of Political Activity and Political Change in Highland of Orissa*, London: Oxford University Press.

Bakshi, S.R. and Kiran Bala (2000). *Social and Economic Development of Scheduled Tribes*, New Delhi: Deep and Deep Publications Pvt. Ltd.

Balakrishna, S. and K. Hanumantha Rao (ed.) (1998). *Database on Rural Poverty Indicators*, National Institute of Rural Development, Hyderabad.

Banerjee Sukumar (1969). *Ethnographic Study of Kui Kandha*, Anthropological Survey of India, Kolkata.

Bajpai Peeyush, Laveesh Bhandari and A. Sinha (2005). *Social and Economic Profile of India*, New Delhi: Social Science Press.

Behera, M.C. (1994). *Planning and Socio-Economic Development of the Tribals*, New Delhi: Commonwealth Publisher.

——— (2018). "Resource-Tribe-Power Complex and Exclusion: A Scrutiny", in Rashmi Pramanik, Uwe Skoda and Lidia Guzy (eds.),

Vulnerability, Marginalization and Culture, New Delhi: Concept Publishing Company Pvt. Ltd., pp. 43-74.

Behera, K.K. (2000). *The Impact of Weekly Markets in Tribal Region — A Case Study of Koraput District*, Unpublished Ph.D thesis, Utkal University, Bhubaneswar.

Behera, M.C. and J. Basar (eds.). (2010). *Interventions and Tribal Development — Challenges before Tribes in India in the Era of Globalization*, New Delhi: Serial Publications.

——— (2014). *Resources, Tribes and Development*, Jaipur: Rawat Publications.

Behuria, N.C. (1965). *Final Report on the Major Settlement Operation in Koraput District (1963-64)*, Cuttack: Govt. Press, Odisha.

Bell, R.C.S. (1945). *Orissa District Gazetteers*, Koraput: Govt. Press, Cuttack, Odisha.

Best, John W. (1982). *Methodology in Research*, New York: The Ronald Press.

Bijoy, C.R. (2003). "The Adivasis of India — A History of Discrimination, Conflict, and Resistance", *PUCL Bulletin*, February, 2003.

Bhowmik, K.L. (1971). *Tribal India: A Profile in Indian Ethnology*, Kolkata: World Press.

Bose, Nirmal Kumar (1977). *Tribal Life in India* (Revised by C.B. Tripathy), New Delhi: National Book Trust of India.

——— (1967). *Culture and Society in India*, Mumbai: Asia Publishing House.

——— (1971). *Tribal Life in India*, New Delhi: National Book Trust.

Census of India 1961. *Tribes of Orissa*, Vol. XII, Part V-B, Cuttack: Govt. Press, Odisha.

——— (2001). *Tribes of Orissa*, Vol. XII, Part V-B, Cuttack: Govt. Press, Odisha.

Chaudhuri, Buddhadeb (ed.) (1992). *Tribal Transformation in India*, Vols. I-V, New Delhi: Inter-India Publications.

COATS, Koraput (2004-05). *Five Year Perspective Plan under NFFWP (2005-06 to 2009-10) Koraput District*, COATS, Koraput.

Cramer, J.S. (1968). *Empirical Econometrics*, Amsterdam: North Holland Publishing Company.

Dalton, E.T. (1872). *Descriptive Ethnology of Bengal*, Calcutta: Superintendent, Government Printing Press.

Danda, Ajit K. (1981). "Statutory Provisions Safeguarding Interests of Scheduled Tribes and Scheduled Castes", L.P. Vidyarthi (ed.), *Tribal Development and Its Administration*, New Delhi: Concept Publishing Company Pvt. Ltd., pp. 19-28.

Dandekar, V.M. (1981). "On Measurement of Poverty", *EPW*, XVI(30), July, 1241-50.

Dandekar, V.M. and N. Rath (1971). *Poverty in India: Indian School of Political Economy*, Dirubhai J. Desai at States' People Press, Bombay.

Das, P.K. (1975). "A Study of Some Aspects of Tribal Agriculture in Koraput District of Orissa", *Orissa Economic Journal*, July-Dec., Bhubaneswar.

Das, T.C. (1945). "The Purums: An Old Kuki Tribe of Manipur", *Anthropological Papers No. 7*, University of Calcutta, Kolkata.

Dash, S.N. (2001). *A Study of the Problem of Land Alienation in Tribal Areas with Special: Reference to the District of Koraput*, Unpublished Ph.D Thesis, Utkal University, Bhubaneswar.

Daspatnaik P. (1984). "Ownership Pattern, Land Survey and Settlement and Its Impact on the Dongoria Kondhs of Orissa", *Adivasi* (A Journal of Anthropological Research), Vol. XXIII(4), pp. 23-32. The Harijan and Tribal Research Institute, Bhubaneswar.

Datt, Ruddar and K.P.M. Sundharam (2009). *Indian Economy* (Sixtieth Edition), New Delhi: S. Chand and Company Limited.

Debi, Kiran Bala (1963-64). "Kandha", *Adivasi*, Vol. 3, pp. 69-74, THRTI, BBSR.

Deogaonkar S.G. (1980). *Problems of Development of Tribal Areas*, New Delhi: Leela Devi Publications.

——— (1990). *Tribal Exploitation: A Study of Victims of Crime and Bondedness*, Columbia/New Delhi: South Asia Books.

——— (1994). *Tribals Administration and Development*, New Delhi: Concept Publishing Company Pvt. Ltd.

Dev Nathan and V. Xaxa (eds.) (2012). *Social Exclusion and Adverse Inclusion — Development and Deprivation of Adivasis in India*, New Delhi: Oxford University Press.

District Administration, Koraput, Government of Orissa (1988). *Koraput District — A Profile* (Mimeograph).

District Statistical Office, Koraput (1970). *District Statistical Handbook*, Koraput, 1969 and 1970 (Combined Issue).

District Statistical Office, Koraput (2007). *District Statistical Handbook*, Koraput.

Doshi, S.L. (1978). *Process of Tribal Unification and Integration*, New Delhi: Concept Publishing Company Pvt. Ltd.

Dube, S.W. and Ratna Murdia (ed.) (1977). *Land Alienation and Restoration in Tribal Communities in India*, Bombay: Himalaya Publishing House.

Elwin, Verrier (1939). *The Baiga*, London: John Murray.

——— (1943). *The Aboriginals*, London: Oxford University Press.

——— (1944). "Notes on Kandh Tour", *Man in India*, Vol. 24, No. 1.

——— (1965). *The Fundamental Needs of the Tribal People*, Tribal Souvenir, published by Adimjati Sevak Sangha, New Delhi.

——— (1950). *Bondo Highlanders*, London: Oxford University Press.

——— (1954). *Tribal Myths of Orissa*, London: Oxford University Press.

——— (1959). *A Philosophy for NFFA*, NEFA Secretariat: Shillong.

——— (1964). *The Tribal World of Verrier Elwin*, London: Oxford University Press.

——— (1965). *The Religion of an Indian Tribe (Saora)*, London: Oxford University Press.

Fernandes, Walter (ed.) (1992). *National Development and Tribal Deprivation*, New Delhi: Indian Social Institute.

Foster, James E. (1998). "Absolute *versus* Relative Poverty", *American Economic Review*, American Economic Association, Vol. 88(2), pp. 335-341.

Francis, W. (1907). *Vizagapatam District Gazetteers*, Madras: Government of Madras.

Gandhi, Malli (2019). "Approaches to Tribal Development in India, Policy Issues and Concerns: An Overview", in M.C. Behera and Ganga Nath Jha (eds.), *Dimensions of Tribal Studies*, New Delhi: Nation Press.

Ganguly J.B. (1968). *Economic Problems of the Jhumias of Tripura: A Socio Economic Study of the System of Shifting Cultivation*, Calcutta: Bookland Pvt. Ltd.

Ghose, S. K. (1990). *Law Enforcement in Tribal Areas*, New Delhi: Asia Publishing House.

Ghose, Swapnajit (2007). "Sustainable Livelihood of Tribals Through Food Security Programme: A Study of Nabarangapur Block", *Unpublished M.Phil Dissertation*, Berhampur University, Berhampur.

Ghurye, G.S. (1959). *The Scheduled Tribes*, Bombay: Popular Prakashan.

——— (1943). *The Aborigines — so called-and their Future*, Gokhale Institute of Politics and Economics, Poona.

Gordon, David (2005). *Indicators of Poverty & Hunger*, Expert Group Meeting on Youth Development Indicators, UN Headquarters, New York. Available at https://www.un.org/esa/socdev/unyin/documents/ydiDavidGordon_poverty.pdf

Goswami, B. (2003). *Constitutional Safeguards for Scheduled Castes and Scheduled Tribes*, Jaipur: Rawat Publications.

Govt. of India (1960). *Report of Special Multipurpose Tribal Blocks Committee*, Ministry of Home Affairs, New Delhi.

——— (1977). Approach to the Development in the Sixth Plan: A Preliminary Perspective, *Occasional Paper on Tribal Development No. 17*, Ministry of Home Affairs, New Delhi, pp. 99-100.

——— Planning Commission (2009). *Report of the Expert Group to Review the Methodology for Estimation of Poverty*, Government of India, New Delhi.

Govt. of Orissa (1992). *Koraput at a Glance, Report-4*, Cuttack: Govt. Press.

——— (2006-07). *Orissa Agricultural Statistics*, Directorate of Agriculture and Food Production, Orissa, Bhubaneswar.

——— (2004). *Tribes of Orissa*, Cuttack: Govt. Press.

Greer, J. and E. Thorbecke (1986). "Food and Poverty Profile Applied to Kenyan Small Holders", *Economic Development and Cultural Change*, XXX(1), Oct., pp. 117-140.

Guha, B.S. (ed.) (1951). *The Tribes of India*, 2nd Volume, New Delhi: Bharatiya Adimjati Sevak Sangha.

Guha, B.S. (1935). "The Racial Affinities of People of India", *Census of India*, 1931, Vol. I, Part IIIB, Shimla: Government Press.

Guha, B.S. (1955). *Indian Aborigines and Who They Are: Adivasi*, Publication Division, Government of India, New Delhi.

Gutkind, E. (1986). *Patterns of Economic Behaviour Among the American Poor*, New York: St. Martin's Press.

de Haan, Arjan and Sakti Padhi (2003). "Monitoring of Poverty in Orissa: Report from a Workshop", *Economic and Political Weekly*, Vol. 38(50), pp. 5243-45.

Haimendorf, Christoph Von. Furer (1982). *Tribes of India: The Struggle for Survival*, New Delhi: Oxford University Press.

Hardin, Garrett (1968). "The Tragedy of the Commons", *Science*, New Series, Vol. 162, No. 3859 (Dec. 13, 1968), pp. 1243-1248.

Herskovits, M.J. (1940). *Economic Anthropology — A Study in Comparative Economics*, New York: Knopf.

Hutton, J.H. (1933). *Census of India*, Vol. 1, Shimla: Government of India Press.

Jain, P.C. (1999). *Planned Development among Tribals*, New Delhi: Rawat Publications.

Jensen, Hans E. (1983). "J.M. Keynes as a Marshallian", *Journal of Economic Issues*, Vol. 17, No. 1 (Mar., 1983), pp. 67-94.

Joros, Dean (1973). *Socialisation of Politics*, Madras: Higgim Bothem.

Joshi, Dina Krishna, Sasmita Mund and Mihir Prasad Mishra (2007). "The Kanda Revolution in Kalahandi", *Orissa Review*, pp. 76-77.

Joyee, B. and Well, M. (1985). *Different Methods of Experimental Research* (IInd Edition), New Delhi: Prentice Hall of India Pvt. Limited.

Kancha, Ilaiah (1990). "SCs and STs: Systematic Exploitation", *Economic and Political Weekly*, Vol. 25(51), December 22-28, pp. 2771-74.

Koul, Lokesh (1985). *The Research Methodology*, New Delhi: The Starring Pvt. Ltd.

Kumar, Alock (1986). *Tribal Culture and Economy*, New Delhi: Inter-India Publications.

Kumaran, K.P. (2000). *Impact of Economic Reforms on SCs and STs*, National Institute of Rural Development, Hyderabad.

Libenstein, H. (1957). *The Theory of Underemployment in Backward Economies*, Berkley: Institute of Industrial Relations, University of California.

Lipton, Michael (1983). *Poverty, Undernutrition, and Hunger*, World Bank Staff Working Papers, No. 597, The World Bank, Washington DC.

Macpherson, S.C. (1838). "Report on the Goomsur, Duspullah and Boad Zeminderies. Section One. On the Configuration and Superficial Characteristics of the Country in the Plain", *MJLS*, Vol. VII, No. 19 (April), pp. 400-12, Madras.

Macpherson, S.C. (1842). *Report upon the Kondhs of the Districts of Ganjam and Cuttack*, G.H. Hutterman at the Bengal Military Prdhan Press, Calcutta.

Madiath, Joe and Deborah Nelson (2009). *Dignity, Not Charity — Empowering Tribal Communities*, Posted in Internet.

Majumdar, D.N. and T.N. Madan (1956). *An Introduction to Social Anthropology*, Bombay: Asia Publishing House.

Majumdar, D.N. (1937) (1950). *The Affairs of a Tribe: A Study in Tribal Dynamics*, New & enl. ed., Lucknow: Universal Publishers. First published as *A Tribe in Transition: A Study in Culture Patterns*.

Majumdar, D.N. (1944). *Races and Cultures of India*, Lucknow: Universal Publishers.

Malik, R.M. and Rajkishore Meher (1999). *Impact of IRDP on KBK Districts of Orissa* (Seminar paper, unpublished).

Mathur, P.R.G. (1977). *Accountation and Integration in Tribal Life*, New Delhi: Inter-India Publishers.

Mehrotra, Santosh and Enrique Delamonica (2007). *Eliminating Human Poverty: Macroeconomic and Social Policies for Equitable Growth*, London: Zed Books.

Mehta, Basant and Prakash Chandra Mehta (2000). *Dynamics of Tribal Development*, New Delhi: Anmol Publications.

Mehta, B.C. (1993). *Rural Poverty in India*, New Delhi: Concept Publishing Company Pvt. Ltd.

Mirowski, P. and D. Plehwe (eds.) (2009). *The Road from Mont Pelerin: The Making of the Neoliberal Thought Collective*, MA: Harvard University Press, Cambridge.

Mishra, Baidyanatha (ed.) (1991). *Poverty, Unemployment and Rural Development*, New Delhi: Ashish Publishing House.

Mishra, Sujit Kumar (2002). "Development, Displacement and Rehabilitation of Tribal People: A Case Study of Orissa", *J. Soc. Sci.*, 6(3), pp. 197-208.

Mohanty, Biswajita (2008). "Too Much Burden", *Yojana*, September, Publication Division, Ministry of Information, Govt. of India, New Delhi.

Mohanty, Gopinath (1946). *Paraja*, Cuttack: Manamohan Pustkalaya.

——— (1949). *Ambrutara Santan*, Cuttack: Bidyapuri.

Mohanty L.C. (1989). *An Analysis of the Improved Economic Life of the Tribals of Orissa and the Way Towards Integration*, New Delhi: Deep and Deep Publishers.

Mohanty, D.C. (1978). "Bonded Labour in Orissa with Special Reference to Koraput District", in P.C. Mohapatro and D. Panda (ed.), *Tribal Problems of Today and Tomorrow*, Bhubaneswar: Sabari Cultural Society.

Mohanty, J.K. (1998). "Financing Non-farm Sector for Rural Development in District of Orissa — An Empirical Study", Unpublished Ph.D Thesis, Berhampur University, Berhampur.

Mohanty, K.K., P.C. Mohapatro and J. Samal (2006). *Tribes of Koraput*, Koraput: Council of Analytical Tribal Studies.

Mohanty, M.K. (1990). *Tribal Society: Programmes, Planning and Economic Change*, Allahabad: Chugh Publications.

Mohapatra, K. and K. Devi (1973). "Shifting Cultivation in Orissa", *Adivasi*, Vol. XIV, No. 4 (Jan.).

Mohapatra, P.M. and P.C. Mohapatra (ed.) (1997). *Forest Management in Tribal Area*, New Delhi: Concept Publishing Company Pvt. Ltd.

Mohapatro, P.C. (1987). *Economic Development of Tribal India*, New Delhi: Ashish Publishing House.

Mohapatro, P.C. and D. Panda (ed.) (1978). *Tribal Problems of Today and Tomorrow*, Bhubaneswar: Sabari Cultural Society.

Mahapatro, P.C. and J. Samal (1999). *Adibasi-Reeti, Neeti O Arthaniti*, Berhampur: Das Brothers.

Morris, M.D. (1979). *Measuring the Condition of World's Poor — The Physical Quality of Life Index*, Pergamon Press, Oxford.

Nabakrushna Choudhury Centre for Development Studies (2004). *Human Development Report: 2004-Orissa*, UNDP, New Delhi & Planning Commission, New Delhi.

Nag, D.D. (1958). *Baiga Economy of Madhya Pradesh*, Calcutta: M.K. Publications.

Naik, T.B. (1968). "What is a Tribe: Conflicting Definitions", in L.P. Vidyarthi (ed.), *Applied Anthropology in India*, Allahabad: Kitab Mahal, pp. 84-97.

NIEAM (MANAGE) (2001). *Strategic Research and Extension Plan of Koraput District*, Rajendra Nagar, Hyderabad.

Narasaiah, M.L. (2007). *Agriculture and Rural Poverty*, New Delhi: Discovery Publishing House.

Nazer, M. (2004). *A Study of Land Alienation and Indebtedness among Tribals in Tamil Nadu*, New Delhi: Planning Commission, Government of India.

NCAER (1961). *Techno-Economic Survey of Orissa: Appraisal Report on Tribal Area* (mimeo), New Delhi: NCAER.

Niggemyar, H. (1956). "Kutia Kandha Pilara Ekoisa (Oriya)", *Adivasi*, Vol. 1, No. 2 & 3, pp. 5-7, THRTI, BBSR.

Niggemyar, H. (1964). *Kuttia Kond: Dschungel-Bauern in Orissa*, Miinchen: Klaus Reiner Verlag [pp. 226-229: kin terminology.]

Ntibagirirwa, Symphorien (2009). "Cultural Values, Economic Growth and Development", *Journal of Business Ethics*, Vol. 84, Supplement 3: Global and Contextual Values for Business in a Changing World, pp. 297-311.

Omvedt, Gail (1996). "Worst in a Hundred Years: The Kalahandi Drought", *Manushi*, Issue 97, Nov.-Dec. 1996, pp. 22-31.

Orshansky, Mollie (1969). "How Poverty is Measured", *Monthly Labor Review*, Vol. 92, No. 2, February 1969, pp. 37-41.

Ota, A.B. (ed.) (2009). *Development Induced Displacement and the Tribals*, SC and Training Institute, Orissa, Bhubaneswar.

Ota, A.B, and K. Patnaik (ed.) (2009). *Two Tribal Friendly Acts and their Implementations*, Scheduled Castes and Scheduled Tribes Research and Training Institute, Orissa, Bhubaneswar.

Padel, Felix and Samarendra Das (2010). *Out of this Earth: East India Adivasis and the Aluminium Cartel*, Hyderabad: Orient Black Swan.

Padhi, Sakti; Nilakantha Panigrahi and Aswini Kumar Mishra (2005). "Tribal Population and Chronic Poverty in Orissa: A Note on the North-South Divide", *SSRN Electronic Journal*, 10.2139/ssrn.1756811.

Padhi, S.R. and Biswajita Padhi (ed.) (2010). *Tribal Development in India — Contemporary Issues and Perspectives*, New Delhi: Mangalam Publications.

Panda, N.K. (1986). "Fixing Income and Price Targets for the Poor in India", *Journal of Development Economics*, XX(2).

Panda, N.K. (1987). "Poverty in Rural Orissa (1960-83)", *Margin*, XX(2), Oct.-Dec., pp. 42-45.

Pandey, A.K. (1997). *Tribal Society in India*, New Delhi: Manak Publications Pvt. Ltd.

Panagariya, Arvind and Vishal More (2013). *Poverty by Social, Religious and Economic Groups in India and Its Largest States, 1993-94 to 2011-12*, Working Paper No. 2013-02. Columbia University: School of International and Public Affairs, Institute for Social and Economic Research and Policy.

Passi, B.K. Goel and Swarup D.R. (1986). "Research Methodology and Socio Economic Development of People of India — A Monograph", D.A.P.U., Indore.

Patanaik, N. and S. Bose (1976). *An Integrated Tribal Development for Keonjhar District, Orissa*, NICD, Hyderabad.

Patanaik, N. (1976). *Tribes and Their Development — A Study of Two Tribal Development Blocks in Orissa*, NIRD, Hyderabad.

Patel, M.L. (1984). *Planning Strategy for Tribal Development*, New Delhi: Inter-India Publications.

——— (1987). *New Dimensions of Tribal Developments*, Bhopal: NBS Publications and Distributors.

Pathy, J. (1984). *Tribal Peasantry: Dynamic of Development*, New Delhi: Inter-India Publications.

Pathy, Jagannath (1988). *Underdevelopment and Destitution: Essays on Orissan Society*, New Delhi: Inter-India Publications.

Pati, Biswamoy (ed.) (2011). *Adivasis in Colonial India — Survival, Resistance and Negotiation*, New Delhi: Orient Black Swan.

Patnaik, N.F. Bara and A. Mall (1986). " Herbal Medicines of Dongrias", *Adibasi*, 26/1-4.

Patnaik, Nihar Ranjan (ed.) (1997). *Economic History of Orissa*, New Delhi: Indus Publishing Company.

——— (1989). *The Kondh*, Tribal and Harijan Research-cum-Training Institute, Bhubaneswar.

Patnaik, L.K., H. Egnens and S.S. Das (ed.) (1989). *Social Forestry Handbook for Orissa*, SIDA, Bhubaneswar.

Patnaik, N. (1988). *The Kandh*, Tribal and Harijan Research-cum-Training Institute, Bhubaneswar.

Patnaik, N. and P.S. Das Patnaik (1980). *The Kandha of Orissa*, Tribal and Harijan Research-cum-Training Institute, BBSR, Orissa.

Patnaik, Nityananda (1957-58). "Orissara Bivinna Prakara Kandhs (Oriya)", *Adivasi*, Vol. II, No. 4, pp. 26-31, THRTI, Bhubaneswar.

Patnaik, U.N. (1964-65). "Reminiscences of an Administrative Officer in Kandha Hills", *Adivasi*, Vol. 2, pp. 22-36, THRTI, Bhubaneswar.

——— (1970). "Religious Ceremonies, Ordeals and a Legend about Oriya Infiltration in Kandha Hills", *Adivasi*, Vol. XI, No. 4, pp. 76-84, THRTI, Bhubaneswar.

——— (1984). "Kui Kondhs: Observation of an Administrative Officer in the Kondh Hills in the Early Forties", *Adibasi* (A Journal of Anthropological Research), Vol. XXIV, Nos. 1 & 2, pp. 1-29, Tribal and Harijan Research-cum-Training Institute, Bhubaneswar.

Phillips-Fein, K. (2009). *Invisible Hands: The Making of the Conservative Movement from the New Deal to Reagan*, Yayasan Obor, Indonesia.

Piaget, J. (1970). *The Science of Education and Research Methodology*, New York: Viking Press.

Planning Commission, Govt. of India (2009). *Report on the Expert Group of Review of the Methodology for Estimation of Poverty*, New Delhi: Govt. of India, Planning Commission.

Polanyi, K. (1957). *The Great Transformation: The Political and Economic Origins of Our Times*, Boston: Beacon Press.

Pullen, John (2001). "Henry George's Land Reform: The Distinction between Private Ownership and Private Possession", *The American Journal of Economics and Sociology*, Vol. 60, No. 2 (Apr. 2001), pp. 547-556.

Prasada, K.N. (1991). *India's Rural Problems*, New Delhi: Concept Publishing Company Pvt. Ltd.

Raghavaiah, V. (1971). *Tribal Revolts*, Andhra Rashtra Adimjati Sevak Sangha, Nellore, Andhra Pradesh, New Delhi: Ashok Printing Press.

Ramamani V.S. (1988). *Tribal Economy — Problems and Prospects*, Allahabad: Chugh Publications.

Rao, N. Gopal. (1978). "Land Alienation, A Menace of Tribal Economy", *Tribe*, Vol. X, No. 4.

Rath, N. (1983). "Measuring Rural Unemployment in India: A Methodological Note", in A. Robinson; P.R. Brahmananda and L.K. Deshpande (eds), *Employment Policy in a Developing Country: A Case Study of India*, Volume 1, International Economic Association Series, Palgrave, London: MacMillan.

Rath, N. (1985). "Garibi Hatao — Can IRDP Do It", *Economic and Political Weekly*, Vol. 20(6), pp. 238-246.

Reddy, G. Prakash (1987). *Politics of Tribal Exploitation*, New Delhi: Mittal Publication.

Reddy, Y.R.H. (1987). *Bonded Labour System in India*, New Delhi: Deep and Deep.

Risley, Herbert H. (1908) (1915). *The People of India*, 2nd ed., Calcutta: Thacker.

——— (1891). *The Tribes and Castes of Bengal*, Calcutta: Bengal Secretariat Press.

Rout, Jitendra Kumar (1963-64). "Tribal Welfare in Orissa", *Adivasi*, Vol. 3, pp. 17-22, THRTI, BBSR.

Rout, Siba Prasad (1964-65). "Dom Exploitation in the Kandh Villages of Koraput District", *Adivasi*, Vol. 6, No. 1, pp. 21-28, THRTI, Bhubaneswar.

Roy Burman, B.K. (1973). "Modernization of Tribal People in India's Borders", in K.S. Mathur (ed.), *Studies in Social Change*, Ethnographic and Folk Culture Society, Lucknow.

——— (1979). "Some Dimensions of Transformations of Tribal Studies in India", *Journal of Social Research*, Vol. XXIII, No. 3.

Roy, S.C. (1912) (reprinted 1950). *The Mundas and their Country*, Calcutta: City Book Society, reprinted in Asia Publishing House, Bombay.

——— (1922). "Ethnography in Old Official Records (Kandh Human Sacrifices)", *Man in India*, Vol. II, pp. 67-81, Ranchi.

Saha, Vimal (1969). *Tribal Economy in Gujarat*, Jaipur: Well Print Publications.

Sahoo, A.C. (2009). "The Scheduled Tribes and Other Traditional Forest Rights Act, 2006 — A Critical View in Forest Policy, Practice and Operational Issues", in Ota and Patnaik (eds.), *Two Tribal Friendly Acts*, SC and ST, THRTI, BBSR.

Sahoo, Basudev (ed.) (1989). *Backward Classes and Economic Development*, Satanetra Publications 6, BBSR-12.

Sahu, L.N. (1942). *Hill Tribes of Jeypore*, Orissa Mission Press, Cuttack.

Sen A. (1973). *On Economic Inequality*, Oxford: Clarendon Press.

Sainath, P. (1996). *Everybody Loves a Good Drought: Stories from India's Poorest Districts*, New Delhi: Penguin India.

Samal, J. (1985). "Tribal Economy — A Regional Study: A Case Study of Koraput District", *Orissa Economic Journal*, Vol. XVIII, No. 1 & 2, Bhubaneswar.

——— (1985). "Tribal Economy and Forest Ecology", in P.S.B. Rao (ed.), *Tribals and Forest Eco System*, Koraput: DAV College.

——— (1979). "Problems of Tribal Agriculture in India", Unpublished M.Phil Dissertation, University of Poona (GIPE), Poona.

——— (1992). "Some Aspect of Tribal Economy — A Case Study of Koraput District", Unpublished Ph.D Thesis, University of Poona, Poona.

Samantaray, A.K. (1985). "Tribal and Forest — A Status Review", in P.S.B. Rao (ed.), *Tribals and Forest Eco-System*, Koraput: D.A.V. College.

Sarva Seva Sangha (1960). *Report on Koraput Gramdans*, Sarva Seva Sangha, Wardha.

Saxena, R.P. (1964). *Tribals Economy in Central India*, Firma, K.L. Mukhopadhyaya, Calcutta.

Sen, Amartya (1981). *Poverty and Famines: An Essay on Entitlement and Deprivation*, New Delhi: Oxford University Press.

——— (1976). "Poverty: An Ordinal Approach to Measurement", *Econometrics*, Vol. 44, No. 2, 219-231.

Senapati, N. and N.K. Sahu (1966). *Orissa District Gazetteer*, Koraput, Cuttack: Orissa Government Press.

Sengupta, Nirmal (1990). "The Social and Economic Basis of Current Tribal Movements", *Social Action*, October.

Shanti, George (1985). "Operation Flood and Rural India: Vested and Divested Interests", *Economic and Political Weekly*, Vol. 20, No. 49 (Dec. 7, 1985), pp. 2163-2170.

Shashi, S.S. (1994). *Tribal World in Transition (Encyclopaedia of Indian Tribes)*, Vol. 1, New Delhi: Anmol Publications Pvt. Limited.

Shishkov, Iurii V. (1993). "Exploitation of Labor: History *versus* Marxist Theory", *Problems of Economic Transition*, 36:6, 7-20. Available at "https://doi.org/10.2753/PET1061-199136067" _10.2753/PET1061-199136067.

Shoobert, W.H. (ed.) (1933). *Census of India, 1931*, Vol. XII, Central Provinces & Berar, Part-I, Report, Nagpur.

Shrivastava, B.N. (1968). *Exploitation in Tribal Areas*, New Delhi: Bharatiya Adimjati Sevak Sangh.

Singh, R.S. (1986). *Changing Occupational Structure of Scheduled Tribes*, New Delhi: Inter-India Publications.

Singh, A.K. (1984). *Tribal Development in India*, New Delhi: Amar Prakashan.

Singh, K.S. (1982). "Transformation of Tribal Society Integration Vs. Assimilation", *EPW*, Vol. XVII, No. 33, Aug.

——— (ed.) (1982/2002). *The Tribal Situation In India*, Shimla: Indian Institute of Advanced Study.

Srichandan, G.K. (1998). *Tribal Development and Welfare Legislation in Orissa (Under Indian Plan) Perspective*, New Delhi: Pratibha.

Stedman-Jones, D. (2012). *Masters of the Universe: Hayek, Friedman and the Birth of Neoliberal Politics*, Princeton: Princeton University Press.

Sundaram, K. and Suresh D. Tendulkar (2003). "Poverty among Social and Economic Groups in India in 1990s", *Economic and Political Weekly*, 38(50), pp. 5263-5276.

Tendulkar, Suresh D. and Jain L.R. (1995). "Economic Reforms and Poverty". *EPW*, Vol. 30(23), pp. 1373-1375+1377.

THRTI, BBSR (1973). "Shifting-Cultivation in Orissa" *Adivasi*, Vol. XIV, January.

Thakur, Devendra (1986). *Socio Economic Development of Tribes in India*, New Delhi: Deep and Deep Publishers.

Townsend, Peter (1979). *Poverty in United Kingdom: A Survey of Household Resources and Standard of Living*, Harmondsworth: Penguin Books.

Tripathy, S.N. (1999). *Tribals in Transitions*, New Delhi: Discovery Publishing House.

Tripathy, D.P. (1952). *Shifting Cultivation in Orissa — Its Causes, Effects and Remedy*, Cuttack: Orissa Government Press.

Trivedi, Madhusudan (1991). *Entrepreneurship among Tribals*, Jaipur: Printwell Publication.

UNDP (2004). *Human Development Report 2004 — Cultural Liberty in Today's Diverse World*, New York: UNDP.

Vaid, N.K. (2004). *Who Cares for Tribal Development*, New Delhi: Mittal Publication.

Verma, R.C. (1990). *Indian Tribes Through the Ages*, New Delhi: Hindusthan Offset Press.

Vidyarthi, L.P and B.K. Rai (1976). *The Tribal Culture of India*, New Delhi: Concept Publishing Company Pvt. Ltd.

Vidyarthi L.P. (ed.) (1981). *Tribal Development and Its Administration*, New Delhi: Concept Publishing Company Pvt. Ltd.

——— (1957). "Anthropology, Authority and Tribal Welfare in India", The *Eastern Anthropologists*, Vol. XI(1).

——— (1960). "Anthropology and Tribal Policy", *Journal of Social Research*, Vol. III(2), Ranchi.

——— (1963). *The Maler: A Study in Nature-Man-Spirit Complex of a Hill Tribe in Bihar*, Calcutta : Bookland Private Limited.

——— (1968). "Some Implications of Industrialization in Tribal Bihar", *The Anthropologist*, Special Number, Vol. 2, Delhi.

——— (1971). "Cultural Diversities in the Andaman and Nicobar Islands: A Preliminary Report", *Indian Anthropologist*, Vol. 1(1).

Vyas, N.N. (1967). *Customs and Traditions of Some Indian Tribes*, New Delhi: Vikas Publishing House.

——— (1981). "Tribal and Forest", in N.N. Vyas (ed.), *Social Forestry in Tribal Development*, MLV Tribal Research Training Institute, Udaipur.

Watts, Neville A. (1970). *The Half-Clad Tribes of Eastern India*, Bombay: Orient Longman.

Wissler, Clark (1923). *Man and Culture*, New York: Crowell Co.

Wolff, Jonathan (1999). "Marx and Exploitation", *The Journal of Ethics*, Vol. 3, No. 2, pp. 105-120.

World Bank (2011). *Poverty and Exclusion in India*, Washington DC: The International Bank for Reconstruction and Development.

Xaxa, Virginius (2018). "Exploring Ideas of Autonomy through Tribal Movements in Eastern India", in M.C. Behera (ed.), *Revisiting Tribal Studies: A Glimpse After Hundred Years*, pp. 61-69, Jaipur: Rawat.

INDEX